Internet Digital Libraries

The International Dimension

Internet Digital Libraries

The International Dimension

Jack Kessler

Artech House
Boston • London

DB# 1535129

Library of Congress Cataloging-in-Publication Data
Kessler, Jack.
   Internet digital libraries : the international dimension / Jack Kessler.
      p.   cm.
   Includes bibliographical references and index.
   ISBN 0-89006-875-5 (alk. paper)
   1. Libraries—Data processing.   2. Online information services.
   3. Digital libraries   I. Title.
   Z678.93.O64
   025.04—dc21   96-46061
                                                                 CIP

British Library Cataloguing in Publication Data
Kessler, Jack
   Internet digital libraries : the international dimension
   1. Digital libraries   2. Internet (Computer network)
   I. Title
   025'.00285'467

   ISBN 0-89006-875-5

Cover and text design by Darrell Judd

© 1996 ARTECH HOUSE, INC.
685 Canton Street
Norwood, MA 02062

International Standard Book Number: 0-89006-875-5
Library of Congress Catalog Card Number: 96-46061

10 9 8 7 6 5 4 3 2 1

Z
678.93
.O64
K47
1996

Contents

Preface

MY FIRST ENCOUNTER with *digital libraries* came courtesy of a Turkish graduate student at the University of California at Berkeley, Yasar Tonta, who described to me something called "email" simply by saying, "You gotta get this thing," one day back in 1989. I went up to the UC computer center the next week, paid $5 for an excellent class, came back to Yasar for a demonstration of how to see Oxford University's libraries from a laptop in Berkeley, and I was hooked.

Digital and I go a longer way back. I spent years—from the IBM 360 on—using punch cards and printouts and spreadsheets and wondering how the whole thing worked but never having the time to find out. *Libraries* and I go back even further, as they do for most people. I have happy childhood memories of the Berkeley Public Library, and I cherish the recollection of years spent in academic libraries in Berkeley and, during college and graduate school years, in various different places.

So the chance for synthesis provided by digital libraries is extraordinary for me. That two interests as apparently disconnected as "bits and bytes" and "books" not only might have a connection, but might fit together very neatly and necessarily, has been a personal revelation. That other people have seen the same connection is comforting, because digital libraries seemed a pretty nutty idea only a few years ago. That so many other people would have seen the connection seems to me to be one of the significant events of this century. Perhaps my own interests blind me in this, but it does look that eventful to me. That so many people are located, in other countries, doing digital libraries each in their own very different ways, is largely the point of this book.

The thanks that any writer bestows can be two-sided. Depending on the composition and perhaps reception of the work, over none of which they have any control, its recipients may want to bask or duck. Thanks are due, nevertheless, not for attribution—that is, a job for footnotes—or for blame, but simply to acknowledge the enormous role that coworkers and friends all play in any composition.

I have had numerous stimulating conversations over a number of years about many of these subjects—conversations that I hope will continue—with François Bar, Ole Jacobsen, Bob Berring, Judy Baker, and recently Walt Crawford and Joan Aliprand. Tom Reynolds has reminded me continually, both in person and in his writing, of the existence in librarianship of both books and good humor. Michel Melot has reminded me by example that good quality does not always come written in American English. Christian Xerri showed me, one day in a San Francisco research laboratory, on a multimedia connection being viewed simultaneously in Marseille, just how immediate and awesome international connectivity can be.

Inspiration and instruction have been derived from sources as varied as Michael Buckland, Mary Kay Duggan, Clifford Lynch, Steve Cisler, Roy Tennant, and John Ober. Ramsay MacMullen taught me how to write and warned me how not to, and I have generally tried to follow his advice about this for over thirty years. I am indebted to my editor, John Garrett, for inspiration and support and to Yvonne and Jaime at Martha's on Church Street for congenial surroundings, a plug for my laptop, and much good caffeine.

This book was not a cooperative effort—some are, this wasn't, I have no one to blame here but myself—and yet it benefited enormously from the cooperation or at least the inspiration of the people mentioned above and many others. I have them to thank for many of its felicities and only myself to blame for any of its faults. Advice about both, from anyone, will be gratefully received by me via e-mail at kessler@well.sf.ca.us.

Jack Kessler, kessler@well.sf.ca.us
November 1996

Introduction

T HERE IS DETAILED understanding today of the term *digital*. At the same time there is little common understanding of the term *libraries*.

The term digital has become the byword of our era. Images and impressions of *computers, networks, systems, information, imaging,* and *telecommunications* dominate our popular press and, increasingly, our general thinking and conversation. Politicians; scholars; people in business, the arts, and the professions; and, above all, school children all now speak knowledgeably about the computers that they use at work, school, or home and about the wondrous things that can be done using computers.

In the case of the term digital, this general knowledge and conversation is supported by established and meticulous science. Terms such as computers, networks, systems, information, imaging, and telecommunications are all backed by large numbers of international researchers and research institutions and by growing bodies of highly specialized technical literature. All of this current digital research and development is constantly producing new ideas and refining those that already exist.

Recently, however, the term libraries seems to have lost its clarity of definition. The term digital has come to symbolize exactness and precision, while the term libraries has become imprecise. The term libraries, today, can refer to unorganized data; or to that same data organized as information; or to containers of that information, such as books and other media; or to the containers of the containers themselves, that is, social institutions that house, organize, and provide both the books and other media and their information.

Increasingly, particularly in its digital incarnation, the term libraries is used to mean *library service*—not a thing or its container or the container of its container, but libraries as the function of getting information to its user. Online services are developing that help users find and use online digital information regardless of where the users, these library service providers, or the information itself are physically located.

At the same time, and in stark contrast, on college campuses the term *the library* continues to be associated with brick-and-mortar buildings—most often, in fact, with a particular building, one normally large, old, covered with ivy, increasingly less-frequented by users, and occupying a prime piece of much-coveted central-campus real estate.

Furthermore, we speak, write, and argue about *university libraries* and *library collections, online library databases, image and text and data libraries,* and even *library service* interchangeably. We do this without distinguishing things made of bricks and mortar from things made of cardboard and paper, or either of these from things made of electronic bits and organizing principles—or even just the bits without the principles or the principles without the bits. Libraries has become a term as amorphous in meaning as its accompanying term digital has become exact.

All beginning philosophy students learn Gilbert Ryle's parable illustrating the *category mistake*. Visitors, Ryle said, particularly those from U.S. campus-style colleges, come to Oxford—an English town dotted with little colleges and other things all of which together compose, loosely, the great medieval university—stand in the center of town, surrounded by shops, pubs, scholars, quaint buildings, and traffic, and ask, "Where is the university?" [1].

The error is one of apples and oranges, that is, of asking for a U.S. college campus using a term that describes something entirely different in the Oxford context. Discussing digital libraries poses somewhat the same problem. The old categories that defined the term libraries have been changed by the digital revolution as much as everything else has been changed. Just as it no longer makes sense to speak of office procedures in terms of scrivening and penmanship, it no longer makes sense to speak of libraries in terms designed exclusively or even primarily for worlds once inhabited by scriveners and by those who produced and read parchment-borne illuminated manuscripts.

This is not to say that the term libraries, despite its current confusions, has not received the attention of rigorous investigation and scientific definition. Library theorists have been at work for a very long time. Library science and information science have been working on information definition and organization and flow for a century. *Documentalists* developed categories at the turn of the last century that now appear modern and relevant at the imminent turn of the coming century [2].

The general result of these efforts, however, has been to broaden terminology that was previously too narrow. Documentalists addressed more than what had previously been addressed by librarians. Library science added rigor to the already broad interests of general library and documentalist studies. Information science has added even more, folding in concerns of fields as diverse as information theory, cognitive studies, and artificial intelligence.

The result has been confusing to outsiders. The general effort to loosen the hard-and-fast concepts used by nineteenth-century librarians has endowed the term libraries, and the various disciplines that have come to support it, with a very twentieth-century approach that is eminently flexible. As befits any changing subject matter, *library studies/library science/information science* presents a changing approach, shifting constantly to try to anticipate, or at least keep up with, radical developments and shifts in the way information is defined, stored, retrieved, communicated, and used. But all this flexibility makes libraries a difficult partner, one as capricious and unpredictable as digital developments are, or currently appear to be, defined and logical.

Why use the two terms together then? Why lump together an inexact term like libraries with an exact term like digital? An answer was suggested by C. P. Snow in his description of "The Two Cultures." At Cambridge, he said, "By training I was a scientist; by vocation I was a writer…I felt I was moving among two groups—comparable in intelligence, identical in race, not grossly different in social origin, earning about the same incomes, who had almost ceased to communicate at all…after a few thousand Atlantic miles, one found Greenwich Village talking precisely the same language as Chelsea, and both having about as much communication with MIT as though the scientists spoke nothing but Tibetan" [3].

Snow's own hope was that, "The clashing point of two subjects, two disciplines, two cultures—of two galaxies, so far as that goes—ought to produce creative chances. In the history of mental activity that has been where some of the breakthroughs came" [4].

There is a mutual tempering wrought by the association of the exact with the inexact. One tends both to moderate and to refine the other, although this is rarelyobvious from either extreme position. On college campuses, engineering faculties have forever shown little patience with literature departments, and literature departments have returned the compliment. But most college administrators, general educators, and students have appreciated the successful melding together of the two, among other intellectual extremes, which a well-administered campus and a good education can bring.

Certainly people in business and the professions and the rest of the outside, practical world—who wind up exasperated at extremes representing either the exact or the inexact academic tradition—appreciate efforts to compromise the two. *Digital libraries* is just such a compromise. As the exact sciences that construct our digital world progress, from academic testbeds to user applications and beyond, they perhaps could not find a better ally than libraries, with all the uncertainty and malleability—but also the user-friendliness, user experience, tradition, and history that the term implies.

Since the term libraries is perhaps too ill-defined at the moment, and the terms digital and digital libraries too new to be susceptible to any single particular definition, the objective here is first to present some examples of how the digital libraries term is currently used in practice. One might call this essays in definition, using the old French sense of the term *essai* as an *attempt* or a *try*. An attempt at defining deductively what all the talk of digital libraries is about could parse the term infinitely. An inductive approach could instead simply try to identify some common strands in the current wide-ranging discussion of the subject. The latter approach is adopted in this book.

The particular concern here, though, is not the discussion and refinement of the term digital libraries for its application "at home," in any particular local arena. A single setting, country or culture, might exhibit more agreement as to the categories and context surrounding the use of a particular term. However, there are two problems with this degree of agreement, particularly in the case of digital libraries.

1. *Parochial interests.* Greater and hopefully more useful contrasts and insights can be derived from greater distance. The farther away one is from a particular local treatment of a problem, the more clearly parochial interests and concerns not necessarily relevant to the problem in its general case become apparent. The trick is to be sure that one is talking, in each case, about essentially the same thing. Digital

libraries experiments in a San Francisco business will show differences from those conducted by an academic department at the University of California at Berkeley due, at least, to the differences in geography and professional orientation, or so runs the premise that underlies any comparative analysis. It is important, though, to identify digital libraries undertakings in San Francisco and Berkeley that have more in common than simply the name, which is one challenge addressed in the present study.

2. *The virtues of removal.* International comparisons make the next step—a "quantum step"—in distance. The idea is that, once again, as long as the projects under examination truly have something in common—that is, are truly digital libraries in more than just name only—the greater distance involved in an international comparison can provide even greater objectivity. Digital libraries in Budapest, as long as they really are digital libraries, should be different in significant ways from similar digital libraries in Berkeley, and the differences should be interesting for anyone from Berkeley wishing to transplant technology to Budapest or vice versa, and perhaps even for the Berkeley and Budapest developers wishing to improve their own locally available products and services.

If what emerges from an international comparison is an improved local definition, so much the better. It will be enough, though, for the present study, if the point is made simply but forcefully that international application will exert some special strains of its own on a technological development that so far has enjoyed untrammeled and explosive growth at home.

Getting online digital information—such as the Internet, the *WorldWideWeb* (W3), digital text, and imaging and econferencing—to *scale up* beyond national boundaries is an adventure fraught with its own special promises, challenges, and difficulties. "We're not in Kansas anymore, Toto," is the argument, generally. Just what this means, in terms of identifiable factors to consider in helping all of this to scale up, is the detail that the following aims to provide.

Digital libraries, finally, as one of the more user-oriented applications of the technology to have developed so far, presents an opportunity for looking at the international scale question through the eyes of users and may, therefore, be of great interest to those who want to reach users, anywhere, through any digital techniques.

NOTES

[1] Ryle, Gilbert, *The Concept of Mind*, New York: Barnes and Noble, c1949, 1967, p.16.

[2] Dewey, Melvil, *A Classification and Subject Index, for Cataloguing and Arranging the Books and Pamphlets of a Library*, Amherst, MA: Melvil Dewey, 1876; Otlet, Paul, *Traité de Documentation: le Livre sur le Livre, Théorie et Pratique*, Bruxelles: Editiones Mundaneum, 1934; Shera, Jesse H., *"The Compleat Librarian"; and Other Essays*, Cleveland: Press of Case Western Reserve University, 1971; Shera, Jesse H., *Documentation and the Organization of Knowledge*, Hamden, CT: Archon Books, 1966; Shera, Jesse H., *The Foundations of Education for Librarianship*, New York: Becker and Hayes, [1972]; Shera, Jesse H., *Introduction to Library Science: Basic Elements of Library Service*, Littleton, CO: Libraries Unlimited, 1976; Lancaster, F. W., *Toward Paperless Information Systems*, New York: Academic Press, 1978; Buckland, Michael K., *Library Services in Theory and Context*, New York: Pergamon Press, c1983; Buckland, Michael K., *Information and Information Systems*, New York: Greenwood Press, 1991; Buckland, Michael K., *Redesigning Library Services: a Manifesto*, Chicago: American Library Association, 1992.

[3] Snow, C. P., *The Two Cultures and the Scientific Revolution*, New York: Cambridge University Press, c1959, 1963, pp. 2–3.

[4] Snow, C. P., *The Two Cultures and the Scientific Revolution*, New York: Cambridge University Press, c1959, p. 17.

Part I: Setting the Stage

Chapter 1

The Internet goes public—a new story, online digital information

I N *cyberspace*, the online world, the new idea is that the general public—the consumer, the average user, the nonacademic and noncomputer scientist, the nonresearcher, the non-"geek"—is at last to have access to online digital information.

1.1 From the Internet testbed to digital commerce

Still only a few years ago, the idea of general public access to the Internet not only was unimaginable, it was illegal. *Acceptable use policies* governed Internet access, and most of the activity that has suddenly made online digital information so interesting and available to the general public—selling sex, entertainment, and anything commercial—was deemed *unacceptable*. The Internet still was an academic testbed, or, more specifically, a U.S. federal government-funded exercise, restricted to a number of U.S. university research sites, to develop a computer communications project designed originally for the U.S. Department of Defense.

Any such project, by virtue of it origins alone, is bound to be riddled with regulation, bureaucracy, and restriction. The Internet was so riddled. Still, in 1991, its exclusively academic users had to acknowledge a personal "acceptable use" responsibility not to use it to develop or purvey anything that even hinted at being commercial.

The change—that is, this *new story*—came quickly. The definitive history has yet to be written [1]. However, simplistically stated, what happened was that the academics petitioned the U.S. government for greater Internet capacity; the government pleaded poverty and went to the large commercial firms that had been providing indirect subsidies; and those firms replied that more money might be obtained but that perhaps the time had come for the applications to *go commercial.*

At the time, the U.S. political climate happened to be undergoing a strong swing toward procommercial and *small-government* stances. This swing is a periodic event in American politics. This particular movement had begun well after the initiation of the Internet as a *big-government* defense project. The U.S.-government decision makers then considered the Internet situation as ripe for the abandonment of government control and *acceptable use* and ready for an infusion of private-sector commercial, rather than government, money.

By 1992, then, in the United States, one could obtain an Internet account without being a member of the academic community that was supposedly testing it, although lip-service was still being paid to acceptable use policies and noncommercial use restrictions. By 1994, however, even these latter restrictions were gone; no one, then, signing up for an Internet account in the United States, bothered to observe the old policies and restrictions.

This transition was accomplished in true U.S. style; that is, these regulations simply withered from neglect—to the great confusion of Internet users in overseas nations, where written laws and regulations are somewhat more sacrosanct.

Progress toward general public access was rapid once the acceptable use policies barrier was broken. By 1994, commercial applications developers had developed interesting ideas for attracting the general public, including *graphical user interface* (GUI) techniques, *online chat* in various flavors, online games, and commercial selling techniques. At the same time, cost thresholds for necessary hardware, software, and systems were plunging through their well-known descent. The general user who needed to invest US$10,000, including elaborate training in arcane techniques, to *go online* in 1990 could get the same and more, with a much more user-friendly format, for $2000 only a few years later.

This hardware/software/systems cost descent has accelerated so significantly that the next step appears to be their virtual elimination from the market (the French use the term *banalisation*). In 1996, the firms that formerly produced all three are going bankrupt or getting out of the market, as their costs plunge to those of the $500 Internet-connected NC/Network Computer/Non-computer, their profit margins drop, and their use becomes literally marginal to the online services that are increasingly becoming the commercial market's greatest source of excitement, concern, and profit.

By 1995, the WorldWideWeb's user-friendly and graphically interesting interface, *Mosaic*, was in operation as *Netscape* and Mosaic's many other incarnations. Currently, the Internet has become a human cultural artifact growing so wildly that its growth curve alone is being studied on some university campuses as an example of sheer system growth in enormous proportions. Total Internet host counts expanded from 1,313,000 in 1993 to 2,217,000 in 1994—up 69%; to 4,852,000 in 1995—up 119%; to 9,472,000 in January of 1996—up 195%; and to over 12 million only six months later [2], with accompanying estimates of total users now ranging from 13 to 30 million and higher [3]. It has been said that some U.S. neighborhoods and certain small countries overseas now have more Internet accounts than they have users, and certainly some extrapolations of current growth curves that can be found in the popular press assume this as a given general global trend.

1.2 The French Minitel and digits for people— community networking

The U.S. Internet does not provide the only model for online digital information growth. France has pursued an online digital information development pattern that, while it has had some similarities with that pursued by the U.S. Internet, has developed basic differences that are particularly timely now in the era of general public access.

The French central government made a policy decision, during the late 1970s, to develop computerization and online digital information as a matter of national strategic policy. The French called the totality *informatisation*. For reasons such as national development and competition with the Germans, the

English, and the Americans, successive French administrations since the 1970s have deemed the development of online digital information to be crucial to the French national interest and, therefore, worthy of substantial central government participation, financial subsidy, and—what is perhaps more important in the French administrative context—bureaucratic priority [4].

Since the 1970s, informatisation has opened doors within the French national government that stay firmly closed to other issues and are generally hard to open in any national bureaucracy. French government agencies and subagencies have been increased—and in some cases created—and given money to spend for anything that would enhance French informatisation [5].

This degree of French governmental commitment to online digital information does have its analog, perhaps, in the private enterprise-fueled development that went into the U.S. Internet during the same period. The monetary amounts, difficult though they are to compute, might be comparable on a relative basis when the far greater size and economic resources of the United States are considered. The differences of approach could simply be due to differences in governmental philosophy; that is, the French favor central government participation, while the United States favors its private sector.

But there was one significant difference that has currently become very relevant. The French developed the *Minitel*, an online digital information service that was general public–oriented from its inception, at the same time as the Americans were pursuing their academic user–restricted, *acceptable use policy* Internet. The Minitel offered a business formula that is now viewed with great longing by commercial Internet developers due to its simple technologies: small, inexpensively produced access terminals that were given away to users; simplistic user interfaces and indexing software; and clean and easy-to-use central billing procedures for content providers. All this was designed to purvey basic commercial goods and services, from retail catalogs to library services, government information, the telephone book, and cinema, rail, and airline schedules and reservations.

For years, U.S. Internet developers, as well as some French Minitel developers, scoffed at the technological inferiority of the Minitel as compared to the Internet. The Minitel used old-fashioned TTY terminals and an eccentric v23bis standard, while the Internet was graduating to sophisticated screens and high-quality graphics; Minitel's 1,200 bps *in* and 75 bps *out* speeds (they designed it initially to suit a typical typist, who they thought never would type faster than 75 bps) could not compare, considering that the Internet's users were progressing through 2,400 bps and 4,800 bps and 9,600 bps to 14,400 bps and 28,800 bps speeds and beyond, and the Internet's backbone speeds were soaring to unimaginable heights. Minitel utilized straight and simplistic, hierarchical indexing, while the Internet developed complex Boolean-to-probabilistic search algorithms, capable of expanding and refining searching seemingly infinitely.

The Minitel has had to play technical catch-up. The French have had to make their standard fit the now omnipresent personal computer and to upgrade their telecommunication backbone to accommodate user speeds of at least 9,600 bps. They have invested heavily in ISDN development, which they call *Numéris*, and are trying hard to integrate this with Minitel system use. At last, as well, France has become a heavy Internet user itself. There were 137,217 Internet hosts in domain ".fr" at the beginning of 1996 [6], and gateway services have now been provided from one technology to the other to enable users to reach the Internet from the Minitel and vice versa [7].

But the Internet only just now is discovering the general public user, with whom the Minitel has been dealing closely for some time. And some, but not all, of the simplicities already offered by the technologically less-advanced Minitel are being found more attractive by this type of user than are the more complex and more expensive Internet approaches: Simple billing, simple indexing, inexpensive and simple end-user hardware and software are all very suddenly becoming interesting to Internet developers.

Internet developers are now trying to capture an enormous user market that is not only technically less sophisticated than the Internet's previous academic testers were, but that, crucially, is also not even interested in the technology. The Internet's new general public market— users who want to "drive the car" but are too busy to care, or simply do not care, about "how the car works"—is a hard sell. The Minitel has been serving such a market for many years, and many of its simplicities are designed precisely to cater to the needs of such a group of *un-interested users*.

1.3   The search for paradigms for general public access

The combination of the Minitel's low-technology, simplistic, minimalist strategy with the Internet's high-technology, complex, stretch-the-possibilities approach may or may not take place consciously as the current trend proceeds toward making online digital information generally available to the general public. Other than saving trouble, money, and duplication of effort, there is no reason why the Minitel might not develop Internet gateways, higher speeds and bandwidth, and more sophisticated graphics and indexing facilities or why the Internet might not develop increasing interoperability, simpler and more user-friendly applications, and more satisfactory commercial arrangements, without Internet developers officially consulting their opposite numbers at Minitel and vice versa.

This appears in fact to be the path under pursuit. The Minitel is upgrading technically as fast as it can. America Online and other commercial developers are simplifying complex Internet procedures, or at least hiding them, in order to reach the general public (and are being castigated for their highly successful efforts by Internet purists)—all seemingly without looking at the Minitel's simple indexing and its 20,000+ online commercial services. Oracle Corporation chairman Larry Ellison is pushing his inexpensive Internet box NC/Network Computer/Noncomputer [8], which threatens and promises to replace—with services—much of what the Internet knows today as user hardware and software, to the great consternation of the now-giant firms that have invested so heavily in the latter two and without regard to the continuing effective presence of over seven million simple little terminals on the Minitel.

Each side is aware of the other. Mutual consultation is to some extent unnecessary, to a certain extent illegal, and to a great extent inimical to the competitive nature of the general marketplace. The general trend may illustrate nothing more than *convergence*, that is, the coming together of technologies and the elimination of duplications, regardless of expensive duplication that might have occurred in their independent developments. U.S. and Western European information technologies may or may not converge, but in either case each may continue to develop in splendid isolation from the other.

But one question that might be asked is which of these development models may be pursued elsewhere, as India, Indonesia, Estonia, Thailand, Japan, and China go online? These places seem most likely simply to be overwhelmed, for now, by the current expansion of U.S. techniques, perhaps as modified in some part by Western European contributions in online digital information. However, it would be naive to assume that U.S. and Western European internet-working dominance will prevail forever and everywhere overseas.

Much of the world's wealth is already located in Asia—along with by far the greatest number of the world's potential consumers of everything, including online digital information—so it must be assumed that Asia will eventually want its say in online digital information's design and development. Which model will they choose? Which paradigm for the design and development of online digital information will they adopt?

Both the Internet and the Minitel began with substantial initial central government subsidy and control. The Internet's subsequent development was chaotic, however, and expensive. Specifically, the U.S. government directly controlled little of what it had subsidized, and Silicon Valley and other development centers in Texas, around Boston, and above all in the Washington, D.C., suburbs spawned great numbers of competing and continually self- and mutually bankrupting private firms that spent a great deal of money and duplicated significant efforts in inventing the Internet.

The Minitel, by contrast, at least appears to have been centrally developed and still to be centrally controlled and to be cleaner, neater, and less expensive. Which model will appeal more to a decision maker, inevitably in these cases a central government bureaucrat, looking for a local development model to transplant to Kuala Lumpur, Shanghai, or Singapore?

The common characteristic of online digital information's current era—in its Minitel or Internet incarnations—clearly is general public access, whatever the future development paradigm is to be, in Internet or Minitel countries or elsewhere. Online digital information is searching for ways of developing its use by general public users. This search may be ongoing, as it is for the Minitel, or it may be entirely new, as it is for the Internet. In either case, the dilemma posed for the system developer is how to cope with *un-interested users*, those users who no longer are interested in the systems or even in the idea of online digital information itself—users who don't have the time to learn, or just don't want to know, "how the car works" and simply want to "drive the car."

NOTES

[1] Quarterman, John S., "The History of the Internet and the Matrix," *Connexions, The Interoperability Report*, Vol. 9, No. 4, April 1995, p. 13. Quarterman's is the best effort that I have seen so far.

[2] Mark Lottor/Network Wizards, http://www.nw.com

[3] For the most careful analysis of total Internet users available (no one really knows), see John Quarterman at http://www.i-m.com/hyper/inet-marketing/archives/ 9503/0402.html, "200M Internet users by the year 2000 is actually a conservative estimate"; see also http://www.mids.org/mids/howbig.html .

[4] Cohen, Elie, *Le Colbertisme "High Tech": Economie des Télécom et du Grand Projet*, Paris: Hachette, c1992.

[5]   See Elie Cohen, supra; see also, Bar, François, *Configuring the Telecommunications Infrastructure for the Computer Age: the Economics of Network Control*, Berkeley: Berkeley Roundtable on the International Economy, University of California Berkeley, Institute of International Studies, c1990; Bar, François, "Télécoms: Seule la Flexibilité est Vraiment Stratégique," *Télécoms Magazine*, No. 3, Jan.–Feb. 1991.

[6]   Mark Lottor/Network Wizards, http://www.nw.com

[7]   Minitel, http://www.minitel.fr, telnet://minitel.fr, or voice telephone from North America to 1-800-MINITEL; Minitel-Internet "gateway" services (not true "gateways" in the technical sense, but they work for users) may be found on the Minitel at, for example (there are others), 3615INTERNET, 3616EMAIL, 3619USNET; the last is the U.S.-based Delphi service, now owned by Rupert Murdoch's News Corporation.

[8]   Oracle Corporation, http://www.us.oracle.com

Chapter 2

Digitization in libraries—an old story, information and libraries

2.1 Libraries, as places for public access to and use of information

The library side of the digital libraries equation is nothing new; and to libraries, the idea of general public access, which is so new to the Internet, is very old. As new as digital techniques are and as new to them, in some cases at least, as is the idea of providing access to the general public, the idea of providing library service to a public unacquainted with and perhaps even uninterested in its techniques is ancient.

They are rebuilding the Great Library of Alexandria [1]—whatever it precisely was and whomever it served [2]. Very long ago—for the Romans—the Alexandrian library served much of their world's recorded knowledge (their own and that transmitted from the Greek tradition), supposedly to a broad range of scholars. It is not known exactly who frequented the Great Library of Alexandria or what they used—time is an even better guardian of "borrowers' records" than a protective librarian. However, it is a safe assumption that the scholar who traveled to Alexandria to consult texts on a particular papyrus roll did not share its librarian's personal fascination for the technique of the roll's preparation and preservation, the system of its classification within the collection, and perhaps even the aesthetic beauty of its calligraphy. Users don't change that much over time. The scholar probably just wanted to read the thing.

Today, the modern version of the ancient Great Library of Alexandria will confront much the same situation as did its ancestor. Users now, like users then, will come from a very broad range of interests and backgrounds. Modern digital media and telecommunications access will ensure that this variety will be great. But the problem will remain the same.

The typical user of the modern Great Library of Alexandria will be as un-interested in most of that library's information storage and retrieval techniques as were the ancient scholars in the techniques of preparing and preserving papyri. Some will be interested; most will not. The modern library will have to serve both groups, and primarily the latter. There will be dial-in remote users of the new Great Library of Alexandria who will want to know how its Web servers are set up, but most will simply want to read some text, listen to some audio, and look at some pictures.

The philistine qualities of the users—their lack of appreciation for the inner workings and implicit beauties of the information storage and delivery systems that they use—have been the distress of some librarians for centuries. This has been so much the case, in fact, that the image of the librarian as the jealous, defensive guardian of the unappreciated systems and objects given her or him to guard has grown. From the keepers of the Alexandrine papyri to the protectors of medieval codices, librarians have been branded with a less than user-friendly image, as Umberto Eco, among others, gently lampoons them [3].

Yet, providing library service to the philistine user has been the primary charge of librarians for all this time. From readers who bent the papyri in ancient Alexandria to medieval French kings who insisted on borrowing books that were "on closed reserve" (the king got his book and never gave it back [4]) to modern-day high-school students armed with scissors and spray-paint cans and modern French presidents who give things away without permission [5], unappreciative users have been the continuing plague, and challenge, of librarians.

2.2 Library service as a paradigm for information

The same might be said, of course, for the distress and challenge of any specialist. The specific parallel being drawn here is between the librarian and the specialist digital media designer. The new challenges to the latter, that is, of serving the general public, are no different in kind from the challenges long provided librarians in serving a public that does not know or care much about library systems and books. But this might also be said of the client and the lawyer, the patient and the doctor, and the car mechanic and the driver. The challenge is common to any specialist who must deal with users who do not know "how the car works" but simply want to "drive the car."

It would be difficult though, for a number of reasons, to build a paradigm for online digital information service upon the delivery of mechanical services in car repair. Auto drivers are distressingly unconcerned with information, while information appears to be central to the concerns of both librarians and their users and digital systems designers and theirs. Doctors and their patients, likewise, have less concern for information than for outcomes. The mystification that characterizes most medical consultation is perhaps justified by the over-whelmingly greater importance of outcome over information (although it shouldn't permit the degree of mystic faith that many patients have and that many in the medical profession promote). As for lawyers and clients, the medical profession is not the only one that often banks more heavily on success-ful outcomes than on imparting full information.

But libraries and librarians throughout their professional history have been primarily concerned with information—its accuracy, its completeness, its ease of access and use, and its preservation. These have been library mandates that have sustained the library profession over many centuries. These are exactly the same mandates that are now being given to online digital information system designers. The parallel is close—closer than one drawn to the specialist/user relationship in any other profession's case.

So the idea offered here is that the similarity of the library/user relationship to that of the online digital information system and its user should be examined to suggest measures that might benefit both. Digital libraries appear to be under way. W3, the Internet generally, the Minitel, and vast numbers of stand-alone systems and academic workstation hard disks are filled with them—a few things that are already called digital libraries and many more involving libraries making increasing use of digital techniques. Some international digital libraries exam-ples are shown in the chapters that follow.

The presentation is aided greatly by recent changes in the status of librarians, with respect to the general online digital information effort. Digital techniques that originated in the minds and laboratories of mathematicians, electrical engineers, and computer scientists have now broadened their reach with the development of actual nonspecialist user applications. Among those "invited to the table" for this recent development have been librarians.

As the U.S. *National Science Foundation* (NSF) projects and other examples that follow bear witness, library techniques and experience have been found useful in organizing and presenting the massive bodies of data increasingly encompassed by digital libraries efforts. The NSF projects now include librarians. Librarians serve, increasingly, on digital information panels and boards and on policy- and standards-making committees at national and international levels. It becomes easier to find informed opinion on digital information activities seen from a library perspective, even if it is still difficult.

Although the general digital libraries effort may be ill-defined theoretically, considering that the term libraries is defined as loosely today as the term digital is defined closely, perhaps the common interest in serving an uninterested public might be the best place to look for common solutions to common problems.

Every multifaceted problem needs a common denominator. Those involved with the most technical aspects of online digital information's development initially perhaps did not need library and librarian contributions. As the technique grew, however, the common problem that emerged concerned how to design digital applications for use by the general public. Specialist public users did not need so much help, but the more general the user-public became, the less interested they became in the information storage and search and retrieval techniques. The phenomenon of the uninterested user emerged—of new concern, gradually, to the architects of the online digital information revolution as it had been to librarians for centuries and, consequentially, the common denominator of the increasingly joint efforts of both.

2.3 The disadvantages and advantages of a paradigm that has a history

There are disadvantages to allying a social construct as old as libraries with an engineering technique as new as digitization. The two have many differences. Comparative age and youth are one. The Great Library of Alexandria was said to have been burned by Julius Caesar, while digitization as thought of today has largely been invented within the lifetimes of most people now living. Libraries have had a longer time to learn—but also to make mistakes. Library communities that would like to contribute to online digital information development perhaps contain much accumulated deadwood from the past, while many digital technique and media developers are beginning, or at least they feel that they are beginning, entirely anew.

There are other differences. One is a technique that only now is spawning institutions; the other is an institution that is engaged in a desperate search for renewal of its technique. The latter is labor-intensive; the former is so much the opposite that it is increasingly blamed for "digitization downsizing" from labor economies that it supposedly creates. Libraries are associated so much with one, printed and textual, form of representation of information that they have to defend their role in respect to others, such as images [6]; while digital media are so general in their grasp of terrain that *multimedia* has become an all-encompassing buzzword, bearing almost no meaning (sound, light, music, video, audio, text, drawing, TV, video games, books, drawings, prints, and virtual reality games, all working together or independently on their own; there is perilously little in human entertainment and, loosely, communication, that is not subsumed under current definitions of multimedia).

Differences, however, can constitute advantages in the search for a paradigm [7]. It is easier to draw distinctive parallels, and to make comparisons, if the two things being compared are different. So long as there is something in common, the differences can be instructive for that common effort.

The compelling commonality between libraries and digital media, I suggest here, stems from the interest of both—new in the one case, ancient in the other—in getting information to the un-interested user. As long as and to the extent that this remains of interest to both, the differences between libraries and digital systems will simply enhance the value of comparisons that are drawn.

NOTES

[1]   Chen, Ching-Chih, "Bibliotheca Alexandrina Comes to Life Again After 2,000 Years: Is There a Place for New Information Technology?", *Microcomputers for Information Management*, Vol. 7, No. 1, Jan. 1990, p. 75.; also a personal communication on April 10, 1996 from Egyptian Consul Nasr in San Francisco.

[2]   http://www.perseus.tufts.edu/~ellen/alexandria/resources.html

[3]   Eco, Umberto, translated from the Italian by William Weaver, *The Name of the Rose*, San Diego: Harcourt Brace Jovanovich, c1983; see also Eco's very funny speech: Eco, Umberto, translated from Italian into French by Eliane Deschamps-Pria, *De Bibliotheca*, Caen: Echoppe, c1986.

[4]   Franklin, Alfred, *Précis de l'Histoire de la Bibliothèque du Roi, Aujourd'hui Bibliothèque Nationale*, 2nd ed., cor. et. très-augm., Paris: L. Willem, 1875.

[5]   Kessler, Jack, "EXTRA—The Korean Manuscripts Caper," *FYI France*, gopher://infolib.berkeley.edu_72- path: 3.Electronic Journals/6.FYI France/5.1995/10. September 29, 1993, ISSN 1071-5916.

[6]   Collard, Claude, Isabelle Giannattasio, and Michel Melot, *Les Images dans les Bibliothèques*, Paris: Editions du Cercle de la Librairie, 1995, ISBN 2765405778.

[7]   Kuhn, Thomas S., *The Structure of Scientific Revolutions*, 2nd ed., Chicago: University of Chicago Press, 1970.

Chapter 3

Incunabula—the development of digital libraries in the United States

MANY ASPECTS OF modern digital libraries development began in the United States. Much of the work that has formed the modern digital universe began in Canada, Europe, and elsewhere on its own or in conjunction with U.S. partners. Libraries, moreover, are older than the United States itself; Europeans had libraries when the United States was still largely forest, and Asians had libraries when forests covered Europe.

Still, digital libraries, as we now know them, owe much to a series of developments in a number of academic and research and development fields that took place in the United States primarily during the last three decades.

Histories of all of this sort of work might one day be written for any particular country, as the experience of each is somewhat different. A history of digital libraries development in the United States should have been written by now [1].

What follows is not a history but merely a historical sketch, intended only to give the reader some sense that a history in fact exists for online digital information and digital libraries. The inundation of detail involved at present, in any kind of digital learning or work, normally obscures this. People are so busy reading arcane computer manuals, mastering unnecessary keystroke commands, and grappling with completely unfamiliar conceptions of time and space that they have little time for context. The idea that important aspects of all of this existed before—that they themselves might have encountered some of this before and might use what they learned then in problems that they face today—becomes submerged in the detail and dazzle of the supposedly new technology.

It would be useful to remember, for example, that there have been libraries and information and users—and categorization and classification and user interface questions and search-and-retrieval and communication—for a very long time. There have been transitions in media in the past that, while they were not necessarily digital, were considered every bit as revolutionary and irreversible and inexorable, at the time, as is the supposed revolution in digital media that is taking place today.

Television, radio, telephony, the telegraph—even the printed book itself, the parchment page, and the codex format—each had its day in the sun, a day that accomplished many objectives but failed to achieve others that ultimately never happened. A little historical analysis, which we do not attempt here, might complement the comparative analysis that generally is being addressed in the present work.

This U.S. chapter, however, is presented somewhat historically. It at least suggests an immense effort by a vast number of people, most of whom inevitably will go unrecognized. The point is that digital libraries in the United States did not spring suddenly one day, fully clothed and armed, from the head of some lone brilliant researcher, from some MIT or Berkeley computer science laboratory, from a government agency, or from a commercial development house. This is the impression given, certainly to non-U.S. outsiders, by so much of the dazzling publicity that currently surrounds online digital information and the Internet.

Digital libraries instead developed in the United States over a very long period of time, building upon a vast array of efforts undertaken by a great variety of people. Perhaps no technical or social development of any significance has a simple beginning, and the development of digital libraries in the United States has been no exception—many different actors, in many different arenas, contributed.

3.1 Origins and pedigrees

Computer people invented, developed, and then largely perfected the sciences of storing and manipulating data electronically. Telecoms people patiently elaborated the elegant art of transmitting electronic data over telecommunications channels. Information scientists developed techniques of representing, storing, and retrieving meaningful information as electronic data.

Cyberneticians, social psychologists, government regulators, commercial entrepreneurs, economists, politicians, and graphic designers all played roles. Research scientists, hardware manufacturers, software and systems designers and developers, professors, graduate students, campus administrators, and even research and industrial park property developers were also involved.

Librarians, archivists, records departments, museums, and research collections were the traditional information gatherers, of every stripe, who shared a common twin concern for preserving and making accessible information stored on various different media.

The various stories that might be told about these different actors also are very old in the United States as they are elsewhere. Librarians, for example (and archivists and the other traditional media people), have carried their twin worries about information preservation and access on their shoulders for centuries.

Information scientists claim a pedigree that extends back to theoretical work done in the late 1940s [2], building on "content analysis" work developed during World War II [3], which grew in turn out of still earlier psychological and social analysis.

Telecommunications—the science and the art—has developed in the United States, as it has elsewhere, for well over a century. In the United States, credit is given to Guglielmo Marconi, Alexander Graham Bell, Thomas Edison, and Samuel F. B. Morse, among the earliest inventors and developers. But they themselves built on even earlier serious work—and much fiddling, dabbling, and occasional catastrophes—of phlogiston and electricity enthusiasts dating back to Benjamin Franklin and beyond.

Even computer science has a long history. All of the recent events and excitement about computing machines often obscures the fact that they now are decades old and that the first personal computers appeared in the U.S. commercial market twenty years ago, the first business mainframes thirty years ago, and the earliest electronic computational devices half a century ago.

Several generations of digital library workers have been born and have developed since the enormous ENIAC computer at the University of

Pennsylvania in 1946 [4] or the discovery of the first computer *bug*, a little moth, stuck to a circuit, by Grace Hopper in the Harvard Mark 1 during the early 1940s [5]. The perhaps apocryphal but often told tale of how mathematician John von Neumann first connected the binary on/off mechanisms of the human nerve synapse and the electric light switch, during an excited dinner with a brain surgeon, is supposed to have taken place during the 1930s. If one extends computer science back to Charles Babbage, Blaise Pascal, and certain Greeks, the history of this cutting-edge field has a pedigree as long as the others [6].

What was needed to create digital libraries out of all of this—out of library and communications and computer and other long-standing work—was a catalyst.

3.2 The 1970s in the United States

As of the 1970s, all of the eventual digital libraries players already were hard at work in the United States.

The minicomputer—a marketing package of features and capacities of the larger and more expensive mainframes and designed for less-expensive applications—had been developed and was beginning to be sold widely, even to small businesses.

The U.S. telecommunications infrastructure, which had long been a highly sophisticated and internetworked system of systems, experienced growth, consolidation, and evolution that eventually saw the 1984 breakup of the giant national monopoly, AT&T, and the development of the *BabyBells*. Information science was enjoying some of its most fruitful years of theory development, with pioneers like Gerard Salton [7] and the work of the newly christened *American Society for Information Science* (ASIS).

(ASIS changed its name from *American Documentation Institute*, on January 1, 1968, to reflect increased membership, interest, and activities in the *information explosion* of the 1960s and a conviction that information science at last had emerged as an "identifiable configuration of disciplines" [8]. The earlier Institute traced its founding back to 1937 [8].)

Libraries were among the earliest customers for the minicomputers, acquiring them, as businesses had, first for financial and accounting purposes and eventually for inventory control—*cataloging*, in the librarians' world—which was eventually to lead to *Online Public Access Catalogs* (OPACs), remote access, and online search and retrieval.

It was during the 1970s, as well, that the ideas of two researchers, Vinton Cerf and Robert Kahn—building upon defense-related work for the U.S. government's *Advanced Research Project Agency* (ARPA) of the 1960s—led to procedures that would permit digitized information of any type to be sent, safely, easily, and very quickly, over telecommunication channels. The eventual *Transmission Control Protocol/Internet Protocol* (TCP/IP) was to be the catalyst—the "glue" in the digital libraries parlance of a later generation [9]—that would meld together the various different activities described here to produce digital libraries on the Internet.

3.3 The 1980s in the United States

The 1980s saw a revolution in the computer science field as great as that of the AT&T breakup that shook telecommunications during the same period. Another computer marketing package—the *personal* computer, this one smaller and still cheaper than the minicomputer of the 1970s—was introduced and immediately took hold, this time among ever-broadening computer markets that, for the first time, included general consumers.

By the 1980s, information science had progressed to the point where sophisticated information storage and search and retrieval systems were in operation. In libraries, these systems took the form of enormous and growing OPACs, some already equipped with public access and even with the development of remote dial-in access by general public users.

Traditional-media libraries' use of digital systems for cataloging became great during the 1980s. New methods for sharing bibliographic records were developed that used the TCP/IP protocols developed originally by Cerf and Kahn and other telecommunications techniques for linking different remote systems together.

Regional and national consortia had formed, such as the *Ohio Colleges Library Consortium* (OCLC) [10], the *Colorado Association of Research Libraries* (CARL) [11], and the *Research Libraries Group* (RLG)[12], to pool resources and avoid duplication of effort, much as time-sharing and other computer utilities had done for businesses. Tape-loading procedures gradually gave way to telecommunications, in the TCP/IP case using the NSF's supercomputer and research connection backbone, the *Internet*.

Traditional-media libraries were not the only users of telecommunications techniques during the 1980s, of course. The *database*, one of the triumvirate—

with *word processing* and particularly the *spreadsheet*—of basic computing applications that were achieving popularity, was proliferating in nontraditional media libraries as well. Research scientists, including computer scientists, were assembling very large collections of data, realizing the opportunity offered by computers to comb through large data sets in ways and with speeds never before possible.

Businesses and government agencies were gathering and preserving large quantities of data for much the same reason. These databases were called libraries, particularly when there were databases of databases, and sometimes databases of databases of databases. Within the U.S. government and on research-oriented academic campuses or in research-and-development commercial firms, huge agglomerations of data began to be assembled. Very rarely were all equipped with underlying organizational structure and search-and-retrieval engines that would be adequate to handle the tasks imposed by the even more giant, complex, and public access services that they very shortly were to become.

All of this was libraries, and all of it was digital. Digital libraries were born in the United States in the 1980s, out of a congeries of originally disassociated efforts, all of which appeared to lead in a similar digital and libraries direction. The key term that emerged toward the end of the decade was *convergence*. Various digital techniques, hitherto considered dissimilar and unassociated, were seen by then to be *converging* upon common applications goals; a symptom of the maturing of the technology, the effort to establish digital libraries was to become one of these convergence goals.

3.4 The 1990s in the United States

By the early 1990s, the term digital libraries itself had begun to emerge.

Digital libraries were both actively under construction and already in intensive use by traditional-media libraries by the beginning of the 1990s. Many thousands of individual libraries' catalogs already contained records for vast portions of their institution's modern collections, with *recon/retrospective conversion* projects under way in many places to construct digital records for the remaining older items.

Cooperative *union* cataloging efforts, which combined the records of several locations or institutions into a single database, such as the University of California's multicampus MELVYL system [13] or Harvard University's

HOLLIS [14], already contained many millions of bibliographic records. Regional and national efforts, including the *Ohio College Library Consortium* (later renamed the *Online Computer Library Center*) (OCLC) and (RLG), were developing records counts in the tens of millions.

By the early 1990s, the Internet had found common acceptance in the traditional-media library community's digital libraries efforts. The use of tapes, for both loading and output—which had been the rule for large jobs during the 1970s and even the 1980s—was increasingly being abandoned in favor of online and particularly Internet access. Internet use became more and more the practice, not only for those maintaining databases but for the public wishing to reach and use them as well.

The addition to library OPACs of ancillary services was a step further, made during the early 1990s, in the direction of the full digital libraries picture. Services other than cataloging—other than the old inventory control function long performed by traditional-media libraries—were developed either within the traditional library itself, or outside elsewhere in the institution of which the library was a part, or, increasingly, even outside the larger institution, in the growing general information market.

Early additions to the OPACs were composed largely of general library information, such as access hours, addresses, telephone numbers, and borrowing policy information. Gradually other non-library-specific campus information was added, such as campus telephone directories, campus calendars, job postings, and even student course catalogs.

The final step was taken when the library systems went off-campus, finding and loading outside information resources deemed useful to campus communities, including off-campus databases, academic and commercial publishers' offerings, and indexing and abstracting services of various types. As Internet use became more accepted and more popular during the 1990s, libraries' own digital libraries implementation of its capacities increased.

In their first ventures off-campus, library systems merely acquired data to load. Gradually, though, more imaginative systems provided gateway connections to their users to reach and use the off-campus systems themselves. Protocols were designed that enabled users familiar with a single system to conduct searches using familiar command structures in the remote systems. When the WorldWideWeb finally arrived—with the bright colors, hypertext format, and immense user-appeal of its Mosaic and other graphical user interfaces—the library community was prepared. They redesigned the access to multiple remote services, which they already were building, as WorldWideWeb *links*.

The database efforts assembled by those not originally a part of the traditional-media library community have followed this same general pattern in the 1990s in the United States. Many large science, government, and business databases that were reached and used originally only on mainframes, then via minis, and then via networked and increasingly powerful personal computers and workstations also took advantage of 1990s developments in interconnectivity and interoperability. Like library services, other large database efforts developed connections to other databases and services within the firm or institution, progressing from tape-loading of outside resources to providing online gateways to establishing graphically appealing WorldWideWeb links.

Where both the digital libraries assembled by libraries and the digital libraries assembled by others are today in the United States is one of the great and exciting unknowns of the digital revolution. References to the term digital libraries abound in online conversation. Indexes, such as the WorldWideWeb's Altavista [15], list thousands of occurrences of the term. These refer to a vast range of activity, from casual online email discussions to enormous, formal, institutionalized database and service efforts. Both these numbers, and the variety of efforts that they describe, are increasing. The effort to differentiate and define amid all this activity is an undertaking of which this book is a part.

Much of the cutting edge of the digital revolution now resides with digital libraries. Digital libraries have positioned themselves to absorb and take advantage of every new development, whether that development stems from the efforts of computer science, telecommunications, information science, or libraries themselves.

This is so much the case, in fact, that the danger no longer is that digital libraries will be behind in their technological progress but so much ahead as to lose sight of some of the fundamental reasons for having embarked on the development in the first place and to lose touch with some of the reasons for which and clients for whom they in fact exist.

3.5 Roots

Along the way, for example, at least two fundamental changes have occurred in what digital libraries thought they were doing at their origins.

3.5.1 Bibliographic records versus fulltext

Libraries, like other organizations, automated in the United States during the 1960s and 1970s to bring computers into the accounting department. At that time, most people thought the single function of computers was to compute. Computers calculated numbers. The greatest marketing step that guaranteed the broad acceptance of the personal computer during the 1980s, for example, paving the way for the popular acceptance of word processing and database management and other PC-based applications, was the Lotus Corporation's introduction of the numbers calculation and "what if scenario" capacities of the spreadsheet.

The computing application that really caught on in libraries, really attracted the eye of users and administrators, and into which most U.S. library computing funds eventually would be poured, was the database application of inventory control, or cataloging. Traditional librarianship was, in business terms, an inventory-heavy industry. The collection, which consisted of the accumulated mass of books, periodicals, and other things, was the largest library asset and, next to personnel, the most difficult to manage.

In addition, libraries, unlike businesses, did not have the luxury of trimming inventory. Where a retail merchant might minimize inventory storage and management costs simply by discounting and selling slow-moving inventory, the same could not be done easily by a librarian with the books; librarians' consciences and the protesting howls of users normally prevented effective *deaccessioning* of little-used books, at least in any quantity sufficient to salve a librarian's inventory headaches. Enormous library book inventories—the dead stock along with the live stock—remained in the book stacks and grew enormously and inexorably in volume and in cost of organization and management. Computer databases used for library inventory control assisted greatly in coping with this situation.

However, the advent of the OPAC complicated this picture for U.S. libraries greatly in another way. Once public users were able to see the inventory records, libraries experienced an explosion in user access demand that never could have been met by traditional paper card catalog techniques. Greater visibility meant greater use, at least of the cataloging and sometimes of the collection. In some cases, user traffic to the library increased, at least initially. In all cases, remote access eventually enabled users to do great amounts of research without undertaking the time-consuming and often prohibitive trip to the library building to consult the card catalog.

Few library buildings and card catalogs could have been conceived, much less constructed, that might have accommodated the volumes of user searching logged during the 1990s. The University of California's MELVYL service logged over one million user sessions during May 1996—over 180,000 user sessions that month just for the UC Davis campus alone [16]. This traffic volume would have dog-eared the catalog cards badly and produced unacceptable waiting lines for reference desks and restrooms, had all those users shown up at library buildings in person.

These library catalog databases, however, were databases that contained bibliographic records. They were literally digitized versions of the paper card catalogs that they were replacing. There were internal links, immense standardization efforts, and various other improvements that made the online catalog database in many ways far superior to the paper card catalog that it has now effectively replaced in U.S. libraries. However, it was still a catalog and, crucially, the information that it contained was only bibliographic, that is, an abbreviation or, rather, primarily a description of only the container of the information being sought by the user.

One irony of the development of digital libraries, then—for the traditional media libraries that themselves have been active in this development in the United States—has been that digital fulltext increasingly has become available. The irony involved is the immense investment that the library community has made in bibliographic description, both traditionally and as carried over into digital libraries, an investment that is somewhat at odds with digital fulltext.

Once in the digital environment, libraries encounter difficulties with traditional bibliographic description due to its inadequacy for describing new digital media formats that are highly changeable in nature and its irrelevancy for users who are less and less concerned with the medium being described. Increasingly, the books do not matter; digital information is being freed from structures that hitherto have hindered but to some extent also have defined and contained text—books, and textual ordering and restrictions of various types, break down in digital libraries, and all that users often have left is the text. This poses problems for librarians trained only in traditional bibliographic description and for library systems built around simply describing books; specifically, there is precious little left to describe using traditional bibliographic methods if there no longer is a book.

This may, however, be a temporary phenomenon. During the *Age of Incunabula*, the period just after Gutenberg's invention, printers experimented with new formats and methods that even then caused a special kind of bibliographic chaos. There was no pagination, no title pages, and no orthographic regularity, and there were basic presentation approaches that were inconsistent and that contradicted each other wildly. The post-Gutenberg Age of Incunabula contained all of these; and the chaos that it presented has provided ample material for intensive bibliographic and historical scholarship for centuries [17].

The present digital age is not unlike that predecessor Age of Incunabula. Digital libraries—which grapple with text that sometimes is or is not in books, sometimes contains images and even sound, jumps back and forth among any and all of these unpredictably, and always appears in various and conflicting formats—might best be viewed as a recurrence of the chaotic but ultimately highly productive ferment of the printed book's own Age of Incunabula.

It might be useful to observe, then, that the Age of Incunabula eventually produced standardization and quality control in print publishing that endured for several centuries. The same may happen with digital media, particularly with fulltext. The current decade is going through a flurry of such activity in developments such as *Standard Generalized Markup Language* (SGML), *Hyper Text Markup Language* (HTML), *Text Encoding Initiative* (TEI), Unicode, and even a *Virtual Reality Markup Language* (VRML), all of which are designed to provide standardization and quality control in online digital information in the decades to follow.

For now, though, the problems and confusion in the fulltext area are many. Library efforts are understandably perplexed at the daunting prospect of providing user access to such an amorphous, volatile, and, for now, unstructured body of material and information.

3.5.2 Multimedia

Fulltext itself, moreover, currently is deemed but a small part of a much larger digital phenomenon. Into the pot containing text and all of its problems—including bibliographic description, fulltext, the structure of same and the lack thereof, multilingual access and the difficulties of non-Latin character sets, and problems of versioning and of the general malleability of digital text—are now being dumped scores of other non-text-based digital techniques and problems, all masquerading under the supposedly general name of multimedia.

A popular saying in academia has it that, said of a particular field of study, "If it's everything, then maybe it's nothing." The term multimedia, in the immediate digital libraries context, is a term said to subsume text—both bibliographic description and fulltext—and images, sound, and anything else that can be digitized. The difficulty with the definition is that increasingly nearly anything, it seems, now can be digitized and made available to users.

Digital library files, archives, and services are being built that offer information, stimulation, and simply entertainment to people in so many different ways that simply to call the totality multimedia increasingly begs the question of what multimedia really is. The term might describe everything that the current digital revolution is producing. But it also might describe, and has been used to describe, any combination of media from performance art to grand opera to the ballet of Louis XIV, to printed books containing pop-up art and images, to illuminated manuscripts and the written transcription of oral traditions of the Homeric poets. If multimedia is everything, then truly perhaps it is nothing—although it may have been this for a very long time.

The simple use of the term, however, indicates at least an awareness of some sort of change that is occurring in the way in which information is being perceived and used. An awareness that new digital media formats might be amenable to the combination of a number of traditional forms of expressions, forms that previously have been used separately, would not be the smallest contribution of the current use of the multimedia term.

At least, then, this combinatorial sense of the multimedia term is causing a significant part of the digital libraries revolution. Traditional printed book libraries once loosened a bit to admit departments of *periodicals,* prints and drawings, and in some cases even medallions (France's Bibliothèque Nationale has found room for all of these for a long time) just as, long ago, they allowed printed books into the spaces reserved previously for handwritten and illuminated manuscripts. Libraries now must accommodate video, audio, CD-ROM, and, increasingly, the Internet's WorldWideWeb access and other techniques that combine functional aspects of all of these.

Keeping up with all of this is a challenge. Traditional print libraries in the United States that are bravely trying to do so are confronting all sorts of teething problems, from bitter contests for space allocation to encounters between elderly patrons of the print collections and purple-haired and body-pierced teenagers monopolizing library WorldWideWeb terminals [18].

The totality constitutes a change. What change, precisely, remains to be seen. It seems sufficient to observe for now, though, that the change—to digital online fulltext, to multimedia, to other digital innovations—is not one easily foreseen by the original developers of U.S. digital libraries.

3.6 Summary

Digital libraries in the United States, therefore, developed, like any other significant social phenomenon, from a combination of many different efforts, originating in apparently disparate undertakings but all of which converged eventually upon a common goal.

Two agents worked as catalysts in engineering this convergence. The first undoubtedly was digital technique. Despite its perhaps ancient origins, or at least its development over a period of fifty years, the idea that all sorts of information, be they textual, image, sound, or combinations thereof, might be represented simply by recorded binary zeros and ones really took off in development work in the United States during the 1970s and 1980s. The pure theory long antedated this period. But practical applications began really developing during this time, as the broad implications of digital information technique and their possibilities began to be realized.

The second catalyst, which arrived about a decade later during the late 1980s and the early 1990s, was the expansion of digital techniques to reach the general user. IBM's marketing of the original *personal computer* (PC) initially led the way, along with the development of the word processing/spreadsheet/database triumvirate of user-friendly software applications, the introduction of Apple's computer products and style, and finally access to the Internet, Mosaic, and the WorldWideWeb by the general public.

The combined force of these public-access developments has altered the thrust of digital libraries developments in ways probably unforeseen by the contractors who developed packet-switching techniques for the U.S. Defense Department during the 1960s and certainly unforeseen by the engineers who tinkered with giant vacuum tube–equipped mainframes during the 1950s and the 1940s.

3.7 Implications

Beyond general public access, then, lies the world. The international expansion of online digital information techniques is accompanying the expansion to general public access and is somewhat its logical although highly complex extension. Just as, within the United States itself, the expansion of the Internet to general public users is bringing in all sorts of new and interesting problems to the hitherto hermetically sealed Internet testbed development environment, so too, outside the United States, the Internet's international expansion is prompting unique problems of its own.

Both sets of problems—that is, those of reaching the general public and those of reaching international users—are dramatically illustrated in a consideration of the digital libraries application of digital information techniques. Questions of general public access within the United States are complex and the subject of a separate book or of an ongoing series of same. The question taken up here instead is the second, more general, and somewhat more removed query: whether and to what extent the digital libraries techniques, which in large partly evolved in the United States as just suggested, will scale up in the current flood of international applications? The chapters that follow describe a variety of such experiences developing in different nations. The reader will see that the answer to the question, like most things about digital libraries and online digital information, is complex.

NOTES

[1] Several not-so-careful attempts at recording the Internet's history have been made in journal articles. One careful effort is found in Quarterman, John S., "The History of the Internet and the Matrix," *Connexions, The Interoperability Report,* Vol. 9, No. 4, April 1995, p. 13; A large collection of W3 sites—some good, some not—devoted to pursuing Internet/computer history may be found at http://www.yahoo.com/Computers_and_Internet/History/.

[2] Shannon, Claude Elwood, *The Mathematical Theory of Communication,* Urbana: University of Illinois Press, 1949.

[3] Lasswell, Harold D., *Propaganda Technique in the World War,* New York: Alfred A. Knopf, 1927; Lasswell, Harold D., Nathan Leites, and associates, *Language of Politics; Studies in Quantitative Semantics,* New York: G. W. Stewart, 1949; Lasswell, Harold D., *The Analysis of Political Behaviour; an Empirical Approach,* New York: Oxford University Press, 1947.

[4] ENIAC 50th Anniversary Celebration, http://www.seas.upenn.edu/~museum/history.html .

[5] Editors of Time-Life Books, *Understanding Computers—Software,* Alexandria, VA : Time-Life Books, c1985, p. 17 (complete with pictures of both Ms. Hopper and the famous moth).

[6] The University of Pennsylvania's history of computing online service, http://fx.comm.upenn.edu/pennprintout/html/v12/4/abacus.html.

[7] Salton, Gerard, *Information Storage and Retrieval,* Cambridge, MA: Computation Laboratory, Harvard University, 1964; Salton, Gerard, *On the Development of Information Science,* Ithaca, NY: Cornell University, Computer Science Dept., 1972.

[8] The American Society for Information Science, http://www.asis.org/AboutASIS/the-society.html.

[9] The Stanford NSF Digital Library Project, http://Mjosa.Stanford.EDU:80/diglib/pub/abstract.html; see also Chapter 14.

[10] The Online Computer Library Center, Inc., formerly the Ohio College Library Consortium, http://www.oclc.org.

[11] Colorado Alliance of Research Libraries, now a Knight-Ridder company, http://www.carl.org.

[12] The Research Libraries Group, Inc., http://www.rlg.org.

[13] The University of California's MELVYL system, telnet://melvyl.ucop.edu.

[14] Harvard University's HOLLIS system, telnet://hollis.harvard.edu.

[15] Digital Equipment Co.'s AltaVista W3 service, http://www.altavista.digital.com.

[16] The University of California's MELVYL system, telnet://melvyl.ucop.edu; enter SHO MONTHLY STATS.

[17] One of the best, among a very broad-based and distinguished literature on the subject, is Febvre, Lucien et Henri-Jean Martin avec le concours de Anne Basanoff [et al.], *L'Apparition du Livre*, Paris: Editions A. Michel, 1958; Febvre, Lucien, and Henri-Jean Martin, translated by David Gerard ; edited by Geoffrey Nowell-Smith and David Wootton, *The Coming of the Book: the Impact of Printing 1450–1800* [New ed.], London: N.L.B., 1976.

[18] Kessler, Jack, "Libraries—to Internet or not to Internet?", *PACS-L econference*, pacs-l@uhupvm1.uh.edu, May 7, 1996; see also PACS-L archive, telnet://a.cni.org.

Part II: Specifics—national

THE ATTEMPT BEING made here is to reconcile the apparently common concern of two professions—that is, the very new one of online digital information and the very old one of librarianship—in the process of helping information users. The approach is inductive and international, looking at several examples, from several widely scattered nations, of things that either have been called or might be considered to be digital libraries and discussing common elements that these examples exhibit.

A note about nations and cyberspace categories in general

The choice of the *nation-state* as a unit to use in examining the vast assortment of international factors to consider in digital libraries development is arbitrary. Entities like France, Vietnam, China are somewhat fictional, as additional examples like Europe, Lesotho, or Singapore perhaps illustrate: A wide range of shapes and sizes and characteristics as well as an immense range of histories, cultures, and claims to political viability are represented in any list of nation-states.

Comparing France to the United States is difficult enough. Beyond obvious size, location, economic, and social differences, each nation may be said to be either much younger or much older than the other, and each might claim more or less of various relevant historical, cultural, and educational traditions. How much harder, then, is a comparison drawn between Mexico and India or between other nations that are even less similar to one another.

So the intention here is not to suggest any direct comparisons among digital libraries based on physical presence in a given nation-state. The nation-state simply is a convenient boundary that represents the least restrictive alternative in a search for some sort of comparative criteria.

Furthermore, in some cases, nation-state boundaries and definitions change repidly. The city of Lyon, France now calls itself a pôle Européen and, for some purposes, claims to have more in common with Frankfurt and Milan than it does with France and than either of the latter two do with Germany or Italy. Hong Kong, which is an anomalous city/nation-state to begin with and which plays a significant role in digital libraries development, is in the process of a radical change of its nation-state status at the moment. The identification of any activity in the former USSR or Yugoslavia with any particular national boundary is, for the time being, suspect.

The differences among national digital libraries approaches, however, are the important things here. The malleability of nation-state boundaries merely accentuates and increases the differences; national neighbors most often strive to be different. If this study were a search for similarity, there might be more of a problem in relying on current national boundaries. Similarities between Chechnyan and Sri Lankan digital libraries might disappear quickly with the political disappearance of Chechnya and Sri Lanka.

The differences, however, would remain. They might, in fact, become a little greater as formerly small and international projects become integrated into larger and perhaps more strongly defined national efforts. A small but independent country like Sri Lanka, for example, might feel very comfortable in a large international consortium, cooperating with other members in order to share and obtain joint benefits, as small countries often do. But a Sri Lanka incorporated at some point into a larger Indian neighbor would be more subject to that larger country's status and role; larger countries are not known so well for flexibility in international consortia and political arenas as smaller countries are. The smaller actor normally has more to lose from rigidity.

So differences among digital libraries efforts might increase as small national efforts merge into larger efforts; just so, though, they also might decrease, as the political Balkanization so much in vogue in Europe now takes hold more firmly and spreads, and larger national digital libraries efforts break up into smaller efforts. It is hard to tell where, in balance, current political consolidation and Balkanization trends will end up, but both can affect the course of digital libraries development.

Furthermore, cyberspace is an area that until now has developed somewhat innocently of the existence of any political boundaries at all. These boundaries are being discovered, certainly as the Internet "goes international." Recent controversies pitting German sensitivities to pornography and pseudo-Nazis against U.S. free speech ideals have created an initial international skirmish in what promises to become a long battle [1].

There are a few, still, who feel fervently that information that "wants to be free" inevitably will be so, in other nations as it supposedly is in the nation in which it was created. There are far more, and these numbers are increasing, who are searching for means of control, both of information coming from abroad and of information being generated at home.

In the international case, despite the uncertainties and malleability of nation-state definitions and boundaries and despite much progress and a certain amount of wishful thinking in international relations, these things still are seen in terms of nation-states: French applications of techniques designed in Germany, Chinese efforts to control information generated in Japan, Singapore's efforts at information infrastructure compared with those of Finland, whatever nonnational links might exist or be forged between Bangalore and Kobe or Silicon Valley and Sophia Antipolis or an online bulletin board in Savoie and its user-base in the outside cyberspace world.

What follows, then, is in many senses an arbitrary choice of current digital libraries experiments. The grouping by nation-states is not the least arbitrary factor. The inclusion of an effort as a library is based on the loosely defined congeries of library characteristics suggested earlier here, plus the fact, in some but not all cases, simply that its creators call it a library.

The methodology is one adopted in the absence of a better one. If there is little agreement at a national level as to what constitutes a library, there is even less internationally; intrinsic definitions fail all round. But definitions themselves are derived from usage and from users. When James A. H. Murray compiled the *Oxford English Dictionary,* he looked at how the words were used, not just at other dictionaries [2].

Here, in the same spirit, what is hoped at most to be a beginning compilation of international digital libraries efforts is presented. This book and its readers must undertake the task of distilling what these efforts have in common, perhaps eventually arriving at a satisfactory, one-size-fits-all definition of digital libraries.

The most that might be said for the choice presented in what follows is that, by the list's end, if it has illustrated a few interesting international differences among essentially similar digital libraries efforts, it will have achieved its purpose.

NOTES

[1] The Germany/Compuserve/hate-group incident was widely reported throughout the world. It is perhaps most fascinating to see it discussed on a Thailand-based (Suranaree University of Technology) W3 server at http://wtech.technopolis.or.th/news/ia/latest.html.

[2] Murray, K. M. Elisabeth, *Caught in the Web of Words: James A. H. Murray and the Oxford English Dictionary*, New Haven: Yale University Press, 1977.

Chapter 4

France—flexible centralization

FRANCE WAS HOME TO 137,217 Internet hosts as of January 1996: one Internet host per 422 French people (per Network Wizards, http://www.nw.com, and CIA World FactBook 1995, http://www. odci.gov/cia/publications/95fact/index.html).

The idea of library in France has a long and special history. The French record with their *bibliothèques* is not only political but is intimately interrelated with the historical development of the French monarchy and the political viability of the French state [1].

Some of the oldest and still often repeated stories of the French Bibliothèque Nationale concern a medieval invasion of France by the English and the seizure and dispersal of the collected books by the invaders. In most cases, modern French book collections trace their existence to political upheaval, such as to Viking invasions and the flight of manuscripts from one monastic "armarius"/bookchest to another, to threatened and real burning at the hands of some faction during the Wars of Religion, or to liberations of First and Second Estate collections by the Third during the Revolution.

This political history, one might say political and national and generally governance-oriented history, is still very much in mind among the modern French. Provincial library collections jealously guard their independence of Paris, remembering the political dangers in the capital from which their collections were spared by having been sequestered in the provinces during the Revolution. In Paris itself, decisions that might never be made in the provinces are made and executed with alacrity. For example, Parisians are moving one of the world's largest libraries across the city in 1996 as a result of a policy being executed only eight years after it was first suggested. Such speed on such a major project rarely is found in other national capitals elsewhere in the world, much less in a French provincial government center.

As with book libraries, so with online services and other things in France, one always must be aware of an active political component, such as the active involvement of government and the governors and not just of the usual political process. Moreover, in France, the central government exerts a strong and direct control. An online bulletin board service physically located on a mountain top in Haute-Savoie has much to be concerned about in the government debate and policy making in Paris. That such central government policies have been flexible enough to permit and in fact to promote much of the digital libraries activity described in what follows does not suggest that French developments in this area have been any less centrally controlled or any less political.

The Bibliothèque Publique d'Information

The Bibliothèque Publique d'Information (BPI) offers general purpose, central city, general public access digital libraries service. It is located at the Centre Georges Pompidou, in the center of Paris, and was founded in 1977 with a mandate to expand French library services in a nontraditional way. Its architecture alone was revolutionary. But even more revolutionary were its open access, overt appeal to the general public, and commitment from its beginnings to nontraditional information media. The BPI went online early on the Minitel at 3615BPI

**Bibliothèque
publique d'information**

- 3615 BPI ———————————————————-

1 Recherche de documents

2 Manifestations de la B.P.I.

3 Accès à la B.P.I.

4 Horaires

5 Services particuliers

6 Comment mieux utiliser les
  resources de la B.P.I.

and on the Internet: at telnet://terminus.bpi.fr:2300—

164 BIBLIOTHEQUE GENERALE - CATALOGUE GEAC - INTRODUCTION

BONJOUR

VOUS ETES DANS LE CATALOGUE

DE LA

BIBLIOTHEQUE PUBLIQUE D INFORMATION

Today it has an established online presence, linking its numerous services, on W3 at http://www.bpi.fr (Figure 4.1).

The first thing that any user notices upon connecting to the BPI now via its service on W3 is the inline image of the enormous, high-technology barnlike, very unlibrary-like interior of this now very popular Paris library.

The second thing that a foreign user notices, however, is that an English-language version of the BPI's online access is available via a link that is tucked in immediately after the initial image. An American particularly notices this because one does not find French or, for that matter, any non-American-English abilities appearing on American libraries' online services at all, much less as an initial feature. A first thought is that France, which is known so well for its jingoistic approach to language, seems to be an unlikely candidate for such linguistic flexibility; yet the link exists, and choosing it leads to a very good rendering of the main library entry point, thus accessible to foreign English language users.

A third initially noticeable feature of the BPI online W3 service is the variety of resources that it offers in addition to that which an online user normally seeks in consulting a library. A traditional library contains printed books and their bibliographic records—the initial entry point for most users is the catalog of these records. Yet the BPI features many other resources on its opening online screens. There is a general description of the BPI itself (how many library users have read books in a library for years without knowing much about the library itself?). There are announcements, a calendar of events, lists of other libraries in France and elsewhere—with live links to them—BPI publications lists, and an online images database.

Figure 4.1   The BPI—a truly "public" French library. © 1996 Netscape
Communications Corporation.

Most of these resources and announcements have been presented by
printed book libraries in the past, but in a service ancillary to their basic
occupation of providing the books. These extra services were items posted on
thumbtack-filled bulletin boards at which users at best glanced as they waited
for their books. One wonders whether with increased online usage the tables
might be turned, and the "community bulletin board" library function will
become more of a primary digital libraries activity, taking precedence over an
increasingly ancillary function of providing access to the old printed book
collection?

The BPI online library catalog, finally, also is available, that is, the bibliographic records of the printed books and other documents in the collection. For
this, by contrast to the BPI W3 page, a foreign user notices initially a lack of
non-French access. The screens obtained via the telnet link for the catalog do
not resemble the screens obtained on the W3 service or on other telnet-available

library catalogs. There is a similar library logic to the command structure that a user must follow to find an item such as the familiar title (TIT), author (AUT), author-title (A-T) typology. But it is clear that the exact procedures, and the format of the bibliographic records thereby obtained, are unique, perhaps to France and perhaps to this BPI institution alone.

So, by contrast to the immense standardization of its initial W3 access (so much of the WorldWideWeb appears to a user still to be standard, if only because of the continuing domination of the single Mosaic/Netscape browser), the BPI catalog access, with its specialized vocabulary, command structure, and interface, appears positively eccentric to a foreign user.

Institut National de l'Information Scientifique et Technique

The Institut National de l'Information Scientifique et Technique (INIST) offers PASCAL/FRANCIS, a leading example of the stand-alone database.

Like the science establishments in other countries, the French scientific community was an early user of online digital information. Researchers associated with the giant Centre National de la Recherche Scientifique (CNRS) have had access to most digital technology as it has developed and evolved in France and elsewhere. Traditional library functions have been among those developed in French scientific online digital information. The Institut National de l'Information Scientifique et Technique (INIST) was established in 1988—building upon a precursor that had been established in 1970—to coordinate these French science information activities.

An initial view of the INIST W3 service (Figure 4.2) shows the immense range of digital information and services that it provides online, including descriptions of pan-European cooperative research projects in the sciences, thesis and general gray literature bibliography and publication, documentation collections (periodicals, scientific reports, conference proceedings), document delivery and translation and research services, newsletters, and online conferencing.

Among the various INIST projects has been the digitization of the large citation and abstract service provided since the World War II by the printed series Bulletin Signalétique, rechristened for its digital and online incarnation as PASCAL (sciences) and FRANCIS (humanities). These contain a combined total of over 13 million citations, with multilingual searching and abstracts.

via W3 to http://www.inist.fr

Bibliothèque Municipale de Lyon

The Bibliothèque Municipale de Lyon is a *local* French state library effort.

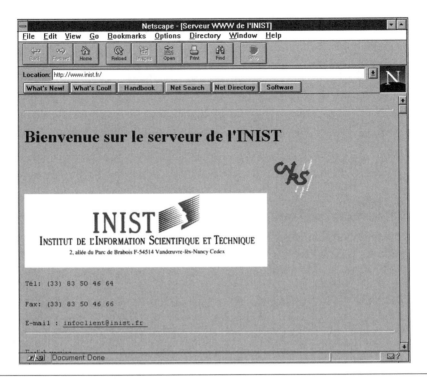

Figure 4.2   INIST—scientific and technical information online. © 1996 Netscape
Communications Corporation.

Other early leaders in the provision of digital libraries information in France
have come from the ranks of the bibliothèques municipales. This term, often
mistranslated as *public library* in the United States, in fact refers to very large
research institutions and collections, located in most of France's major cities,
that house some of the oldest and rarest books in the country, books that most
certainly are not provided in open access to the general public. A French
bibliothèque municipale is more like the New York Public Library than it is
similar to normal public libraries in U.S. cities.

Moreover, French bibliothèques municipales benefit from national and
international prestige, and French central government participation and direct
financial support, which public libraries elsewhere lack. From its beginning in
France, the digital libraries effort has seen the involvement of numerous bibliothèques municipales.

As with other online digital libraries offerings, that of the Bibliothèque Municipale de Lyon strikes the user first with an image devoted to its

monumental architecture (Figure 4.3). Like national efforts, in the French capital, the BM Lyon is concerned with non-French-language access and is developing an English-language option.

The BM Lyon is just as concerned as is the BPI to show users all the nonprinted book resources that it has to offer, such as links to Lyon's remarkable Musée de l'Imprimerie et de la Banque (Figure 4.4) and to various online databases and fulltext publishing experiments, community announcements, detailed online exhibits of the library's varied special collections, rare books (the BM Lyon's oldest book was given to a predecessor collection by Charlemagne), new acquisitions and exhibitions, and modern and ancient documents of Lyon and its region (Figures 4.5 and 4.6).

The BM Lyon online catalog, however—like that of the BPI, also online via Minitel and telnet—suffers from the same standardization drawbacks that confront the BPI online catalog. As with the BPI online catalog, the foreign user confronts a seemingly familiar command structure that retrieves records markedly unlike those found in similar online catalog efforts in Asia, the Americas, and even in the rest of Europe. From the great standardization of Mosaic/

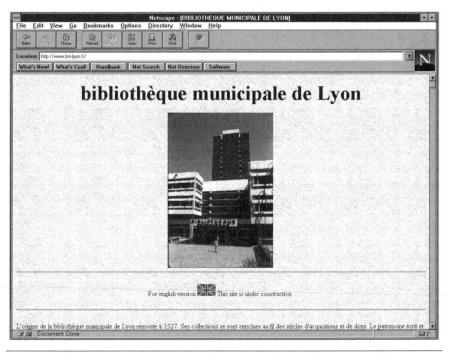

Figure 4.3 The BMLyon—a French "state" library. © 1996 Netscape Communications Corporation.

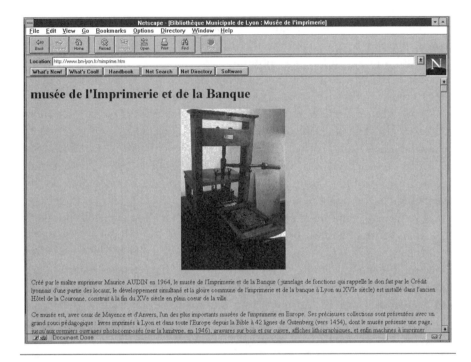

Figure 4.4 Lyon's remarkable Musée de l'Imprimerie et de la Banque—the History and Art of the Book, online. © 1996 Netscape Communications Corporation.

Netscape pointing and clicking, the BM Lyon digital libraries effort proceeds to a highly nonstandard basic cataloging resource—nonstandard, that is, to any user unfamiliar with Lyon or with basic French online cataloging technique—which describes most of the potential BM Lyon digital libraries users on the Internet.

> via W3 to **http://www.bm-lyon.fr** , Minitel to 3615BMLYON, catalog via telnet to telnet://134.214.24.3

(A full list of other French bibliothèques municipales that may be found online appears in the appendix.)

FRANTEXT/ARTFL

FRANTEXT/ARTFL offers fulltext online digital information techniques.

One great logical conundrum of the digital libraries effort—as yet unaddressed, let alone solved—is whether and to what extent digital libraries will have to adapt traditional, predigitization, information-finding techniques, like

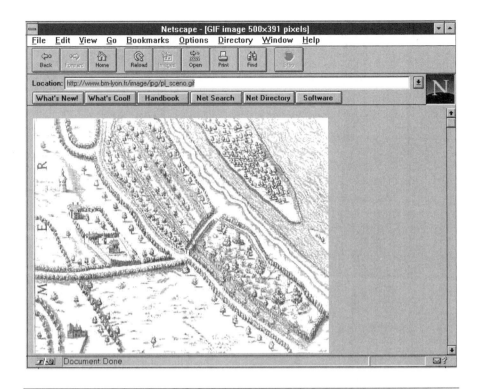

Figure 4.5 An example of what libraries are doing now online—a sixteenth-century map of Lyon. © 1996 Netscape Communications Corporation.

the *MAchine Readable Cataloging* (MARC) formats or simply ignore them and proceed directly to providing fulltext to the user online, without any bibliographic records that merely describe and represent them. "All this leads one to think that, in a short while, access to fulltext might render useless any new work on the MARC format," wonders the president of the French Conseil supérieur des bibliothèques, Michel Melot [2].

The French are forging ahead with both. The BPI and the BM Lyon show examples of the traditional approach, although this is perhaps imperfect for its lack of standardization. But there also is French fulltext, hampered or not by traditional bibliography as an intermediary, to be found at FRANTEXT.

FRANTEXT

FRANTEXT offers digitized fulltexts assembled for the massive French dictionary effort—Trésor de la Langue Française (TLF)[3], by the Institut

Figure 4.6   Another example of what libraries are doing now online—an 1871 Lyon newspaper. © 1996 Netscape Communications Corporation.

National de la Langue Française (INALF) (Figure 4.7)—nearly 2000 French fulltexts drawn from various centuries and disciplines.

>   via W3 to **http://www.ciril.fr/~mastina/FRANTEXT**

>   And then, in addition or perhaps instead, ARTFL.

ARTFL

ARTFL is a project at the University of Chicago: the "project for American and French Research on the Treasury of the French Language," which includes the

Figure 4.7 Online fulltext—FRANTEXT and the INALF. © 1996 Netscape Communications Corporation.

FRANTEXT fulltexts with a different search engine than that used by FRAN-TEXT itself, along with many other French scholarly resources such as a Provençal poetry database, linguistic tools for FRANTEXT, a project to mount Diderot's Encyclopédie online, a number of ARTFL imaging projects, and links to others (Figure 4.8).

As with the printed-book libraries—the BPI and the BM Lyon—one notices immediately questions of standardization and language. What standard will be used in providing online fulltext? What language—whose, and which version of that? ARTFL even has seen it necessary to provide an entirely different search engine, presumably in some part to suit the different needs of its essentially North American users. The question of multilingual access is answered by ARTFL but not addressed by the French language–only Frantext.

via W3 to http://humanities.uchicago.edu/ARTFL.html

Institut de Recherche et Coordination Acoustique-Musique

The *Institut de Recherche et Coordination Acoustique-Musique(IRCAM)* offers online sound techniques (Figure 4.9).

Lest anyone forget, sound as well as text and images is being digitized and provided online actively by digital libraries. The IRCAM is part of the giant Centre Pompidou cultural complex in Paris, which also contains the BPI. Its online offerings include a music software users' group, music and sound software evaluations, bibliographic access to a library of books, music scores,

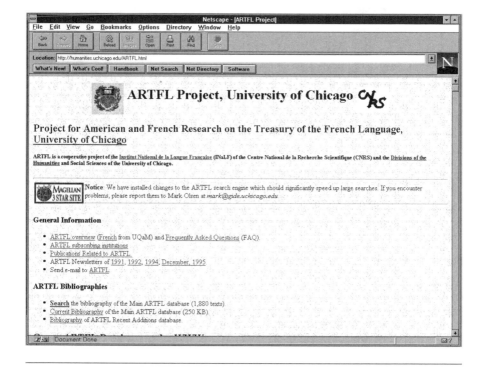

Figure 4.8   Different versions in Cyberspace—FRANTEXT on ARTFL at the University of Chicago. © 1996 Netscape Communications Corporation.

recordings, multimedia resources, and descriptions of projects such as "Le tunnel sous l'Atlantique," for interactive music between Paris and Montréal.

Like the other institutions of the Centre Pompidou, and of France generally, IRCAM presents its online information in English as well as in French, and it is very much a product of the French central, national, government—created in 1969 by the French President Georges Pompidou and the composer Pierre Boulez and continuing under government ministry aegis.

via W3 to **http://www.ircam.fr**

Minitel

Minitel is an online service that provides for the organization and delivery of information (Figure 4.10).

Minitel is an integral part of the French digital libraries infrastructure and one of the largest and earliest global providers of online digital information generally, having preceded the Internet by a decade. Today over 7 million

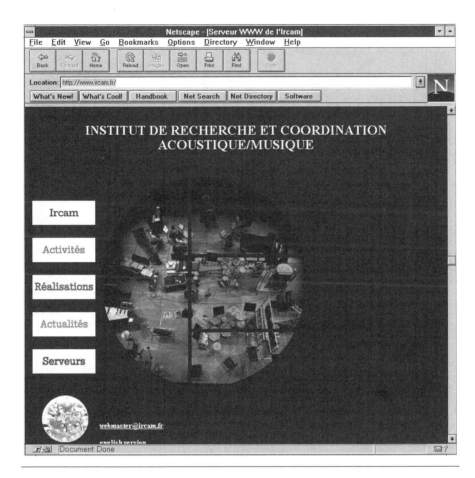

Figure 4.9 Online digital sound libraries—the IRCAM. © 1996 Netscape Communications Corporation.

Minitel terminals and several million more terminal-emulation hookups, world-wide, provide general public users access to nearly 20 thousand online digital information products and services, including hundreds of library resources. (A list of the Minitel library resources is provided in Appendix A. There are hundreds of other resources, however, such as documentation centers, archives, booksellers' services, and thousands of general reference resources, that also provide library service on the Minitel.)

The Minitel was developed, during the late 1970s and early 1980s, by the national French telephone monopoly, France Télécom, as France's entry into the race for computerization/automation/informatisation. This is a race keenly felt by the French, surrounded as they are by European high-technology

Figure 4.10   The Minitel—online digital information for the general public, long before the Internet. © 1996 Netscape Communications Corporation.

competitors, such as Spain, Italy, Switzerland, the United Kingdom, and, above all, Germany, and over-shadowed as they feel themselves to be, in this and other fields, by "le défi américain"—the American Challenge, posed by the United States.

An early Minitel application was the French national telephone book, which was loaded online onto Minitel while, unconfirmed marketing legend has it, the printed version became "very hard to obtain" for a while in France. Early developments included the growth of the infamous Minitel Rose, with its sex chat and various sex services. Eventually, however, public sector and commercial service activity replaced both the annuaire and Minitel Rose as the most important engines of Minitel's growth.

Among the services rendered by the national government in mounting Minitel was the provision of universal access to general public users. The well-organized Minitel "kiosk" system also effectively subsidized the billing component, one of the largest and most difficult portions of any retail mail order or distribution operation, by allowing consumers to charge service usage to their normal telephone accounts.

Less easy to see at the time, however—and certainly less easy to see then as a goal of public policy—was the provision of Minitel as a basic, simplistic, but highly user-friendly service for general public online information usage, anticipating the development of similar techniques for the Internet today. The relatively primitive state of Minitel's *videotex* technology at the time was more than counterbalanced by the foresight of France Télécom and Minitel's creators in aiming the service at the un-interested general public user at a time when the Internet was used only by engineers. Now that the Internet at last is opening, its development of Mosaic/Netscape interfaces and hypertext/WorldWideWeb links and general public-oriented commercial applications represents a prime example of high-technology convergence—in this case of Internet technique with the original Minitel general public orientation and approach.

> via W3 to http://www.minitel.fr; or via telnet to minitel.fr, or (in North America) via voice telephone to 1-800-MINITEL, or through any France Télécom office.

Ministry of Culture

The Ministry of Culture might be known as "French Culture, Inc." online.

The French National Ministry of Culture is perhaps the best place to visit online to appreciate the *flexible centralization* that characterizes digital libraries efforts in France. Few countries anywhere even have a high-level Ministry of Culture—even fewer have one also devoted to its national language, as the official title Ministry of Culture and Francophonie indicates. This particular central government ministry not only has one of the most comprehensive and best-presented online presences itself, but it was an early leader in online work generally.

The projects that the Ministry of Culture encourages and often directly supports include most of the library, museum, and archival experiments in digital media going on throughout the country. Most remarkable, for a government ministry officially devoted to linguistic nationalism, the French Ministry of Culture itself offers online access to its resources and services in, of all things, the much-maligned Anglo-Saxon language, English. Few more dramatic proofs of the flexibility of the French, even in their intense centralization and jingoistic tendencies, might be provided than this. Even if the United States had a Ministry of Culture, one somehow doubts that it would bother to translate all of its W3 homepage screens into French, into any other non-English language, or even into British English for that matter; "color" never would become "colour," "catalog" would not be "catalogue." French relative flexibility in language matters is a seldom-recognized thing.

> via W3 to http://www.culture.fr

BIBLIO-FR

BIBLIO-FR offers an electronic conference discussion online and its archives.

One new and virtually unrecognized resource of the global digital libraries effort is the well-run online electronic conference and its invaluable archive. In an age when so much is being invented anew, very little exists yet in traditional media—in print or on film—that can inform a user about digital libraries. Online e-conferences, however—when they are well-disciplined efforts, governed by special *Listserve* or *List Processor* software and a flexible but firm human moderator—have been assembling enormous stores of accumulated knowledge and often wisdom about digital libraries efforts.

Online archives of these e-conference discussions, which in some cases take place among thousands of individuals located in dozens of countries, are stored and searched easily. BIBLIO-FR, the French librarians' e-conference, was created in 1993 and since has grown to include membership and postings from most librarians and archivists in France who use digital media at all, substantive discussion of most digital libraries issues, enthusiastic participation by franco-phone librarians (most francophile, a few francophobe) located in various countries, and even an occasional posting by a French ambassador and by the Minister of Culture himself. There are few better starting or continuation points for any pursuit of French digital libraries knowledge than a free-of-charge subscription to BIBLIO-FR.

BIBLIO-FR has not chosen, as have so many other French digital libraries resources, to make its discussions available in English-language translation. The BIBLIO-FR intent is, after all, to be a professional discussion group for librari-ans in France, and the primitive state of machine translation is such that the task of keeping up with the extemporaneous style and the enormously rapid growth of something like an e-conference discussion appears for now to be impossible. An e-conference might manage such an effort relying on volunteers, however; e-conference email communication is informal enough that subscribers simply might translate each other's postings.

Two versions of both the BIBLIO-FR current postings and the archives are maintained—one with the French diacritical marks, which requires special software to be read at terminals, and one without. This is done to some extent to accommodate French users who simply do not possess the necessary soft-ware. To a greater extent, however, such accommodated users are non-French people online who have no other need for the software but still would like to read the messages. It is interesting that even BIBLIO-FR has tried its best to accommodate the outside, nonfrancophone world. Multilingual e-conferences, and even monolingual e-conferences that go to this length to accommodate foreign users are still a very rare thing online.[1] The BIBLIO-FR archive may be consulted via keyword searching at http://www.univ-rennes1.fr/ listes/. A full list of the various e-conference archives housed there—a fairly complete picture of virtual digital libraries in the process of being created in France—is shown in Appendix B.

The Bibliothèque Nationale de France

One of the world's largest traditional print libraries, the French Bibliothèque Nationale—newly rechristened the Bibliothèque Nationale de France (BNF)—is making a serious bid to become a world-class one-stop shopping place for information, both offline and online (Figure 4.11).

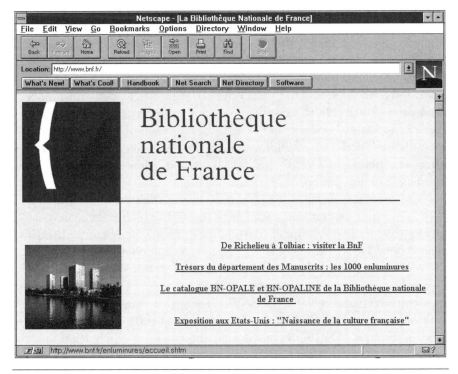

Figure 4.11 The new BNF—bricks-and-mortar, books, and online. © 1996 Netscape Communications Corporation.

---

1. To subscribe to BIBLIO-FR—the same pattern pertains, generally, to any online e-conference—send a simple email message to listserv@univ-rennes1.fr, saying, exactly, subscribe BIBLIO-FR Yourfirstname Yourlastname

The BNF possesses, depending on which account and definition are used, between 10 and 12 million printed books, all of which are being physically moved during 1996 and 1997, to the entirely new, gargantuan, and highly controversial edifice constructed to house them at Tolbiac, just upriver on the Seine from the Paris Left Bank and Latin Quarter.

The BNF project—which involves the construction of the new building at Tolbiac, the move of the collections from one site to another, the retention of some things at the old site and the decision as to what to retain and what to move, and the provision of high-technology organization and access in all of this—is to some extent the product of former French President François Mitterrand's love of literature and books, and to some extent the result of decades of growth and crisis at the former Bibliothèque Nationale (BN) on the Rue Richlelieu.

The old BNF outgrew itself many times during this century. Each time, just when cramped conditions, shelving space, and book damage became insufferable (the French call book mold, curiously to foreign gastronomes, "champignons"; the Paris Right Bank, on which the old BN is built, is an ancient flood plain, and the BN books grew plenty of champignons), a solution was found. But by the 1980s, at least according to then-administrator Emmanuel Le Roy Ladurie, no further "way out" remained; shelf space simply would be exhausted soon, he said, and a new building was needed. Various reorganizations and plans were developed. A "BN bis" was discussed. All were rejected as being insufficient or impractical.

The impetus to do something finally came from then-President Mitterrand. He was an author himself, and a man proud enough of his literary achievements to have his official photographs taken holding fine books and against a backdrop of fine books. He announced, during a remarkable interview held in 1988 in his Elysée Palace garden, that the construction of a *très grande bibliothèque*, promptly rechristened by the irreverent Paris press the "TGB," to rhyme with the French high-speed Très Grande Vitesse train's acronym "TGV," and just as promptly rendered into U.S. journal-ese as the slightly ridiculous-sounding "very big library." The President was right, though; by anyone's definition, this new library was to be "very big."

For digital libraries purposes, however, the most remarkable portion of President Mitterrand's announcement, and of the ensuing BNF mandate, was his intention that "This great library will cover all the fields of knowledge, will be at the disposition of all, will use the most modern technologies of the transmission of knowledge, and will be able to be consulted at a distance and to enter into relations with the other European libraries." (Letter of mission from the President of the Republic to the Prime Minister, August 1988) [4].

This was the mandate to spend money on informatisation, the French term for the congeries of library automation and telecommunications and information search and retrieval and general access hardware, software, systems, and service that underly digital libraries. The idea that President Mitterrand had was that the French would lead, not only with a truly very big library, but with the very latest and very best in online digital information technology.

The project that resulted has consumed much of the imagination, energy, and aggressiveness of the French intelligentsia and most of the budget of the Ministry of Culture for nearly a decade. From original estimates of US$200 million, the construction costs perhaps predictably soared to over US$1 billion, and the building is not yet completed. It has easily become the most expensive among a series of costly central Paris monumental building projects built since the 1970s—which includes the Louvre Pyramid, the Musée d'Orsay, the Centre Pompidou, the Opéra, the Grand Arche de La Défense, and others—known to those most supportive of them as the *grands travaux* and to their critics in the French press by many far less-complimentary epithets. Among the BNF project's greatest supporters have been foreign, non-French, francophiles and French scholars who look forward to improved access to the collections and always enjoy a trip to Paris to view the latest monument.

The great danger of the BNF as a project has been that the new building might so exhaust the budget as to become merely a warehouse for seldom-used printed books. The French have been acutely aware of this danger. To avoid it, much attention has been devoted both to coordinating the Tolbiac site's resources and services with those of other BNF sites and to establishing and maintaining a BNF digital libraries presence. At the BNF online, one already can find digitized texts, digitized images, brave announcements of more of both to come, and immensely helpful services of various types (Figure 4.11).

Online access to the BNF catalog now is available as well, although this particular effort—like any other library cataloging effort—still is subject to the usual criticisms of its lack of standardization. The French are engaged in enormous projects to standardize their bibliographic practices—as are the British, as are the Americans, and as are most librarians—but the standardization is not in place yet, and the entries that one obtains online resemble, but do not match, what is most familiar to a foreign user.

Remarkably for this national and nationalistic BNF library project, its online presence is available in English; one need only point and click to reach a full presentation of this French digital libraries effort in a foreign language.

via W3 to http://www.bnf.fr

La Bibliothèque Nationale d'Art

The Bibliothèque Nationale d'Art is one of the most interesting possibilities for imaging and, thus, for digital libraries of the future. Perhaps ironically, the outstanding source of potential competition for the BNF digital libraries effort already under way comes from within France itself from an entity that may even ultimately become a part of the BNF itself.

Back at the old site, on the Paris Right Bank's rue Richelieu, all the old nonprint BN collections, which now will have the great added benefit of a lot more physical space, are being reorganized into what very hopefully is being called La Bibliothèque Nationale d'Art. This would include the famous BN collections and administrative departments devoted to manuscripts, prints and drawings, coins and medallions, and everything that this enormous institution accumulated over the centuries that did not happen to be a printed text—all this perhaps combined with several other central Paris art library collections and even a new school dedicated to the teaching of art and art documentation.

At a time when *imaging* has become the leading key word in online digital information—everything, it seems at times, that can be digitized can be considered as an image, even text [5]—an institution could do worse than to become a leading world center for nearly everything that up until now has been associated with the term *image*. Online digital information techniques brought to bear, as they necessarily will be, on the collections and concerns of the Bibliothèque Nationale d'Art potentially could eclipse in importance even the enormous efforts in the digital libraries area currently being undertaken by the Bibliothèque Nationale de France.

4.1 Some common themes in the French case

The common themes suggested by these examples of digital libraries in France are several.

The first is a common interest in the exhibition of what is a remarkable national cultural heritage. French pride in their nation's cultural achievement, particularly the long history of this record, is enormous and well-illustrated in the development of the French approach to the construction of digital libraries.

A second strand, though, somewhat modifies the first. Multilingual access is of great concern to the French; almost all of their digital libraries efforts that can be found online provide some form of multilingual access. This perhaps is an admission of the degree of difficulty and limited reach of their own national language—the French themselves at times are even less confident in this regard than foreigners are. But it also shows an understanding of the role of their nation in a multinational world, an understanding not shown by English-language nations. The rest of the world does not speak the French language, and the French appear to realize that if they are to communicate with the non-French world they at least must do so in the language of the users.

A third, particularly French, strand in digital libraries development is the enormous prestige accorded there to digital affairs as a national priority. Interest in the digital revolution is high in most places in the world now, but few have placed it so high on the national development agenda as have the French. It takes the form of a personal crusade in Paris among some decision makers. For example, the French ambassador to the United States and the national Minister of Culture both have posted messages to BIBLIO-FR, the French librarians' e-conference, and the prime minister of the country himself chaired the October 1995 meeting that decreed that the Internet would be brought to all French citizens for the price of a local telephone call in 1996. Politicians elsewhere give Cyberspace much lip service, but few outside those in the United States have become this personally involved.

Libraries and librarians in France never have been considered separate from governmental functions and concerns as they have in the United States. In France, culture is a national concern, with its own national Ministry, civil servants, statutes, and administrative structures. The French would not consider libraries to be a matter for uncontrolled private enterprise any more than they would consider this for hospitals or schools. They even have difficulty imagining telecommunications, originally considered a national security matter of high priority, to be a candidate for privatization and reduced government control.

The general attitude toward government control and active participation is very different in France from the United States but perhaps is more similar to its situation elsewhere. France and other countries did not have a Thoreau who taught "that government is best which governs least." Digitization, insofar as it became a French national priority, logically would be imposed upon French schools, hospitals, and libraries, following a political logic found elsewhere and considered strange perhaps only in the United States.

There is, finally, central government involvement and support in France for digital libraries and online efforts generally. In the United States, where the national central government sponsored the earliest Internet beginnings, subsequent developments have been funded largely by private industry, and now private industry seems to be taking over the enterprise as a whole. The French model, then, insofar as nations elsewhere also have strong central government participation in anything digital or networked—at least in its beginnings over-seas—may be highly relevant to other non-U.S. cases, and perhaps even more relevant.

NOTES

[1] See the online version of the exhibit at http://www.bnf.fr/loc/bnf0001.htm and Tesnière, Marie-Hélène, and Prosser Gifford, eds., *Creating French Culture: Treasures from the Bibliothèque Nationale de France,* New Haven, CT: Yale University Press, c1995, ISBN 0-300-06283-4; although this thesis is, like anything by or about the French, controversial, see Kessler, Jack, "Treasures of the Bibliothèque Nationale at the Library of Congress, and now on W3/the WorldWideWeb," *FYI France,* January 15, 1996, gopher://library.berkeley.edu:72/00/ejrnls/FYIFrance/1996/FYIFrance.01.15.96, ISSN 1071-5916.

[2] Melot, Michel, "Les Nouveaux Enjeux de la Normalisation," *Bulletin des Bibliothèques de France,* Vol. 38, No. 5, 1993, p.10; the text extract appearing here has been translated by Jack Kessler.

[3] Trésor de la Langue Française, http://www.ciril.fr/inalf-bin/wncgi/tlf-showps?main.tlf

[4] http://gopher.well.sf.ca.us:70/0/Publications/FYIFrance/fyi.93.05.15

[5] Collard, Claude, Isabelle Giannattasio, and Michel Melot, *Les Images dans les Bibliothèques,* Paris: Editions du Cercle de la Librairie, 1995, ISBN 2765405778.

Chapter 5

Singapore—rigid centralization

S INGAPORE BOASTS 22,769 Internet hosts as of January, 1996: a phenomenal one Internet host per 127 Singaporeans (per Network Wizards,
http://www.nw.com, and CIA World FactBook 1995, http://www.
odci.gov/cia/publications/95fact/index.html).

One might compare Singapore's administrative centralization with that of
France in examining the two nations' respective online digital information
activities. The comparison, at first glance, might seem to fall victim to the
fallacies suggested in the prefatory warnings made earlier here about the nation-
state—in this case, that a relatively young and tiny, isolated city-state, on the tip
of a peninsula in Southeast Asia, might not easily be compared to a much larger
and centuries older political entity located in and firmly enmeshed in the politics
of Western Europe.

Yet France is not so old, which in some senses is very relevant to its online
digital information management. Its Fifth Republic dates from only 1958, while
Sir Stamford Raffles established Singapore and many of its modern political
institutions in 1819. Tiny Singapore, moreover, is not so isolated from political

entities, and groups of at least potential digital libraries users that are far greater in size than the populations of France and indeed of all of Europe might represent.

The most densely populated large island in the world is a part of an enormous archipelago-nation located physically just across a relatively narrow shipping channel from Singapore, and Singapore's "overseas Chinese" population retains and now actively is nurturing its historical and social contacts with a Chinese mother country that contains a billion people and has a development agenda that may become the economic miracle of the coming century.

Singapore is trying to position itself to become the agent of the digital libraries and other developments of Indonesia, Malaya, Thailand, and China. This small, seemingly isolated city-state might have much to learn from, and perhaps even more to teach, such supposedly larger and greater states as France and the United States in digital libraries development.

But they do things very differently in Singapore than they do them in perhaps most other places on the planet. This tiny Asian city-state has been variously described as the "Switzerland of the Orient" and "Disneyland with the Death Penalty" [1].

The recent Singapore past of puritanical antilitter and other stringent laws, enforced by canings, is perhaps better known than the murkier and further distant past that it succeeded—and that it was invented to solve—of severe civil unrest and instability. Much of the current sensationalist news of this recent past that the outside world sees of Singapore obscures the remarkable social achievement that the tiny nation represents.

That a multiracial, multilingual, relatively enormous mass of people literally crammed onto a tiny and somewhat unhealthy peninsula, physically isolated from any wealthy or even well-intentioned neighbors who might significantly help, might educate and organize themselves to become one of the world's leaders in per capita output and well-being is certainly one of the modern world's social miracles.

Whatever the criticisms that might be made of certain Singaporean excesses, simply the political achievement—certainly compared to the political chaos that has reigned generally among its neighbors during the same period—has been admirable. The more recent Singapore success story now is being enforced upon Singapore's online digital information presence.

Singapore's "Vision of an Intelligent Island"

Singapore has a "Vision of an Intelligent Island" that forms a key feature of its overall thinking about its national future (Figure 5.1).

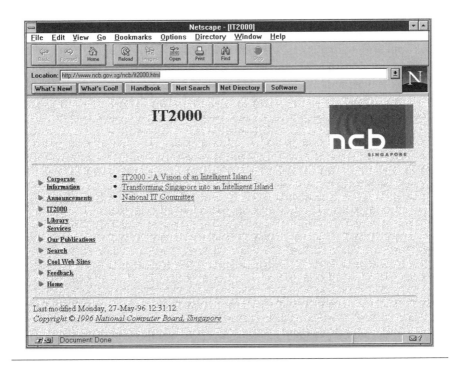

Figure 5.1   Visions of the future—a nation online, and perhaps more.
© 1996 Netscape Communications Corporation.

The basic idea is, and has been since its 1992 formulation, to build a *National Information Infrastructure* for Singapore, similar in concept to the same idea being developed in the United States, but far different in the greater direct activity foreseen for the Singapore version's *National Computer Board* (NCB) [2].

The general strategy calls for projects to promote the use of digital *information technology* (IT) in government; in major industrial sectors (that is, education, health care, tourism, and manufacturing); in *IT Culture,* meaning for school-aged children; and in the IT industry itself and its human resources development [3].

The general hope and vision is that, once accomplished, "Singapore, the Intelligent Island, will be a global centre for science and technology, a high-value location for production, and a critical node in global networks of commerce, communications, and information" [4].

Critics like Sandy Sandfort point out that Singapore's dream of an "Intelligent Island" may depend on the political biases of the islanders: "The paternalistic policies that seem to have worked for Singapore in the past may not be appropriate in tomorrow's information age" [5].

True, but they may be, and in any case Singapore is less concerned with "tomorrow's information age" than it is with Asia and is closer and thus may be in a better position to judge what will work in Asia for Asians than are the U.S.-based inventors of the "information age" as developed so far. We will see. For now it certainly does appear that Singapore will develop, as it has before, into a prime laboratory of the confrontation between Western and Eastern methods, this time as mixed together with the supposedly "neutral pipeline" of online digital information.

via w3to: **http://www.ncb.gov.sg/ncb/it2000.html**

Singapore's Regionalisation 2000

"As Singapore's external economy develops, Singapore companies and Singapore-based MNCs [Multinational Corporations] can participate in the region's growth by distributing their resource-dependent operations to resource-rich countries while maintaining and upgrading their Singapore operations to higher-end activities... The *Regionalisation 2000* (R2000) programme aims to build a strong external economy which is closely linked to and which enhances the domestic economy." (See Figure 5.2.)

Higher end activities have higher profit margins than *resource-dependent operations* do—a lesson taught with bitter result to Central America by the United Fruit Company earlier in this century when Boston got richer and Honduras got poorer. One has to wonder at the Singapore general approach, which this R2000 service mounted by their government *Economic Development Board* (EDB) pointedly defines and which appears not to mince words in describing the overall intention.

Other examples shown here (below, for Indonesia) will illustrate the extent to which Singapore in fact speaks, or at least tries to speak, for much of Southeast Asia. The enormous disparities in income, technical knowledge, capital resources, and general outlook on life between Singapore and most of its Asian neighbors perhaps inevitably make for wariness and jealousy on the part of the latter. There is a further question, however, of rubbing salt into the wound. Whatever the intention of the Singapore effort, any hostile reaction to it on the part of its less industrious and/or perhaps less-fortunate neighbors should be understandable.

via W3 to **http://www.sedb.com/aboutEDB/reg2000.html**

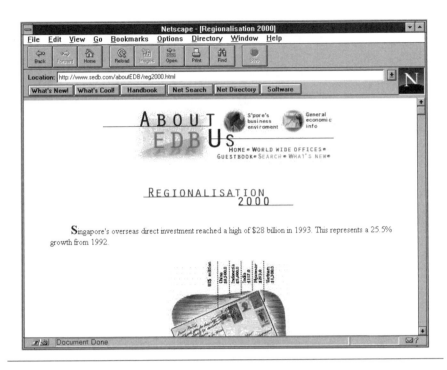

Figure 5.2   Online digital information as national/regional/international policy.
© 1996 Netscape Communications Corporation.

Singapore National Library

Singapore does offer one of the most comprehensive, and peppy, digital libraries available (Figure 5.3). Their W3 service shows announcements, including children's services in Chinese, Malay, and Tamil; links to general Singapore information; a "new books" service; catalog access; and a broad array of other library resources and services. In spite of the multilingual children's' program announcement, though, the W3 service appears only to be offered in English. English is widely used in Singapore, but one wonders how an English-only medium will fare in any Singapore R2000 effort to reach their neighbors.

via W3 to http://www.livewire.ncb.gov.sg/library/main.html

5.1 Summary

The case of Singapore illustrates, perhaps better than the case of any other nation, the immense importance of politics and political structures in

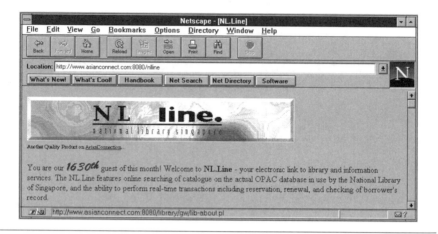

Figure 5.3   A digital library for a digital nation. © 1996 Netscape Communications Corporation.

international digital libraries efforts. The Singapore city-state, surrounded by relatively impoverished, envious, and very different neighbors, simply is not in the political position of a library in the United States—even a large library with a national reputation—to impose its approach and resources upon its neighbors, no matter how excellent that approach and those resources and how greatly they are needed by those neighbors.

Political jealousies exist within the United States as well—among states, between state and national authorities, among universities, and between branches of the same university. But the seriousness, and the degree of fundamental difference, are nowhere near the same when one considers such rivalries against the international crises in which entire European and Asian nations often find themselves involved. An American librarian or online digital information developer might appreciate the difficulty of the Singapore situation better by imagining that any expansion of her digital libraries effort—beyond her immediate city—might be an opportunity or the cause of an international incident for her entire nation. That is a responsibility that rarely arises in Nevada but is an everyday combined opportunity and threat for Singapore.

via W3 to http://www.livewire.ncb.gov.sg/library/main.html

NOTES

[1]   Gibson, William, "Disney Land with the Death Penalty," *Hot Wired*, http://www.hotwired.com/wired/1.4/features/gibson.html

[2] National Computer Board, Singapore, *A Vision of an Intelligent Island: IT2000 Report*, Singapore: National Computer Board, March 1992, ISBN 981-00-3642-6; see also http://www.ncb.gov.sg/ncb/it2000.html

[3] http://www.ncb.gov.sg/ncb/thrust.html

[4] http://www.ncb.gov.sg/ncb/transform.html

[5] http://www.hotwired.com/wired/1.4/features/sandfort.html

Chapter 6

China—Chinese uniqueness

CHINA HAD 2146 Internet hosts as of January 1996: one Internet host per 560,623 people in China (China's superlatives always are bigger—the world's Texas) per Network Wizards, http://www.nw.com, and CIA World FactBook 1995, http://www.odci.gov/cia/publications/95fact/index.html.

China is not so much big as it is unique. Certainly the nation is large, although it is large in ways that Westerners and particularly many Asians do not really appreciate. The land mass is huge, but little of it is arable. China's enormous population—over 1 billion people, one-fifth of all the people on the planet (there are W3 services that recalculate the world total—currently 5,808,828,179, on April 9, 1996 at 00:37:40 GMT—every 30 seconds, if that is something that you need [1])—in fact, is squeezed into only 10% of China's land, which consists of only two major river basins and a small number of enormous urban agglomerations.

China's population mass lives *on* a land mass the size of the United States or Australia, but it lives *from* a land mass—China still is primarily agricultural—that is only the size of France plus Germany. Imagine those latter two nations housing over 500 million people each—France, in fact, has about 58 million, Germany about 80 million—or think of China as being nearly the same size as the United States but with half the useful land and five times the population.

So one enduring genius of the Chinese, among the many possessed by this very talented group of people, has been their ability to administer the affairs of a large population crammed into a tiny amount of space. Administration—the politics of it but, even more, its actual operation—is an art formulated theoretically long ago in China [2] and studied and practiced there for many centuries. Westerners have recognized Chinese administrative talents. For example, eighteenth- and nineteenth-century reformers, seeking models for the improvement of top-heavy and influence-based European government administrations, turned to Chinese models [3].

It is misleading, then, to judge China as non-Chinese so often do, that is, as simply a large nation and certainly as one unduly conditioned by the terrible events of its modern history. China today possesses, and uses, continuous traditions of art, philosophy, social structure, and political beliefs and practices that extend not only back before very recent *Cultural* and *Communist* revolutions but further to centuries and entire ages that antedate the very founding of Europe, much less of modern European nations, or of such relative historical infants as the United States of America. There are practices and beliefs alive today in Chinese villages that evolved before Charlemagne and even before the Europeans' earlier Greeks and Romans; any vestige of Confucianism or Taoist beliefs—of which there are many—or of archaizing influences in modern Chinese painting that draw on (or oppose) Shang and Chou models, can give evidence of this [4].

Chinese administrative talent shares this longevity, just as it does not partake of the image held by many of China as being simply a giant, indeed monolithic, "nation-state," something like an oversized France, England, or United States. There are other fundamental differences though, several of which specifically affect the ability and approach, of outsiders and the Chinese themselves, in constructing digital libraries or any sort of digital information networking in China.

For example, the Chinese army, long the largest but per capita perhaps the most impoverished major army in the world, recently has taken steps to reverse this impoverishment and has become one of the leading entrepreneurial forces in the country. This is not so unimaginable for Internet workers, who at least can remember the days of ARPA and Department of Defense support of networking's birth in the United States. But the idea that the People's Liberation Army now should control large hospitals and significant industries inside China, much less commercial establishments that have direct effects upon China's external relations, seems strange in the U.S. context (the "PX" system became large in the United States, but never threatened Sears or Safeway) and is very foreign in the context of other nation's control of their own armed forces.

A second unique factor in China's current situation is the overwhelming influence of foreign capital in the nation's economic growth. Foreign and "overseas Chinese" investment in China, much of the latter from Taiwan, Singapore, and Indonesia and much denominated either directly or indirectly in Japanese yen, constitutes the capital foundation of China's now rapidly growing economy. Chinese decision makers in Beijing discovered their difficulties in controlling this foreign investment when they tried recently, desperately, to stem severe inflation. U.S. decision makers and their Beijing counterparts are discovering the problem anew, now, as they try to discipline copyright and trademark piracy in China, much of which is financed by this same, uncontrollable, overseas money.

China also has severe social and political dislocations looming as a direct result of its enormous economic growth. These are the same old lessons explored in great detail by students of East Asian and Latin American economic growth during the 1950s and 1960s that include population growth, the breakup of extended and even nuclear families, the breakdown of local and traditional social support systems, and above all an urbanization explosion [5].

In the Chinese context, with more than a billion people involved and much more money than the Third World of the 1950s ever could have imagined, these dislocations promise to be more enormous than they were before. Politically, the problems of gerontocracy in the Chinese hierarchy (Mr. Teng still is not the only very old man left at the top of Chinese national decision making); the inability to control provinces like Tibet, Guangzhou, and Hong Kong (and, in Beijing's eyes, still, Taiwan); and the looming political problem of the growing economic power of the world's largest army all pose severe internal problems. What foreign investor, interested in digital libraries or other ventures, can make plans now for a return on investment that must extend beyond the 1997 takeover of Hong Kong, the imminent death/succession battle of Mr. Teng, or the dénouement of the PLA's seemingly inevitable contest, with others in the country, for political control?

Externally, too, China faces a unique situation hard to appreciate for Americans, Europeans, or any others interested in its development. Japan is just across a very small sea. The bitterness of Sino-Japanese relations—both the history and the present feeling—is hard for any Westerner to appreciate. It is ancient, composed of very old but never-forgotten incidents and supplemented with racial and ethnic legends and slurs learned in both nations from early childhood. Reconciliations, of the type currently taking place in Europe among the contestants in recent wars there, seem far from political reality in East Asia.

Recent events, furthermore, have only fueled the Sino-Japanese enmity. Japanese expansionism since the end of the last century, a long period of unbelievably cruel colonialism and exploitation capped off with a severe war and aggravated further by current competition with and resentment against Japanese economic might have not helped relations. And the Japanese have not helped matters by assembling the world's second largest navy; this by a nation still bound legally not to spend money on armaments.

To make external political matters worse for the Chinese, two of the world's potentially most dangerous renegade nuclear conflicts are developing rapidly just outside its borders in the Koreas and between India and Pakistan. Add to this the many threats poised by the continuing crumbling of the Soviet Union—also as close to the Chinese as it seems far and removed from the United States and Western Europe—and you have a fairly clear-cut recipe for national political paranoia.

So online digital information work in China, like any investment in the Chinese future, must take into account several uniquely Chinese considerations. The army, perhaps the last candidate in the United States or Europe to be looked to now for support in an investment effort, is a major and growing factor in China. Overseas investment appears to be a principal tool as well, so much so that arrangements for investment in China often are more easily made in Singapore, Jakarta, or even Taipei—and certainly, for now, Hong Kong—than within China itself.

The fall, or at least radical restructuring, for which all this is headed shortly, must be anticipated. Internal shifts in political power, perhaps to the People's Liberation Army or growing cities like Shanghai or provinces like Guangzhou, or reactions against them, must be considered. China's foreign relations, which have been generally bad during the past century and now suddenly appear to be growing radically worse—with growing tensions with nearly all of its neighbors and the latest of several looming trade wars with the United States—likewise are a problem.

China's uniqueness lies primarily in the ignorance of outsiders, that is, in the inability of Westerners, primarily, to grasp that it is not just another Western-style nation-state but a very complex, very old, and very systematic culture that contains many distinct subcultures, all of them simply very different from those in the West. Investment and development in China now, with so many unpredictable influences and factors at play there, are matters for gamblers, with far more to be gained than in other political arenas and far more to be lost.

This said, China has digital libraries. Can these be very similar to digital libraries in Kansas or Oxfordshire or Limoges, given the immense cultural differences that exist between China and the United States, the United Kingdom, and France? Certainly the techniques may appear at first glance to be the same. Apple Macintosh computers may, for now, look the same in Beijing as they do in Cupertino; the same flavor of TCP/IP may operate in Shanghai and Stepney; MARC formats may be similar in Chinese and U.S. library online systems; and SGML might even be used to mark up texts in both places.

But Singapore might be closer to China, if only for being Chinese. A nation many times smaller than China than even the United States or France, and perhaps further behind in specific technological developments, might have more that might usefully be compared, in its current digital libraries development, to similar work being done in "giant" China.

This is for others to judge. For now, merely the suggestion is made that the differences not be ignored. And for now, China has some digital libraries online and some efforts that others might call digital libraries.

Institute of High Energy Physics

China's *Institute of High Energy Physics* (IHEP) offers an example of entrepreneurship in a people's republic—and of logic in both Western and Chinese varieties (Figure 6.1).

Perhaps one part of China's uniqueness is illustrated by the fact that its most developed entry point for general online information has been for some time, and is still as of this 1996 writing, the Chinese Institute of High Energy Physics.

Figure 6.1   The Middle Kingdom and the People's Republic online. © 1996 Netscape Communications Corporation.

This W3 service is the source for an array of nonphysics resources and services, including maps of China, tourist and commercial information, and a curious inline image of a Chinese acrobat (Figure 6.2).

These are resources and services that no other Institute of High Energy Physics located elsewhere in the world ever would provide or think of providing. The mysteries of Chinese politics, to a Westerner, would make the politics of ancient Byzantium seem straightforward. Why and how an Institute of High Energy Physics became the Middle Kingdom's leading general-purpose Internet service provider may someday be published. For now perhaps it is sufficient to observe that political structures—the entire permissions system

Figure 6.2 New combinations in China—online digital tourist information and the IHEP. © 1996 Netscape Communications Corporation.

through which an Internet service provider must operate to bring online digital information to China—are perhaps not better nor worse but are definitely different, in this People's Republic, from anything in operation online elsewhere.

Similarly, the content of online digital information offerings in China is unique. The IHEP service provides categories devoted to General Information on China (sections, apparently under development, devoted to Acrobatics, Scientific and Technological Development, and presumably other topics), The Chinese Nation (sections devoted to each of several national ethnic minorities in the country), and New Women in China (a service designed for the 1995 UN Fourth World Conference on Women, held in Beijing).

The Home Page of Peking University

This resource (Figure 6.3) includes two interesting-looking but rarely available online services—PKU Library Home Page and DataBase of Science and Intellectual Property Law in China—and two promising-looking but as-yet-unconnected research tools for Chinese scholarship—Journal of Peking University

Figure 6.3 The Home Page of Peking University. © 1996 Netscape Communications Corporation.

(Natural Sciences) and Journal of Peking University (Philosophy and Social Sciences).

One point about Chinese online digital information resources that must be made is that which is often made about Chinese development generally. Within this generation, only 20 years ago, the political structures of this nation, which for so long has been permeated with one of the most complex and often very difficult political systems of any nation, were rigid, paranoid, and impervious in the extreme to any outside, non-Chinese, influence whatsoever.

The appearance of acrobatics and New Women in China on an IHEP W3 homepage contains superficial ironies that can make foreigners smile. Far deeper ironies are involved, however. For a nation this massive and this complex to have opened itself this far in this short a time—particularly against a recent political background as disastrous as China's has been in this century—is extraordinary in a way in which perhaps younger and simpler and definitely more stable cultures such as those of the United States and Western Europe cannot begin to appreciate.

A Note: Hong Kong, and Singapore and Chiapas, Mexico—the Chinese Diaspora

The Chinese inside China are not the only people concerned with bringing online digital information to the Middle Kingdom. Singapore has already been mentioned. Hong Kong, an area and an entrepreneurial resource of global importance, which importantly is due to become legally and officially Chinese within a matter of months, now boasts hundreds of online digital information resources and services, including dozens of different and competing Web and general Internet service providers [6].

The situation in which China finds itself with respect to online digital information in fact could be used to illustrate the greatest communications advantage offered by the Internet, Cyberspace, and telecommunications in its most general sense. The *Chinese Diaspora* has dispersed Chinese populations, over the course of several hundred years, to every corner of the globe. Such is the force and attraction of Chinese culture, however, that Chinese people who have lived outside of China itself for many generations retain their identity with China, to the point that even the complexities of the Chinese language are preserved overseas.

There are "pockets" of Chinese culture—culture that is Chinese in practice today and not just descended from it—in Chiapas, Mexico; Lyon, France; San Francisco; New York; and London as well as in Singapore and Hong Kong. Much of this loyalty is to local regions within present-day China, that is, to "the village" to which money and devotions have been sent from overseas for centuries. But much more of the overseas Chinese loyalty is directed to the larger, greater, eons-older, and almost mystical "Chinese civilization" that is not necessarily and in fact rarely is associated with whatever the current Chinese political regime happens to be. One of the greatest challenges posed to the current Chinese transition—to the transition in Hong Kong and to the economic, social, and political transition under way in China generally—is to preserve this latter loyalty and exploit it for the jobs at hand, whatever lack of enthusiasm there might be "overseas" for the regime currently in Beijing.

The unification of all of this common global culture, a goal devoutly wished for by many in China—by some only culturally, by some politically—is rendered far easier by the Internet, and is an integral part of digital libraries development inside China. So much of the economic development going on inside China now is financed, at least, by overseas Chinese investment. If mutual communication has anything to do with such development, it would seem that the enhanced ability of China to communicate with its globally scattered populations, provided by the Internet, could make China one of the world's primary beneficiaries of online digital information in the coming century. Digital libraries there stand to benefit greatly, and not just financially, from China's preservation of these loyalties of the overseas Chinese.

The potential political impact of the Internet in China—both its promise and its threat—is more unsettling than the delivery of modern Xerox printers to the citizens of Martin Luther's Germany might have been. It is said that Gutenberg's printing press revolutionized Europe [7]. But the trouble with revolutions, as the French found out with theirs, is that the outcomes are unpredictable. They bring change for the sake of change, but rarely change for the sake of anything else, including the programs of the revolutionaries. They are the last refuge of the desperate, but they represent a brave and dangerous step for those not so desperate who have something still to lose.

There is much to be lost in China now by a wrong move. So much has been gained there since the many low points which that nation has achieved, or to which it has been thrust, in the last few centuries. The starvation appears to be over; the international domination and neglect and isolation have ceased. There is pride, once more, and ambition.

The injection of radical steps into any of this would be done at significant risk. It is not like adding a new factor to the California business climate, for things have been steady in California for a long time—no wars, no revolutions, no starvation, no colonization, no massive oppression, and no cruelty, all of which are both long-standing and recent memories for most living Chinese.

The injection of the technical capacities of the Internet, and all of the implicit social and political values that it carries with it, is very much to the credit of the Chinese. Many problems and questions remain. Who will provide the information access in the Chinese context, to whom, at what price, and what will be the content of the information and the prohibitions are as-yet unanswered questions in China, as they are in most places. The Chinese answers may not be those obtained in other places, perhaps at least for several of the uniquely Chinese reasons suggested here. It may be promoted primarily by foreigners, it may fall victim to the political vicissitudes currently changing China, and it might ultimately become owned by the army. It certainly won't resemble the Internet in California.

But whatever they eventually decide to do with it, the fact that the Chinese have opened the door this far to what promises to be a revolutionary development in any national context does them a great deal of credit.

NOTES

[1]   http://sunsite.unc.edu/lunarbin/worldpop

[2]   Sun-tzu, translated with introductions and commentary by Ralph D. Sawyer, with the collaboration of Mei-Chun Lee Sawyer, *The Art of War = [Sun-tzu ping fa]*, Boulder, CO: Westview Press, 1994.

[3]   Balazs, Etienne, translated by H. M. Wright and edited by Arthur F. Wright, *Chinese Civilization and Bureaucracy: Variations on a Theme*, New Haven, CT: Yale University Press, c1964.

[4]   Cahill, James, *Fantastics and Eccentrics in Chinese Painting*, New York: Arno Press, 1976, c1967; Cahill, James, *Chinese Painting*, [Geneva]: Skira ; New York: Rizzoli, c1977.

[5]   Urquidi, Victor L., *The Challenge of Development in Latin America*, New York: F. A. Praeger, 1964; Hirschman, Albert O., *The Strategy of Economic Development*, New York: Norton, 1978, c1958; Prebisch, Raul, *Latin America: a Problem in Development*, Austin: Institute of Latin American Studies, University of Texas at Austin, 1971.

[6]   See http://www.cuhk.hk/hkwww.html for a well-maintained list of Hong Kong-based W3 resources and services.

[7]   Eisenstein, Elizabeth L., *The Printing Press as an Agent of Change:
Communications and Cultural Transformations in Early Modern Europe*,
Cambridge [England], New York: Cambridge University Press, 1979; Eisenstein
does not say this herself but instead presents an erudite analysis of what often is a
simplistic historical controversy.

Chapter 7

India—Asia's awakening giant

INDIA HAD 788 Internet hosts as of January 1996: one Internet host per 1,188,509 people in India (India sometimes beats even China at superlatives) (per Network Wizards, http://www.nw.com, and CIA World FactBook 1995, http://www.odci.gov/cia/publications/95fact/index.html).

The Indian subcontinent contained monolithic nations before the British era but never an "India." One of the greatest ironies of Asia is that its nation second largest in population—and potentially now among the most powerful economically in the world—is, in fact, a European creation. Ashoka and the Mauryas had large empires long ago, but what we know today as India was created by the stroke of a British civil servant geographer's pen in 1949 [1].

None know this better than the Indians themselves. National unity has been the greatest single national priority since the devastations of *Partition*, the occasion for the bitter and bloody division of India from Pakistan, only a generation ago. The divisiveness of interregional, interracial, interethnic, interlinguistic, and interreligious conflict has been the greatest single fear of Indian national politicians since Mahatma Gandhi toured burned Moslem villages in Bengal 50 years ago. Moslem extremists still kidnap tourists in Srinigar, Buddhists and Hindus battle each other at religious sites in the center of the country, and Tamil separatists wage overseas wars from the South—all somewhat heedless of so-called national policies announced in New Delhi.

Yet, India today works, is stable, and is growing economically at rates as phenomenal as were the legends of India's mass starvations and economic inabilities of the 1950s. Western mothers cautioned their offspring then to, "Think of all the starving children in India"; today, Bangalore, which at most produced sandalwood handicrafts back then, makes software of its own design for computer users in Tokyo.

Indian divisiveness remains, however. There is little sensation in discussions in Madras that national policy set in New Delhi will have direct effects in either promoting or inhibiting Talmil Nadu affairs. Kerala in the South, with its long Communist political tradition and phenomenal high literacy rate at 98% (women are included in the total, as they still often are not elsewhere in the country) has little in common with the great and sprawling and impossibly impoverished city of Calcutta in the East.

One can feel the atmosphere of the Middle Ages and the Silk Route sitting by the Jhelum River in a teahouse in Srinagar and the aura of the twenty-first century coasting through the sprawl and immense wealth of the international movie colony of Bombay's Malabar Hill. Srinagar's and Malabar Hill's languages, diets, smells, air qualities, political traditions, religions, histories, and basic ways of thinking are fundamentally and perhaps irreconcilably different. The one might be and often considers itself to be more a part of Afghanistan, and the other more a part of Beverly Hills. In neither place does one sense any unifying element of a common India that will bridge the obvious gaps, certainly not one emanating from New Delhi.

Perhaps Indian divisiveness is a national virtue, however, at least for the purposes of its rapidly growing online digital information technology. If one can build an industrial plant in Orissa or Bihar, relatively unconcerned about New Delhi much less the rest of India, then perhaps India has avoided a degree of overcentralization that might stifle local development, at least depending upon the character of the administrators at the center. There are cases elsewhere, in fact, where such has been the deliberate policy; *benign neglect* has a time-honored role in administrative policy in most places, and perhaps India is no exception.

Nehru pursued strongly centralized and firmly national restrictive development policies during his administrations in India's early 1950s. Today, though, it seems that the restrictions, certainly those exerted from the central government, are less.

How very different this approach is from the flexible centralization of France, or the more rigid centralization of Singapore, or this last as it may or may not be exported to China and other Sinic cultures and non-Sinic Singapore neighbors, all as described above. Any of the Indian digital libraries developments, described in what follows, must be considered at least against this general Indian difference from several of its more significant neighbors in the online digital information world.

The WWW Virtual Library: Asian Studies: India Subsection (in Pasadena and Argentina)

The India W3 service illustrated here is housed on a computer physically located in Pasadena, California, but is produced by one "Sergio Paoli" who may be found at the Observatorio Astronomico de La Plata, in Buenos Aires, Argentina (Figure 7.1).

via W3 to: **http://webhead.com/WWWVL/India/**

Infoservers and Libraries in India (in Bangkok, Thailand)

This second resource is located physically on a computer in Bangkok, Thailand. It is an excellent effort, offering a full range of India-based digital libraries resources (Figure 7.2).

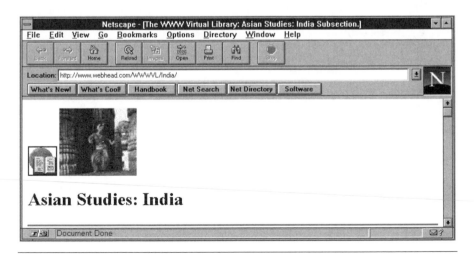

Figure 7.1 Global Reach—India in Buenos Aires via Pasadena. © 1996 Netscape Communications Corporation.

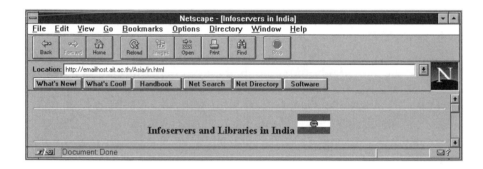

Figure 7.2   Global Reach #2—India in Bangkok. © 1996 Netscape Communications Corporation.

via W3 to: **http://emailhost.ait.ac.th/Asia/in.html**

The Tamil Nadu Home Page (in Tennessee)

This service (Figure 7.3), which is part of a broader online digital information effort concerning all of India, offers a wonderful array of resources and services concerning anything Tamil, from its food to its dancing to its very ancient

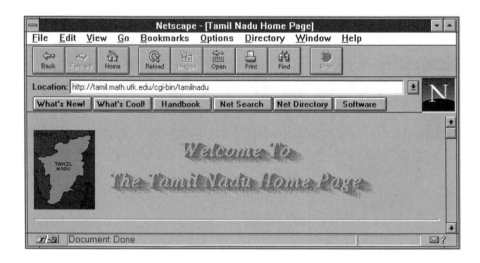

Figure 7.3   Global Reach #3—Tamil Nadu in Tennessee. © 1996 Netscape Communications Corporation.

poetry. Most of the material is in English, but much of it is in the visually very beautiful written Tamil language.

via W3 to: http:tamil.math.utlc.edu/cgi-bin/tamilnadu

7.1 Summary

So one initial observation might be that the *Indian Diaspora* appears to have been every bit as great as that of the Chinese, at least in online digital information. Valuable digital libraries efforts for India appear to be scattered from Pasadena to Buenos Aires to Bangkok and Tennessee. Now, perhaps, those of this Diaspora are coming home to help, both digitally, in the form of digital libraries activity, and physically, as increasing numbers of Indian graduate students turn down Oxford and MIT for schools in Bangalore and Bombay.

The same vast assortment of resources and services may be found, however, among online digital information applications physically located within India itself. Among the organizations in India that one finds online are the Birla Institute of Technology and Science, the Coimbatore Institute of Technology, the Delhi Institute of Technology, the Indian Institutes of Management and of Science at Bangalore, the University of Bombay, Jadavpur University, Haryana Agricultural University, the University of Baroda, and the universities of Calcutta, Hyderabad, and Roorkee.

NOTES

[1]   Collins, Larry, and Dominique Lapierre, *Freedom at Midnight*, New York: Simon and Schuster, [1975].

Chapter 8

Australia—the antipodes, and the sheer *reach* of online digital information

AUSTRALIA BOASTED 309,562 Internet hosts as of January 1996: one Internet host per 59 people in Australia (per Network Wizards, http://www.nw.com, and CIA World FactBook 1995, http://www.odci.gov/cia/publications/95fact/index.html).

Australia illustrates, perhaps better than any other country, the true international opportunity of online digital information. One of the greatest attributes of online digital information, certainly in its international application, is its ability to span great distances. The push of a button speeds information over telecommunications lines; for example, a user sitting in California can consult a library catalog located in England as though she were sitting in a reading room in Oxford.

Great distances are a thing with which Australians are familiar. Not only do they have them at home—they live in a country that is among the largest and the least populated in the world—but their nation as a whole has been considered, since its founding over a century ago, to be at an end of the earth as opposite from the English origin of most of its founders as one could get. A nineteenth-century Yorkshire potter—or Devonshire convict—could dream, or have nightmares, about few places in his universe more remote from home then Bendigo or Botany Bay.

So it would seem that few places on the earth would be more interested in using the Internet, with its immense distance-spanning capabilities, than Australia. Not only might it be used to send information back and forth instantly over the more than two thousand miles that span Sydney and Alice Springs and Perth, but it might connect those cities with people and information back in what used to be called the "home" country, over 10,000 miles away [1].

This has proven to be the case. Internet growth in Australia came early and has been enormous. Australian libraries and universities were among the earliest users outside the United States of Internet techniques. Australia now is fifth among nations in total Internet hosts, with over 300,000 total hosts, a figure growing at over 200% per year, and currently with a phenomenal one host per 59 people [2].

There is a looming problem with Australia's Internet position, however, one that makes it a fascinating case for international comparisons going forward. As able as it is to benefit from online digital information's greatest attribute, that is, that of bridging great distances, Australia itself is burdened by what currently is online digital information's own greatest difficulty in scaling up internationally: both are culture-bound and stem from Anglo and specifically English-language cultural traditions to which non-Anglo/English language cultures have difficulty adjusting.

Australia, like the Internet still generally, is a monocultural territory, entirely English speaking, composed of English traditions both explicit and implicit, and offering very little to the foreign visitor in terms of user-familiar accommodation. As one travel expert puts it, "Socially and economically, Australia is still trying to come to terms with its place in Asia" [3]. A French or Chinese visitor to Sydney feels as unfamiliar as one does visiting an *American ASCII* Usenet session discussing American baseball.

Modern Australians, however, are not anxious to accept their prolonged isolation either from each other or from the outside world. Great efforts have been made in Australia recently to adopt and develop online digital information techniques to span Australian internal distances. These efforts are being applied to the bridging of Australian cultural distances from its immediate Asian outside world, as well.

Some of the more interesting and comprehensive work to develop online sources of information about Asia is being done on Australian information servers. What will be most interesting to see is the extent of until-now monocultural Australia's ability to apply an until-now monocultural technology to an increasingly multicultural online digital information market and world. Australia could turn out to be one of the Internet's great laboratories for examining the international scaling up of the technologies. Australian digital libraries efforts are leading the way with sites such as those that follow.

The National Library of Australia

The *National Library of Australia* (NLA) is a national library, online, but this one is "on the other side of the Earth"(Figure 8.1).

One would expect that the national library of a large industrialized country would have a large and elaborate digital libraries presence online by now, and Australia's is no exception. The NLA makes a sophisticated online catalog, a variety of noncatalog information sources about both the library and Australia generally, and links to many other non-Australian information resources easily available to any online digital information user physically located anywhere.

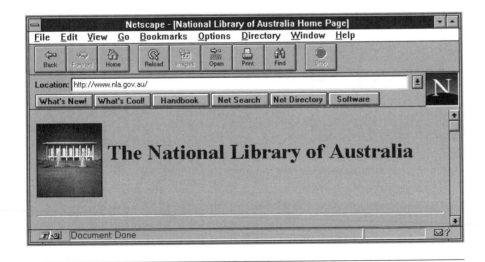

Figure 8.1   The NLA—digital libraries in the Antipodes. © 1996 Netscape Communications Corporation.

All of these Australian resources are subject to the usual digital libraries praise and pitfalls. The NLA's online graphics and bibliographic organization are very up to date, and connectivity to all of them generally is rapid and smooth, despite the great distances. There are the usual problems (noted elsewhere here) of the lack of bibliographic description standardization in the library community generally; Australian MARC formats will marry well with the MARC formats of some but not of all other nations.

There also appears, however, to be a lack of anything but the English language in this Australian case. The NLA has impressive projects under way in *Chinese-Japanese-Korean* (CJK), *Asian Collections,* and *Chinese Library Resources.* But these still are buried; one has to dig to find them online. This Australian digital libraries service does not display its initial information—its W3 service, its gopher, its telnet catalog access—in foreign languages or offer initial foreign language options to the user as do most European and Asian digital libraries services; there is no Chinese or Japanese version of the login screens as there is English at the Bibliothèque Nationale de France.

One would think that with sizable populations (both resident and transient) of non-English speaking people—officially as much as 5% of the population, although unofficial estimates range much higher—and with a historical shift within Australia itself from an identification and preoccupation with Europe to an interest now in neighboring Asia, that Japanese or at least Chinese might show up on Australian digital libraries screens sometime soon.

The truly unique thing about this particular digital libraries service, though, is that it is so very far away. The most impressive demonstration of the power of online digital information is its ability to span distances, and Australian applications certainly demonstrate this.

via W3 to http://www.nla.gov.au

State Library of Tasmania

The State of Tasmania is the antipode of the antipodes—the truly global reach of online digital information in digital libraries (Figure 8.2).

Perhaps even more dramatic than the idea of Australian online digital information being instantly available anywhere in the world is the idea of Tasmania—the antipode of the antipodes, even to most Australians—being more easily reached now, from most places—more easily than the neighborhood store, any nondigital library, or even the bookshelf downstairs.

Tasmania's State Library has mounted an excellent digital libraries service in English only, inevitably limited by resources available to this small, offshore Australian state, and subject to all the library cataloging standardization

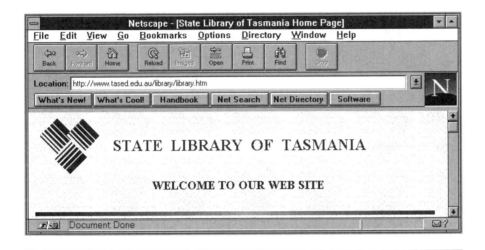

Figure 8.2   Tasmania—digital libraries in the Antipodes of the Antipodes. © 1996 Netscape Communications Corporation.

problems confronting most libraries—nevertheless now accessible from anywhere, including modems in western China, Russia, Kansas, Scotland, and Tibet.

via W3 at http://www.tased.edu.au/library/library.htm

Australian National University—Coombsweb Social Sciences Server

The *Australian National University* (ANU) provides Australian digital libraries outreach, to Asia and further (Figure 8.3).

Australia has gone much further, however, than being merely the farthest away. The profound shift in Australian interests from the extreme Eurocentrism that prevailed through the 1960s, to a broad internationalism and increasing interest in neighboring Asia, is reflected directly in the ANU's superb digital libraries effort, *Coombsweb*.

Coombsweb is among the oldest and most comprehensive attempts to provide online digital information to global digital libraries users. As of the Spring of 1996 it boasted, "Last week this site was accessed 53,110 times. Since the start of its operations (25 January 1994) until the end of last week, the Coombsweb server was accessed 2,617,228 times . . . Currently the Coombsweb server offers over 4800 hypertext links to the best available online resources developed by research institutes, libraries, and universities from all over

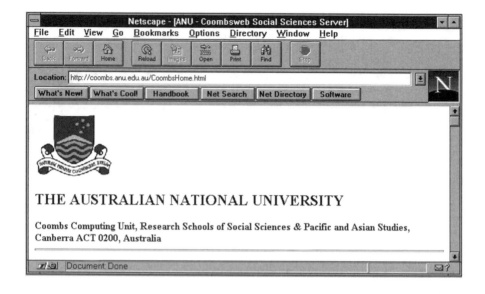

Figure 8.3   Coombsweb—Australia goes Asian. © 1996 Netscape Communications Corporation.

the world. New links are inspected and evaluated before being added to the Coombsweb suite of information facilities" [4].

Even more significant than Coombsweb's popularity, history, and rigorous technique, though, is its particular internationalist approach. Coombsweb offers *WWW Virtual Library* services, which is a part of a more general project overseen by the *W3 Consortium* [5], in Asian Studies, Buddhist Studies, Indonesia, Pacific Studies, Papua New Guinea, Tibetan Studies, and Vietnam. Coombsweb's efforts are currently among the leading digital libraries resources, in each of these areas, to be found anywhere in the world. On them one can see and use not only very complete descriptions and information links to online efforts in each of the areas addressed. In a couple of cases, Coombsweb services are the only adequate, or even the only, online services in their subjects—Coombsweb's digital libraries work in Vietnam and certainly in Papua New Guinea, for example, both appear still to be unique.

via W3 at http://coombs.anu.edu.au/CoombsHome.html

NOTES

[1]   http://www.indo.com/distance/

[2]   Mark Lottor / Network Wizards—http://www.nw.com

[3]   Lonely Planet Publications—http://www.lonelyplanet.com/dest/aust/aus.htm

[4]   Coombsweb—http://coombs.anu.edu.au/CoombsHome.html

[5]   The WWW Consortium—http://www.w3.org/hypertext/DataSources/bySubject/Overview.html

Chapter **9**

Thailand—the blending of worlds, third and other

T HAILAND HAD 4,055 Internet hosts as of January 1996: one Internet host per 14,863 people in Thailand (not yet the Developed World, although getting there rapidly) (per Network Wizards, http://www.nw.com, and CIA World FactBook 1995, http://www.odci.gov/cia/publications/95fact/index.html).

There was a time, not so long ago, when international development was a simple thing. There were three worlds: one euphemistically described as *First*, meaning the *Developed World*, or us; the *Second*, or the *Communists*; and the *Third*, meaning the *Underdeveloped* or, a little later, the *Developing*, or everyone else. Conventional wisdom, in the 1950s, the 1960s, for much of the 1970s, and even still into the 1980s, was that the nations of the Third or Developing World would strive mightily, with much outside First-World monetary and good-will assistance, to attain a quasi-mystical threshold known as the "takeoff into sustained economic growth" [1], and become somewhat like us, the First

World. Now, though, in the 1990s, things no longer are so clear, and there are few places in the world—First, Second, Third, or other—where all of this is less clear than in Thailand.

Thailand very certainly was a part of the Third or Underdeveloped/Developing world in the 1950s. The nation's economy was nearly entirely agricultural then, its population largely rural, its infrastructure largely undeveloped, and its international presence largely nonexistent. Today, Thailand boasts and complains of enormous cities, thriving and rapidly growing industries, and an increasing role as a stable regional leading force in a Southeast Asia that otherwise seems to be perennially unstable. Formerly ancient and serene Bangkok today boasts modern industry, international banking presence, and highways—and traffic jams—that equal those of cities of any other formerly developed nation.

Thailand's development, moreover, now relies largely on investment increasingly not from the United States and Western European Developed world but from a source that itself was in dire straits in 1955: Japan. Thailand's growth has been helped by many factors, including international and "Western" loans. But its primary sustenance today is Asian. In a trend that is increasing in Asia and is being reflected in more and more of its national economies, increasing proportions of Thai capital sources—and its suppliers and its customers—are being found not in the United States and Western Europe but elsewhere in Asia. Americans and Europeans who view Thailand—or for that matter any other Asian state, including those just emerging from the aftermath of the Vietnam War—as being merely potential clients for a renewal of the old East-West trade and influence patterns of the 1950s, had better look again.

Thai Internet and W3 presence, much less sophisticated applications of both such as the digital libraries shown here, are about as unthinkable to a 1950's national development mentality as is the idea that Japan would be motivating Thailand's economic growth. But the world has changed, and the Thais are online. The question appears no longer to be whether "the West" will be the primary player, but whether "the West"—or even Australia, which is a Western nation with an Eastern presence, and very much would like a role—has any role to play at all in Thai and general Asian development going forward. Thai digital libraries, from here on in, may well be Thai.

Asian Institute of Technology (AIT)

Anyone with notions at all preconceived about Asia and its degree of technological development would do well to visit the AIT's site online. Their *Center for Library And Information Resources* (CLAIR) offers nearly everything that might be sought from an online digital information resource located in Mountain View, California, such as help lines, online resources, training programs, and a galaxy of online Internet search engines. There even is an online coffee break—called *no_retur.html*—presented as a recreation center, with images and links to a vast variety of entertaining image services, movie sites, games, and other cyberspace relief, even "Monty Python's homepage," available here via Bangkok (Figure 9.1).

AIT's CLAIR offers online access to the AIT library catalog and a reference section containing links to a wide array of global digital libraries sites and experiments.

via W3 to **http://emailhost.ait.ac.th/clair/**

Chiang Mai University

Chiang Mai University is an example of provincial digital libraries, but in provinces in Asia? (See Figure 9.2.)

What is true in the development story generally for Thailand also is true in its own provinces. Digital libraries development in this former Third World country has taken place in sites located far from its capital. In Chiang Mai,

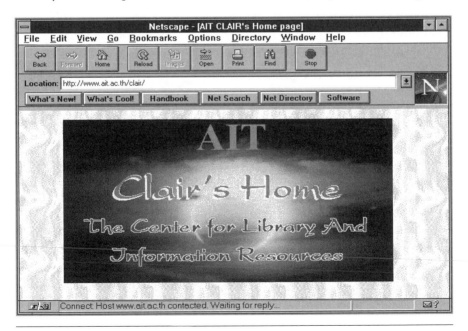

Figure 9.1   The AIT—digital libraries in Thailand. © 1996 Netscape Communications Corporation.

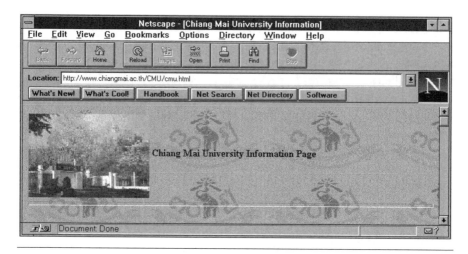

Figure 9.2 Chiang Mai University—the deep reach of digital libraries, already, in Asian provinces. © 1996 Netscape Communications Corporation.

Thailand's very beautiful northernmost province, the local university has mounted a full W3 service, complete with full descriptions of the university, a campus map, links to information resources, and even a Cyber Publishing Thailand Project—associated with the Department of Library Science—which publishes fulltext student papers online, in Thai.

via W3 to http://www.chiangmai.ac.th

Chulalongkorn University

Chulalongkorn University offers a full information panoply, as other Thai digital libraries sites do, in this case supplemented even with the sound of the school song, online, which can be heard by online digital information users in Tasmania, China, Kansas, or anywhere (Figure 9.3).

There also is a university Museum of Image and Printing Technology online at Chulalongkorn, in Bangkok, in Thailand (Figure 9.4)—a fact that may astonish some Thais as much as it does Westerners, both of whom still may labor under an image of a Thailand of rice paddies, water buffalo, Buddhist monks, old temples, and water markets. Such an image is taken more from *Anna and the King of Siam* than from anything at all related to the booming Asian industrial and high-technology center that Thailand very recently has become.

One wonders, in fact, whether the Thais are not ahead in the game, because not too many Western European and U.S. cities and universities have had the foresight to establish a Museum of Image and Printing Technology to preserve

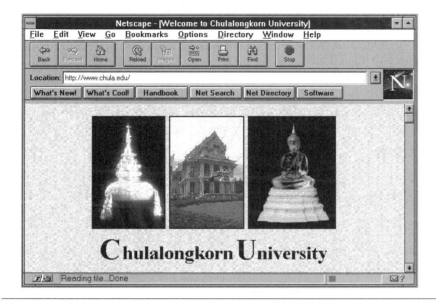

Figure 9.3 Quality work in Asia—Chulalongkorn University. © 1996 Netscape Communications Corporation.

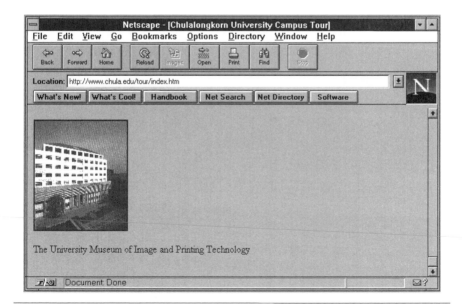

Figure 9.4 A "Museum of Image and Printing Technology" in Asia. © 1996 Netscape Communications Corporation.

these rapidly changing and quickly disappearing techniques, much less to put it all up online in a digital libraries service.

As with other Thai services, linguistic problems loom large just beneath the surface at Chulalongkorn. Initial online interfaces all are in English, but many of the substantive files that may be reached are in Thai already—one wonders when the balance might shift, either to all English as some in the West fervently believe, all Thai, or some other more Asian combination.

via W3 to http://www.chula.edu/

via W3 to http://www.chula.edu/tour/PhotoMuseum/ photo-museum.html

NOTES

[1]   Rostow, W. W., *The Stages of Economic Growth: a Non-Communist Manifesto*, 3rd ed. Cambridge [England], New York: Cambridge University Press, 1990.

Chapter 10

The United Kingdom—crowded pipes

THE UNITED KINGDOM boasted 451,750 Internet hosts as of January 1996: one Internet host per 129 people in the United Kingdom (per Network Wizards, http://www.nw.com, and CIA World FactBook 1995, http://www.odci.gov/cia/publications/95fact/index.html).

The case of the United Kingdom illustrates a particularly technical example of the development of online digital information.

Despite its own occasional protestations to the contrary, the United Kingdom enjoys several affinities to the United States that make it better able to take advantage of a new U.S. technology than other non-U.S. nations. A common command of the English language is only one such advantage.

India has this as well in large part, as do significant portions of Eastern Africa and the educated elites now in most countries. The United Kingdom also has a high level of technical education, very much the equivalent of technical education in the United States, again despite often-cited differences that mask the basic similarity. But, yet again, other nations enjoy this; French, German, Scandinavian, and Japanese technical education are of a high quality as well.

One perhaps unique advantage enjoyed by the United Kingdom, though, is the continuing cultural identification, made by many Americans, with the United Kingdom as their "mother country." There is a nearly parallel idea in the minds of young British, Welsh, Irish, and Scottish engineers of the United States as—if not an ongoing colony—at least a continuing new frontier and land of opportunity, still with some ties to the United Kingdom. The result is what still is referred to as a *special relationship* between the United States and the United Kingdom, offering mutual opportunities for tourism, education, and general cross-fertilization that help a development such as online digital information immensely.

It was far easier, therefore, in the 1970s, to recognize and develop an application of the new digital technology in the United Kingdom than it was in France or Malaysia, despite the presence in Paris and Kuala Lumpur of plenty of people who spoke English. There was more regular travel between the United States and the United Kingdom, more cultural interchange at official and unofficial levels, and perhaps greater understanding of cultural differences and similarities on both sides. The most important factor was the hard work and dedication of the developers, in the United Kingdom as elsewhere. But it also was relatively less trouble in London to get a computer or workstation installed and understood and to establish an information network that might become a node on the then-new Internet (not as much trouble, at least, as in other places).

With unique advantages, however, come unique disadvantages. As U.K. Internet use has grown, U.K. technical telecommunications capacities to handle that use have been out-stripped repeatedly. The pipe that connects the numerous and highly sophisticated U.K. users to the U.S. home base of their technology has had continuous trouble keeping up with the explosive usage growth.

Recently, the problem has been greatly increased by the arrival of general public access and the widespread and rapid adoption in the United Kingdom of the Internet's "killer application," the WorldWideWeb. Some of the most exciting, or at least active, W3 development in the world now is under way in the technically and digitally highly sophisticated United Kingdom, and yet the services and servers that these developers use still largely are located physically in the states.

This great activity, particularly as it increasingly involves the high-bandwidth applications of W3's imaging and sound—literally has brought U.K.-U.S. digital telecommunication in some cases and at some times to a halt. System response time of large U.S. servers, for example, is measured in milliseconds in the United States and can take at most 1 or 2 seconds from continental Europe and elsewhere in the less-cluttered telecommunications world. But recently it has run to a highly unacceptable 10 to 20 seconds along the increasingly crowded U.K.-U.S. telecommunications channels, that is, 20 seconds simply to wait for a response to a single keyed command, which is enough to discourage the most patient U.K. general public user from going any farther.

This U.K. telecommunications traffic problem seems well worth examination and careful consideration by any growing international online digital information channel. Current cabling capacity to Japan, Hong Kong, Hanoi, and Shanghai may be considered far in excess of any future need for now, but so was the NSF-Net relay originally set up in the United Kingdom in the 1980s and the original U.K. universities network [1].

The problem now is that the general public and particularly the commercial Internet users are not as patient with telecommunications traffic slowdowns or with anything else as were the academic testbed users of the 1980s. Technical researchers fascinated with the technology per se might wait 20 seconds, but consumers on the run along Hong Kong's Nathan Road, or parents on their way to pick up the children after school in Bangalore, will not.

Much of the U.K. use seen in what follows may seem impressive—certainly by comparison to the as-yet more limited offerings found in other countries—but the really impressive story of U.K. digital development is the precedent that it offers, no doubt soon to be confronted by other countries, of attempts to keep up with increasingly overcrowded international telecommunications channels.

The British Library

The British Library is the "Portico," as the name implies, the place to start.

The British Library's *Portico* service, somewhat like the Library of Congress for the United States or the Bibliothèque Nationale de France for that country, is the place to begin for an exploration of British digital libraries. From the new and daring logo to the broad-ranging and international selection of online services offered to the warm "We welcome your comments and suggestions" offer on the Portico W3 page, there is little hint now of the august and somewhat forbidding *British Library* (BL) predecessor formerly lodged at the beautiful but now very old Reading Room in Bloomsbury, the library that once made it so hard for readers like Karl Marx even to gain entry therein, much less to use the books. But times have changed (Figure 10.1).

Now Portico offers a vast array of general public–oriented digital libraries services from current news bulletins to public events to great numbers of online

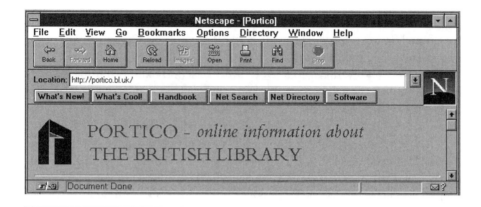

Figure 10.1   The British Library—great libraries online. © 1996 Netscape Communications Corporation.

catalogs and databases to images to descriptions of impressive, new, and almost-completed library buildings. In Portico, the BL has foreseen and adopted nearly every digital libraries technique to have been developed to date, including a very good search service for mining through its own extensive file structure.

Two observations, though, must be made about this leading example of a digital libraries service.

First, the BL, like an other library in Europe, the Americas, Asia, or anywhere else, is very much subject to the general lack of standardization that may be observed in digital libraries services less sophisticated than those offered by Portico. British Library bibliographic records, while they may marry well with formats used by their North American cousins, do not yet marry well with formats used on the continent. The BL, a leader in the effort to standardize in this area, is very aware of the problem, but the problem persists nevertheless.

Second, the BL's digital libraries effort is being made entirely in English. The apparent logic of this practice belies the linguistic diversity and flexibility that one finds in digital libraries efforts elsewhere. In Asia and elsewhere in Europe, the online catalogs and W3 library services speak more than one language, that is, a national language plus at least English, perhaps, but often two or three others, and all with the crucial ability to add still others, as the necessity arises and time and funding permit. One wonders, seeing the BL approach, what linguistic flexibility it might offer to non-English-speaking populations at home in the United Kingdom and certainly in the continental Europe, across the Channel, of which Britain supposedly has become a part.

Thus far, however, the BL digital libraries linguistic medium, whatever its vast technically multimedia capacities might be, is and is only English.

via W3 to **http://portico.bl.uk**

Oxford

This site presents the great medieval university, bibliographic riches told and still untold, information access online par excellence, and superb digital libraries coordination in what, nevertheless, is described as, "an extremely rich, diverse, and fragmented library service provided by over 100 independently managed library units" [2] (Figure 10.2).

Oxford's digital libraries presence, despite the fragmentation of its many independent efforts, offers a variety that perhaps only online digital information techniques are able to organize and present to a user. It certainly is difficult at Oxford. The hundreds of big and little official Oxford libraries, not to speak of the many hundreds of other nonofficial yet invaluable collections of print and nonprint information scattered through the town—on professors' bookshelves, in college common rooms, on researchers' hard disks, and in strange little museum and archival repositories—are nearly impossible to identify altogether, much less to gain access to and use.

All this offers a slightly chaotic information organization, cherished fondly by those who have used it well and remembered bitterly by those whom it has frustrated. Online digital information organization could well represent the first effective means in history of pulling all the many valuable information resources

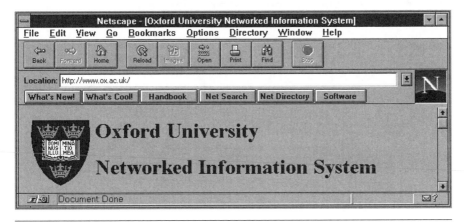

Figure 10.2   Oxford University—great universities online. © 1996 Netscape Communications Corporation.

that exist at Oxford together, the irony being perhaps that it took a technique designed for viewing things from Australia to see what could not be seen conveniently for centuries from central Oxford.

What has been accomplished now, however, could serve as a model for similar situations, in which large numbers of loosely affiliated treasure houses of information are to be associated for a user's convenience, online as they might never be seen together offline. From the Oxford homepage, a user now can proceed to tour through colleges, academic departments, computing services, and a great many libraries.

via W3 to http://www.ox.ac.uk

The Bulletin Board for Libraries

The *BUlletin Board for Libraries* (BUBL) provides meta-information for professionals, online (Figure 10.3).

Among the various sophisticated information services that have been mounted online in the United Kingdom is one that perhaps presages an entirely new development in online digital information—the professional use of it by professionals—led by none other than professional librarians.

BUBL is one of the longest-standing and best-established online information services. It offers:

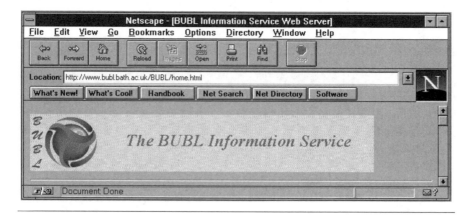

Figure 10.3   Online library service—BUBL. © 1996 Netscape Communications Corporation.

1. *The Subject Tree,* a subject-based service to the academic and research community that indexes all sorts of professionally useful online information resources;

2. *Library,* a highly developed area of The Subject Tree that includes a
   specialist *Library and Information Science* (LIS) service designed to
   help information professionals online;

3. *CATRIONA/*CATalaguing and Retrieval of Information Over Networks Applications, a project based at Strathclyde University to investigate the technical, organizational, and financial requirements for
   the development of applications programs and procedures to enable
   the cataloguing, classification, and retrieval of documents and other
   resources over networks..."

The next development, for the chaos that currently reigns in much of online
information, is for information professions to get online—or to develop anew
there—particularly professionals who will assist general public users in finding
and using online information. This is happening somewhat already—both,
officially, in the enormous grown of the online indexing industry, represented
by services such as Yahoo, Infoseek, McKinley, and AltaVista, and unofficially,
in the equally enormous growth of the information broker and Internet consultant professions. These players realize the tremendous need, and commercial
opportunity, represented by the newly arriving hordes of general public users
who are having great difficulty in finding and using things on the Internet. BUBL
represents one profession's—the existing library profession's—excellent attempt to fill this need.

BUBL also represents, however, an even broader possibility, that is, the
professional use of online digital information by any profession. Attorneys,
doctors, accountants, and members of many other professions all increasingly
are online as individuals. As online digital information sophistication grows,
however, these individuals increasingly are looking to it for applications in their
work—for information, for delivery of goods and services, and for secure billing
and accounting applications.

Just as BUBL is making a good beginning at providing professional services
for the library/information profession, so other online services are evolving to
cater to attorneys, doctors, accountants, qua professionals, and not just in
their current capacities as occasional private users. BUBL's digital libraries

application offers at least part of a model for this professional trend in online digital information.

via W3 to **http://www.bubl.bath.ac.uk/BUBL/home.html**

NOTES

[1]   Stone, Peter, "A Library-Oriented Overview of JANET," *Internet World*, Vol. 4, No. 3, April 1993, p.14.

[2]   Margaret Robb, in—http://www.lib.ox.ac.uk/guides/

Chapter 11

Hungary—phenomenon of the stranger

HUNGARY HAD 11,486 Internet hosts as of January 1996: one host per 898 Hungarians (per Network Wizards, http://www.nw.com, and CIA World FactBook 1995, http://www.odci.gov/cia/publications/95fact/index.html).

One further international development model for online digital information perhaps is presented by the case of Hungary. One of the leaders there is an organization of outsiders, financed by a single individual who, despite his own personal Hungarian roots and identification with its traditions, represents to the country an entirely outside source of capital, expertise, and investment. In Hungary, George Soros, an American investment whiz of Hungarian origin—who was greatly influenced by the late Karl Popper and has named his organization after Popper's most famous book *The Open Society*—has mounted an almost personal crusade to bring Hungary and much of the rest of eastern Europe online onto the Internet.

Figure 11.1   Central European University—George Soros's *Open Society* and the philanthropic model. © 1996 Netscape Communications Corporation.

This effort has involved the establishment of foundations, projects, international organizations of various types, and the *Central European University* (CEU)—an international institution for post-graduate study and research. "Founded by Hungarian-American philanthropist George Soros in 1991, CEU also promotes educational development and policy making throughout Central and Eastern Europe and the former Soviet Union. CEU has a provisional charter from the state of New York and is recognized as a foreign educational institution in Hungary and Poland" (Figure 11.1).

Personal philanthropy as a development model for the scaling up of online digital information, and for digital libraries? Nothing could be farther from the imaginations, perhaps, of those who built the original U.S. government-funded academic testbed Internet. But stranger things have occurred already in the

Internet's growth; no one thought there would ever be commercial applications and general public access either.

Now George Soros's *Open Society Foundation* and *Central European University* present a remarkable and sophisticated digital libraries presence for Hungary online. There are few places now outside of Hungary where one can find out this much about the country, either online or elsewhere.

A personal philanthropy development model—single-minded to the point of being the product of the ideas, organization, and even money of a single individual—perhaps could not be applied to a large or complex development situation such as that of China, Russia, or a smaller yet already industrialized and complex nation like the Netherlands, for example. Eastern Europe, however, represents a well-known anomaly in most of these respects. The nations there are not unduly large. Until recently they were highly centralized and controlled, and their populations still are accustomed to such central control (in some cases they now say they yearn for its return) and are sophisticated and highly educated certainly by comparison with many other developing nations, and they are physically close to the enormous economic production and consumption engines of Western Europe, which still is the world's largest trading bloc if considered as a single entity.

Of these various factors, perhaps the most crucial for any general analysis is Hungary's—and to some extent the rest of Eastern Europe's—history and continuing acceptance of the need for central control. This would appear to augur well for Hungary's acceptance of the type of online digital information development solution represented by the Open Society effort and Soros. To Soros' and the Open Society effort's credit, they officially stand for the opposite of centralized control and are doing their utmost to discourage it. The question remains, however, even for Soros and in Hungary, whether the outsiders will succeed at reforming an inside situation that has remained the same for several generations.

Such a single-minded personal effort as Soros is using in Hungary would spread itself quite thin over a nation the size of India or China. It probably would founder completely amid the complexities of a sophisticated and modern nation like The Netherlands. But how many nations are there that, like Hungary, are neither so large nor so complex and sophisticated as not to be amenable to such a centralized or at least single-solution approach? Perhaps there are not many nations in the developing world that have the additional unique Hungarian characteristics of a well-trained workforce and the nearby highly developed resource-assistance pool and enormous consumer market of Western Europe. But if the Open Society/Soros solution now being developed for Hungary could be grafted onto at least the other countries of Eastern Europe, it could become one of the leading development models for the international progress of online digital information by virtue of this success alone.

> via W3 to http://www.ceu.hu/; also, http://www.ceu.hu/library/ budlibes.html, for the CEU library, Budapest.

Chapter 12

Japan—investing versus consuming

J APAN HAD 269,327 Internet hosts as of January 1996: one Internet host per 466 people (per Network Wizards, http://www.nw.com, and CIA World FactBook 1995, http://www.odci.gov/cia/publications/95fact/index.html).

One of the great, looming, still-unanswered questions in all of high technology is the role to be played in online digital information by Japan. Japanese ability to adopt and develop foreign technologies has become the stuff of legend. Japanese inability themselves to innovate unfortunately has become the mythical corollary of that same legend. As with most legends, neither extreme statement is true, that is, neither the legend of Japanese genius in development nor the myth of Japanese inability in innovation are true as often too generally stated, although there seems to be at least a grain of truth in each [1].

Japan certainly appears, at first glance, to be significantly behind the rest of the developed and networked world in terms of Internet utilization, at 269,327 hosts, ranked sixth in the world behind the United States, Germany, United Kingdom, Canada, and Australia but only slightly ahead of Finland, the

Netherlands, and Sweden [2], countries currently smaller and less well-known for their acumen in electronics and high technology than are the Japanese.

For a nation so often touted as representing not only one of this century's leading economic miracles, but even as the spear-carrier for a coming Asian domination of the next, Japan appears at first glance to be incapable of implementing the new online digital information revolution at home in Japan itself.

But this first glance view of Japanese networking ignores at least two factors.

First, information networking itself is relatively new. If and to the extent that Japan truly is an accomplished developer of other people's technologies, then the technology itself perhaps needs a little more time really to take off before a development-skilled Japan can bring its supposed true productive talents to bear upon it.

Online digital information techniques truly are sophisticated already, but their application in the markets that the Japanese know best—in the mass consumer markets, both in the United States and elsewhere—has only just begun. Consumer electronics—perhaps the best-known example of the particular Japanese genius in production organization and marketing—was a well-established if somewhat tired industry in the United States when the Japanese entered and began their literal takeover of it for both the domestic U.S. and other non-U.S. markets. The auto industry, another immense Japanese success, was in a similar state—tired and perhaps grown inflexible and somewhat unimaginative—but definitely not new and undeveloped. Online digital information is at a stage now that is very unlike that of either the consumer electronics or the automobile industries when Japan entered those. Much innovation still is needed in online digital information, precisely the innovation that some observers of Japanese industry so often cite as Japan's greatest development weakness.

Second, any first glance of Japanese networking that criticizes—and perhaps pins its hopes upon—any supposed innovation weakness at home in Japan would also ignore the past quarter-century of East and Southeast Asian economic development, which has seen a spread of Japanese economic and basic business power throughout the region. This has been a development that was unthinkable to the post-World War II generation and is still unthinkable to many observers and decision makers in Asia, the United States, and Europe.

To a great and increasing extent, online digital information development taking place in the neighboring nations of East and Southeast Asia—where such development is becoming as extraordinary as development in Japan itself has seemed extraordinarily laggard—may be attributed to Japanese offshore and overseas investment either directly or, perhaps more often, indirectly.

The extent of this Japanese participation is extremely difficult to tabulate accurately. Japanese-owned and operated firms in East and Southeast Asia are plentiful enough. Japanese equity ownership, both controlling and minority, extends the picture even further. Indirect Japanese investment, finally—yen- and non-yen-denominated investments by Japanese nationals and banks and corporations, in non-Japanese organizations that in turn invest in others—further extends the picture to include perhaps every significant economic player on the East and Southeast business scene today.

Seventy-five years ago such an economic picture of the Asian business scene would have been presented as evidence of a grand conspiracy. Fifty years ago it would have been dismissed as lunacy. Asians were starving, then, Japan was defeated and broke, and Japanese manufacturing was considered so much a laughing-stock that American schoolchildren and some journalists equated the phrase "made in Japan" with "junk." Most importantly, politically, socially, and economically the United States totally dominated the region, and the defeated enemy, Japan, was almost as totally dismissed and derided.

That this all has changed so completely today is not the result of another conspiracy, and there has not been another war to decide things either way. It is the result rather of the undeniable economic fact that Japan has become the largest source of capital for economic investment in the region—of the world's 10 largest banks, all but one (the Deutsche Bank) now are Japanese, and none have been American for many years [3]—and of 25 years of work by an industrious if supposedly noninnovative people, and a relative decline in the Asian fortunes of the United States [4].

The result is that Japanese online digital information work may largely be found outside Japan, elsewhere in Asia. Direct, indirect, and at times even disguised overseas investment is providing for the development of an online digital information infrastructure that perhaps has not yet approached the enormous increase in figures of the United States and Europe but that may eclipse it one day soon. There are, as business people involved longingly repeat to themselves, like a mantra, over a billion people in China alone—approaching three billion in all of Asia, or half of the population of the planet—and if/when all of them become consumers, of online digital information or of anything else, that market will dwarf any other. This may well be a market owned, operated, and run in largest part—at least indirectly—by the Japanese.

The development problems within Japan itself are traditional. From Ruth Benedict to Arthur Koestler, foreign commentators have characterized the domestic Japanese scene as being somewhat schizophrenic [5], that is, characterized by rigid traditionalism mixed with an immense and effective desire to change and improve. Online digital information development there or the lack thereof perhaps merely offers another example: the immense Japanese ability to develop new products and services and even to innovate in this development, abroad, coupled with great rigidity and incapacity to do the same at home.

Structural problems within Japan itself, ranging from the immense conservatism of the Japanese consumer to the rigid control hierarchies that order the lives of corporations and entrepreneurs to territorial turf wars between government entities such as the Ministry of Trade and Industry, the Post Office, and telephone systems [6] are all cited often to explain the difficulties faced by online digital information's development within Japan. It would be best generally to remember, in addition, that this small island nation's economic influence—and its influence over the development of online digital information— now extends far beyond its own borders, in a manner comparable in extent similar perhaps only to that of Britain during the last century.

Tokyo Institute of Technology Library

The Tokyo Institute of Technology Library offers a W3 service (Figure 12.1) that gives an excellent overview of digital libraries services currently available within Japan itself. In addition to its own library services—a guide to its library, a list of current serials received, a description of a special collection, and access

Figure 12.1 Japan at home—the Tokyo Institute of Technology Library. © 1996 Netscape Communications Corporation.

to its library catalog and its gopher service—TITECH Library offers Other Information for Librarians (various Japanese and international professional resources for librarians, such as a link to RLG), a description of its parent institution Tokyo Institute of Technology, a list of library online catalogs in Japan with links, a list of library W3 servers in Japan with links (following), a list of nonlibrary W3 servers in Japan with links, and an interesting offering of mass media links (such as newspaper, TV, and radio stations).

http://www.libra.titech.ac.jp/welcome_e.html

WWW Servers in Japan (Libraries)

There are already a number of digital libraries, or at least libraries that are online, in Japan—enough to impress the most skeptical Japan Internet watcher (Table 12.1).

Table 12.1   Digital Libraries in Japan

http://www.library.tohoku.ac.jp/library-e.html—Tohoku University Library;

http://www.u-aizu.ac.jp/public/www/istc/library-e.html—The University of Aizu;

http://www.tulips.tsukuba.ac.jp/welcome.english.html—University of Tsukuba Library;

http://www.ll.chiba-u.ac.jp—Chiba University Library;

http://w3.mlib.gunma-u.ac.jp/lib-e.html—Gunma University Library;

http://baloo.cc.uec.ac.jp—The University of Electro-Communications Library;

http://www.libra.titech.ac.jp/welcome_e.html—Tokyo Institute of Technology Library;

http://www.higashi.hit-u.ac.jp/library.html—Hitotsubashi University Library;

http://shallot.pine.timis.ac.jp/home.html—Tama University Library;

http://www.lib.shizuoka.ac.jp—Shizuoka University Library;

http://www.tut.ac.jp/english/libraryE.html—Toyohashi University of Technology;

http://www.kulib.kyoto-u.ac.jp—Kyoto University Library;

http://lib.kuicr.kyoto-u.ac.jp/index_e.html—Library of Institute for Chemical Research, Kyoto University;

http://library.mtl.kyoto-u.ac.jp/default_eng.html—Materials Science Library, Kyoto University;

http://www.library.osaka-u.ac.jp/english.htm—Osaka University Library;

http://www.lib.kobe-u.ac.jp/e-index.html—Kobe University Library;

http://www.lib.tottori-u.ac.jp/eng_index.html—Tottori University Library;

http://owl.shimane-med.ac.jp—Shimane Medical University Library;

http://www.lib.ehime-u.ac.jp/HTML/eng.html—Ehime University Library;

http://www.lib.tokushima-u.ac.jp—Tokushima University Library;

Digital Libraries in Japan (continued)

http://www.is.kochi-u.ac.jp/lib/kulibhome.html—Kochi University Library;

http://www.lib.kyushu-u.ac.jp/index.html—Kyushu University Library;

http://www.cc.saga-u.ac.jp/saga-u/lib/libhomepage.html—Saga University Library;

http://www.miyazaki-med.ac.jp—Miyazaki Medical College;

http://mediacenter.sfc.keio.ac.jp—Keio University Media Center;

http://www.nacsis.ac.jp/nacsis.f-index.html—National Center for Science Information Systems.

via W3 to http://www.libra.titech.ac.jp/libraries_Japan_e.html

Stanford Japan Center

Then too, there is the Stanford-Japan Center (Figure 12.2), a joint project of the Kyoto Center for Japanese Studies, affiliated with Kyoto University, and the

Figure 12.2 Japan overseas—the Stanford Japan Center. © 1996 Netscape Communications Corporation.

Center for Technology & Innovation and Institute of International Studies, at Stanford University in the United States. Among the Center's aims are sponsoring conferences and workshops; assisting faculty research; and Research Initiatives, one of which is currently something called "Project on the Promotion of International Research Networks and Specific Digital Archives" and even something called "Links Galore," offering one of the more complete digital libraries online of Japanese information with Images of Japan, Virtual Kyoto, Jobs in Japan, and Current Weather Maps-Movies.

Perhaps few places in the world, including few places in Japan, are more involved in the development of online digital information applications in Japan—including its digital libraries—than is Stanford University in California in the USA. Nearly weekly, now, there is a lecture or workshop or other manifestation of interest, in and near California's Silicon Valley, in the development of online digital information in Japan by groups such as the Stanford University U.S.-Japan Technology Management Center [7] (Figure 12.3).

Figure 12.3 Japan overseas #2—the Stanford University US-Japan Technology Management Center. © 1996 Netscape Communications Corporation.

There is no irony in this, however. Cooperative research is increasingly the model for development in many scientific fields, and there is no reason why this should not be so for digital libraries, aided in this case by certain characteristics of the very scientific techniques being studied, such as the ability of online digital information systems to span great distance, to create neutral arenas in which controversial subjects might be studied, and to assist in multilingual communication. The model being used by the Stanford Japan Center could well provide a cooperative research and development model for use elsewhere.

via W3 to http://kyoto.stanford-jc.or.jp

NOTES

[1] Johnson, Chalmers, and Laura D'Andrea Tyson, John Zysman, eds., *Politics and Productivity: the Real Story of Why Japan Works*, Cambridge, MA: Ballinger, c1989; Scalapino, Robert A., *The Politics of Development: Perspectives on Twentieth-Century Asia*, Cambridge, MA: Harvard University Press, 1989; Morita, Akio, Edwin M. Reingold, and Mitsuko Shimomura, *Made in Japan: Akio Morita and Sony*, New York: Signet, 1988, c1986; Fallows, James, *Looking at the Sun: the Rise of the New East Asian Economic and Political System*, New York: Pantheon Books, c1994.

[2] Mark Lottor/Network Wizards—http://www.nw.com

[3] http://rtk.net/E10660t430

[4] Kennedy, Paul, *The Rise and Fall of the Great Powers: Economic Change and Military Conflict from 1500 to 2000*, New York: Random House, c1987.

[5] Benedict, Ruth, *The Chrysanthemum and the Sword*, London: Secker & Warburg, 1947; Koestler, Arthur, *The Lotus and the Robot*, New York: Macmillan 1960.

[6] Johnson, Chalmers, *MITI and the Japanese Miracle: the Growth of Industrial Policy, 1925-1975*, Stanford, CA: Stanford University Press, 1982; Johnson, Chalmers, *MITI, MPT and the Telecom Wars: How Japan Makes Policy for High Technology*, Berkeley, CA: Berkeley Roundtable on the International Economy, [1986].

[7] http://fuji.stanford.edu—a WWW Virtual Library project, which itself contains complete and beautifully presented award-winning information about Japan.

Chapter 13

Indonesia—the rest of Asia and the world

I NDONESIA HAD 2,351 Internet hosts as of January 1996: one Internet host per 86,595 people (per Network Wizards, http://www.nw.com, and CIA World FactBook 1995, http://www.odci.gov/cia/publications/95fact/ index.html).

Indonesia is a nation perhaps as untypical as any other. This vast archipelago spans an area as great as any large nation, but it consists primarily of water. The islands rest in the tropics, in climates as hot and wet and sticky as anywhere else on Earth. What land Indonesia does possess ranges in human population from nearly deserted expanses of Kalimantan/Borneo to Java, which is the most densely populated area of human habitation on the planet.

Indonesia has varieties of race, ethnic origin, and cultural, social, and political practices that make most other nations seem positively homogeneous. Indonesian Moslems inhabit islands next to Bali, an enclave of one of the world's most famous populations of Hindus. In both cases, the religions are as different as they might be from those elsewhere of which they are said to be a part. Balinese Hinduism looks very little like anything to be found in India. Of the Indonesian Moslem religion, one leader in Jakarta is supposed to have observed that the reason why the Prophet's holy color, green, is not more prevalent in Indonesian decoration is that while Mohammed lived in a desert, where green is a welcome color, in the Indonesian jungles everything already is green.

Indonesia does possess, however, certain qualities in common with many other countries that distinguish both it and them from the nations that have been listed here so far. These distinguishing qualities consist primarily of things that Indonesia is not. It is not wealthy, advanced, or developed. Indonesia is not among the East Asian "tiger" economies that now so rapidly are advancing and developing and have become the darlings of the international investment community. Indonesia has more cultural ties with similarly situated third world/developing Moslem countries than it does with the United States or Western Europe. Indonesia is not Japan; it is not China; and it is not one of those other remarkable Asian nations about which one hears so much in the West.

Indonesia still has, furthermore, a *client-state* status—one inherited from a long period of colonialism and one that it has not yet fully outgrown—that gives it much in common with the rest of the world not so far described. The Indonesian economic and political legacy from their Dutch period is not completely extinguished, yet, as similar colonial legacies have been totally snuffed out in other Asian nations. Indonesian students still yearn for positions at universities in the Netherlands; Indonesian families still speak proudly of elders who studied at Leiden or who know Dutch culture well.

To some extent, moreover, the Indonesian colonial legacy has been transferred now to the Japanese. Japanese investment is omnipresent in Asia. But in other situations—like those of Taiwan, Korea, Thailand, or certainly China—there is a sense, at least, that a joint venture is under way by which local partners and Japanese investors are sharing in a common enterprise in which the local investor, in fact, is quickly gaining the upper hand.

Not so in Indonesia. The discrepancy in degree of development is too great, the cultures too different, and the availability of capital that might compete with the Japanese too absent. In Indonesia, industrial plant built with Japanese capital during the 1930s was reconditioned during the rapid growth period of the 1960s and 1970s and operates today literally as off-shore Japanese-owned and operated development—as nothing resembling the joint ownership and operation that takes place elsewhere in Asia.

So Indonesia is far more like the rest of the world, now, than are several of its Asian neighbors. The same continuation of economic, political, and even cultural client-state status exists that characterizes nations like, somewhat, Malaysia, Burma, and, until very recently, the Philippines and most of the nations of Latin America, Africa, and the Moslem Middle East.

There are many nations, besides those just listed, that currently are candidates for digital libraries development. Most of them are pursuing online digital information development in some form or another. Many exhibit characteristics found in the nations analyzed here. Some, though, will show characteristics that have not been addressed but could have a profound effect on digital libraries development, such as the religious fundamentalism of devoutly Moslem cultures, the inherent political instability of military regimes, and the severe health crisis of AIDS-infested sub-Saharan Africa—although this last now appears to be a burgeoning problem in Thailand and Vietnam as well. Indonesia perhaps has more in common with these other nations, at least in these first two respects, than any other nation examined here so far.

"From Ritual to Romance"—An Indonesian Online Service

Bali is the island of which Indonesia is most proud, or from which it is at least most willing to profit. The uniqueness of its Balinese religion, general culture, and particularly art is recognized in Jakarta as well as in the rest of the world. Since the conceptual discovery of the South Pacific generally by the Western intelligentsia, at the end of the last century, and particularly since its development as a cultural icon by Covarrubias [1] and other Western artists, earlier in this century, Bali has enjoyed a privileged status.

One thinks of Indonesia, and one thinks of Bali; and even if one does not think of Indonesia, Bali stands on its own, and the Indonesians always are at great pains to emphasize the connection. The From Ritual to Romance service offers 40 online iconographic images from Bali (Figure 13.1). These are contemporary art, and the service offers links to artists' attributions and sketch biographies. The images are in gif format and are easily downloaded and used by personal computers anywhere.

One day Bali might proclaim the independence de jure that would correspond to its current cultural independence de facto from the Javanese mainland and the rest of Indonesia; annexation by Telluride, Colorado, or by Greenwich Village or the Paris Left Bank might be in order, although increasingly the hordes of teenagers sprawled on the Balinese beaches are Japanese. Until then, though, information about Bali and especially images of the island are expected to be leading components of any Indonesian digital libraries effort.

Most interesting to note though, perhaps—certainly for students of digital libraries generally—is that this service is not physically located in Bali itself or

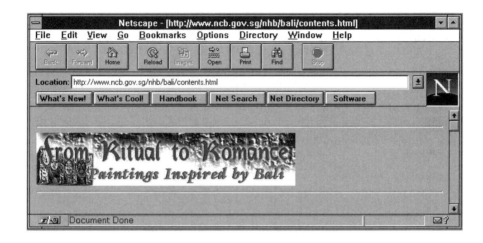

Figure 13.1   Asian neighbors—Indonesia's Bali, in Singapore. © 1996 Netscape Communications Corporation.

even in Indonesia. From Ritual to Romance is mounted on The Online Museum of Singapore Art and History—Government of Singapore, *National Heritage Board* (NHB) server.

This is not the only instance of the offshore application of online digital information. It is the essence of this technology to make distance communication possible. There are many digital libraries applications about the United States lodged on servers that are not themselves physically located in the United States; there are many about France that are not in France.

The situation of Bali, Indonesia, and Singapore is entirely different from those of the United States or France, however. There are cultural and political tensions in the Balinese situation that the United States and France do not enjoy or from which they do not suffer. The United States has little to fear—culturally, politically, or certainly economically or militarily—from any outside power that might, for example, offer a less-than-orthodox version of U.S. culture to U.S. people. The French fear more, for good reason or not.

The Balinese, however, have much to fear, by any account. Bali is a poor island, at least militarily, economically, and politically, if not culturally. It has felt that is has faced great threats in the past from its Indonesian parent; and Indonesia as a whole has felt great tensions for many decades with its fabulously wealthy, ethnically, and culturally very different neighbor just across a very narrow channel, Singapore.

The presence of Balinese digital libraries offerings on a Singapore Internet server carries political, economic, and even military overtones with it that rarely would be thought of in the case of a similar French service located in Luxembourg and never even would be considered for an American Culture offering on a server in Canada or Mexico.

via W3 to   http://www.ncb.gov.sg/nhb/bali/colorplates/
platesmaster.html
http://www.ncb.gov.sg/nhb/bali/contents.html
http://www.ncb.gov.sg/nhb/bali/fount/fountmaster.html

WorldWideWeb Virtual Library: Indonesia

Another friendly neighbor of Indonesia—this one interested more with Indonesia generally than with just its Balinese jewel—is Australia. Many of the same caveats regarding the Indonesia-Singapore relationship apply to the relationship with Australia: the same fears, the same threats real and perceived, the same potential for cross-cultural understanding and misunderstanding—perhaps less benign, perhaps more, than those of the Indonesia-Singapore link.

In this case, the "W3 Virtual Library: Indonesia" service, housed at the *Australian National University* (ANU), is one of a number of digital libraries services organized under the aegis of the W3 Consortium's W3 Virtual Library project [2] (mentioned in Chapter 7) that attempt to give a comprehensive overview of online resources available on their subject. Like many of the other W3 Virtual Library efforts, ANU's on Indonesia is excellent. There appears to be little available elsewhere online on its subject that is not at least mentioned, if not provided with an active link (Figure 13.2).

The service is, however, Australian. It is located, sponsored, financed, and one has to presume greatly influenced in and by Australians and in and by Australian attitudes and economic, political, and cultural opinions. The advantages of such separation have to be weighed against the disadvantages. There are times when an offshore location can bring with it greater objectivity. Voltaire found this at Ferney—a stone's throw, or a mad dash, across a field from refuge in Switzerland—and Hugo found this on Jersey, to cite only the French case.

But objectivity itself can be culturally conditioned. Even an Indonesian staff and good Indonesian contacts and information cannot ensure that an Indonesian service physically located in Australia does not become Australian—perhaps obviously or, more dangerously, subtly and insidiously, in ways that become apparent only during times of cultural and political crisis. There was a time when *Free France* consisted literally only of a single radio microphone located in London; this time has faded for modern memories, but those who

Figure 13.2   Asian neighbors #2—Indonesia in Australia. © 1996 Netscape Communications Corporation.

remember will recall that each side thought that the other was greatly biased in its supposed objectivity about France at the time.

Indonesian digital libraries, located physically in Australia hopefully never will confront a crisis similar to that which highlighted the biases on both sides during the Free France period, but bias of some sort nevertheless could well be present. This is a looming and largely unrecognized problem of online digital information. The supposed freeing of information from its cultural constraints—by enabling telecommuting and distance communication generally—does not free it; it only moves, and new combinations of cultural bias come up in the new location.

via W3 to   http://coombs.anu.edu.au/WWWVLPages/
IndonPages/WWWVL-Indonesia.html

Sekolah Tinggi Manajemen Informatika, Surabaya

One Indonesian digital libraries service that is in fact physically located in Indonesia is that of the *Sekolah Tinggi Manajemen Informatika,* at Surabaya on eastern Java. This is a campus W3 server, similar at least superficially to campus W3 servers of universities and research institutes located in other countries (Figure 13.3).

The similarity is understandable. We still are early in the development of online digital information, and much of the relevant knowledge is acquired internationally, in person and online. The student who set up this service in Surabaya may have copied something similar that was found, either on a visit there or more likely just on W3, at Berkeley.

If and to the extent, however, that one learns at least a different view—if not the true or a more objective one—of Indonesia by seeing what Indonesians themselves say and do about it, this W3 service, which offers campus news, email mailing lists, and links to other Indonesian higher education institutions, is a place to start for making comparisons.

via W3 to **http://www.stikom-sby.ac.id/**

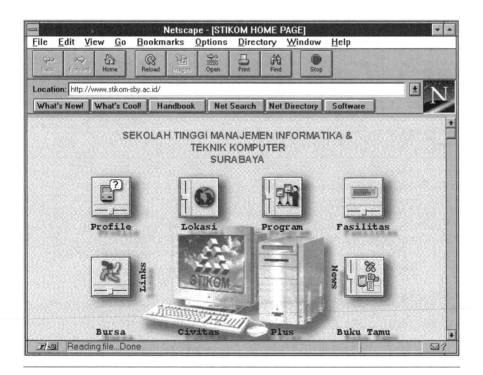

Figure 13.3   Sekolah Tinggi Manajemen Informatika—Indonesia in Indonesia.
© 1996 Netscape Communications Corporation.

Universitas Katolik Parahyangan/Parahyangan Catholic University (UNPAR), Bandung

Another Indonesian digital libraries resource—another one not physically located "in" Indonesia, and, like the other in Australia, subject somewhat to all the same caveats about cultural conditioning—offers a set of tools invaluable for any digital libraries investigation (Figure 13.4).

Someone at this Tokyo-based server has seen fit to mount and provide, among other services, a series of online electronic conferences on Indonesian subjects such as:

- KAMPU (general UNPAR community);
- IPTEK-L (applied sciences and technology);
- PUSKOM-L (informatics, computer sciences, networking);
- WARTA-L (campus news);
- HUKUM-L (law and legal matters);
- ARSITEKTUR-L (architecture and engineering).

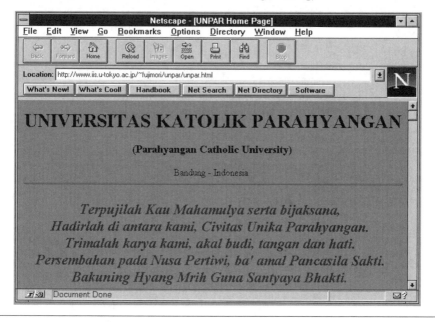

Figure 13.4   Asian discussion—an online digital library of e-conferences on Indonesia, in Japan. © 1996 Netscape Communications Corporation.

One of the greatest problems confronting online digital information is the appropriate use of the new technology. The older term *appropriate technology* referred more to questions of size, its adherents worrying that tendencies to throw money at a problem resulted in tractors being sent when a shovel would do—and horrendous and occasionally funny stories such as that of the snowplow that rotted for several years on a pier in tropical Lagos, Nigeria.

The online digital information appropriate technology problem, however, has more to do with the transition in media of which digital libraries are a part. The analogy often used is that of old wine and new bottles: There is little disagreement that new bottles are in use in the case of the new digital technique, but there is discussion concerning whether the information thereby contained is the same old wine. A recurring problem is that the digital techniques employed in fact often are not very new. Printed books are digitized and made to look just like printed books, only online. Paintings that hang inertly on gallery walls are digitized and made to hang, just as inertly—and with arguably less texture and color resolution—on computer screens. Some things are lost and little is gained in making such a formalistic transition.

The online electronic conference, however, is a quintessential example of the new techniques of the online digital information media. Participants from anywhere in the world are able to exchange information and opinions, in the best cases properly moderated by firm but flexible conference moderators, in ongoing email-based discussions that take place twenty-four hours per day, seven days per week around the globe. Of even greater value than the discussions themselves, for some purposes, the discussions are archived online, and search engines are made available for the convenient search and retrieval of the information that they contain.

In a field of as recent origin as online digital information—in which so little yet is "in print" and conditions change so rapidly that anything that is "in print" is nearly by definition out of date—online searching of a good electronic conference archive is the best and often is the only source of comprehensive and reliable information. This adds value to the electronic conference exercise in addition to the enormous global reach and convenience of online access and the often-political advantages that the anonymity of this access provides.

A user in Iceland can investigate political conditions in Indonesia via a Tokyo-based W3 information server's e-conference, relatively undetected, if she is careful. Electronic conferences typically have hundreds of members and are run by one or very few moderators; in the most successful instances, they may involve tens of thousands of members in many dozens of countries.

The offerings of e-conferences at the Universitas Katolik Parahyangan server offer perhaps the most forward-looking source for online digital information among the various Indonesian digital libraries efforts that are currently available.

via W3 to http://www.iis.u-tokyo.ac.jp/~fujimori/unpar/unpar.html

Sekolah Tinggi Teknik Surabaya (STTS)

One further example of an Indonesian W3 service—this one located in Indonesia itself—presents another application of digital libraries techniques. The W3 service mounted by the Sekolah Tinggi Teknik Surabaya technical institute, in addition to its offering of the usual information about its own institution, provides links to a number of online services of Indonesian printed periodicals, such as ANTARA Online, GATRA Magazine Online, Indonesia Daily News Online, Info Komputer Online, Jawa Post Online, KOMPAS Online, Media Indonesia Online, Republika Online, Surabay Post Online, SWA Magazine Online, and Warta Ekonomi Online (Figure 13.5).

There has been some discussion here already of the appropriate use of the new technology, that is, of the need to take advantage of new techniques of online digital information—such as electronic conferencing—and not just to transfer the old techniques to the new medium, the "old wine" to the "new bottle," the "printed book" to the "online digital book."

But there is, nevertheless, a transition going on. While the change is taking place, there is valuable information in print for which access still is needed. Indeed unless certain extreme positions are believed and adopted, there always will be at least some room for print; just as the written tradition did not stop people from talking and as the printed book did not stop them from writing, so digital information will not necessarily replace all of printing—the day may be long in coming when people willingly will read a paperback novel online [3].

So printed periodicals—and the online services now being designed with painful slowness by those who produce printed periodicals—may be reached online. This means, for the most part still, three things.

1. General information, of the type not constituting news to be printed in the journal—community bulletin board information of various types;

2. Archives, of previous journal issues and other information, equipped with sophisticated search engines for online search and retrieval;

Figure 13.5   Asian e-publishing—an online digital serials library, in Indonesia.
© 1996 Netscape Communications Corporation.

3. "Teasers" for current issues, containing lead articles and issue high-
lights, mounted online as inducements to users to go out and purchase the actual printed version.

Of the three, the archives and their ancillary search services are the most
valuable for now. As with an electronic conference archive, a good periodical's
archive can provide an invaluable reference resource for any research—all the
better if that archive is easy to use via its sophisticated search and retrieval
engine, can be downloaded easily for incorporation into a researcher's text, and
is accessible online though it is physically located halfway around the world.

Increasingly, though, the online teaser services, which now only induce consumers to buy a printed journal, will replace them, particularly in international distribution. Printed journals of various types, especially newspapers, are already failing generally in most countries, for a complicated variety of reasons. Their much-predicted demise in the 1930s and then the 1950s, at the hands first of radio and then of television, perhaps simply has taken longer than was first thought. Then too, the costs of paper and of the printing process have generally not gone down, although this point can be argued.

The availability of online news services merely is a continuation of such substitution arguments. The idea is that, because wire services and other original news sources now may be found online—and, furthermore, may be searched and retrieved and organized by sophisticated software into personalized newspapers—that this, at last, will sound the final death knell of print journalism. Not so, however, still, for all the reasons that defeated or at least delayed the predicted victories of the television and the radio. Print journalists take sometimes-justifiable pride in their professional ability to select, organize, present, and interpret information and themselves credit this with having defeated the onslaughts of other media.

Economics has played a part as well. Radio and television were cheap to the consumer, but they quickly became so successful as to become expensive for the producer—the prices of advertising spots and programming time rose to such an extent that anything at all eccentric, anything at all offering the flexibility necessary to cater to personal taste, became squeezed out of TV and radio.

Then too, there are characteristics inherent in the manipulation of the medium itself that are given credit and blame. People like to hold books, magazines, and newspapers in their hands. They like to write on them, shove them in their pockets, and use them for lining trash containers or decorating dens and studies or propping up the ends of broken tables—and people will continue to pay a price for all this, albeit perhaps less than they paid before.

But other media—radio and television—have the benefit of the same sort of argument: one cannot sit on a couch, with one hand on a beer and the other on a pretzel, and enjoy a book. Ultimately the lesson learned by the advocates of the substitution arguments perhaps simply was that different folks prefer different media for different reasons—always have and always will.

Now, however, comes a new threat: commercial opportunity for the printers themselves. If the transition in media can be made not hard and jolting, as the transitions from print to radio or print to television were meant to be, but smooth, insidious, and, moreover, easy for print producers and consumers themselves to make, perhaps there will be a different result this time around. One key factor appears to be payment. The transfer of cash and its bookkeeping—both the mechanics and the security of such transactions—still have yet to be developed and implemented to everyone's satisfaction online.

Much progress is being made, however. On the day when a newspaper's publisher can be satisfied that a consumer easily and securely can pay for her subscription online, both publisher and subscriber may well decide that the immense reading, printing, searching and retrieving, and archiving capacities of online digital information may well outweigh any supposed convenience of holding a thing printed by someone else in one's hand, particularly if the former is cheaper, as the development of pay-per-use online access appears to promise.

Furthermore, international access makes all of these arguments somewhat easier. In the international arena, the byword of any current discussion of printed journals and periodicals is money. Prices of international journals and periodicals have increased so much recently—at a time when academic, library, and even general subscriber budgets have been reduced by economic recession—that serials budgets everywhere have been cut, particularly for international subscriptions. Libraries in the United States and Western Europe, which are among the largest consumers in the international serials distribution market, have been forced to cut so much that many significant international serials have literally disappeared from access.

So international serials, whatever their eventual development in online digital information applications, have reached a point of financial crisis already, one perhaps resolved only by digital libraries access of the type offered here by STTS online. This may be very old wine in a very new bottle, but at least someone is getting something to drink.

via W3 to http://www.stts.ac.is

Indonesia Meta-Data—a Note

Indonesia has many more university, government, and private online information resources now. For a fairly complete list, with links, see on W3,

http://www.carleton.ca/~hmantiri/universities.html

and there is a good W3 search-tool for Indonesian information subjects available at

http://www.cs.utexas.edu/users/adison/cgi/bimasearch

which accepts simple keyword searches on now over 800 Indonesian-based online resources.

13.1 Summary

There is so much information on Indonesia available now online—and so many new online tools with which to cull through and digest and manipulate it—that the researcher's traditional information problem has become reversed. It no longer is a problem of having too little information but of having too much. There is no more guarantee now than there ever was that all the necessary information is provided; only now there is—or at least there seems to be—so much more information to sort through in order to arrive at this or any other conclusion.

The example of Indonesia points out, furthermore, that information sur-feit—information overload—can be true even of a relatively underdeveloped and in fact neglected subject. It should come as no surprise that there is a great deal of information available online about the nations of Western Europe and North America or about the now very newsworthy and rapidly developing nations of Eastern Asia.

But that Indonesian digital libraries should be as prevalent as they are online should surprise some. There was a time not long ago when a researcher on Indonesian subjects would find very little available in a local library in the United States, Western Europe, or for that matter, in Indonesia itself. The print medium had its own economics and set of priorities. Dutch libraries perhaps had larger collections, but most library entries and shelves anywhere devoted to Indonesian information were relatively limited, certainly by any proportion to that country's size and population.

It is just possible that the advent of online digital information will change some of these information priorities and proportions, as any true revolution does. The economic factor still is present; it still requires economic wealth to mount and serve out information, and most economic wealth still is in the United States and Western Europe; although it seems that much is in the process now of transferring to eastern Asia.

Online digital information, however, is a relatively rootless commodity and service. It attracts investment from a variety of sources, for a variety of reasons, and we have seen here—in Indonesia's example as well as several others—that it can function relatively independently of physical location. Online digital information about Indonesia, which economically is still a poor nation, can locate itself physically in nations as wealthy economically as Australia, the United States, and Japan, and still be just as effective and just as effectively distributed, in Indonesia itself as elsewhere. The same cannot be said of printed journals or of the printed book.

This may constitute a "sea change" in more than just information. When there is a fundamental change in the terms of trade, more than just trade changes. For many years a single U.S. dollar could purchase 360 Japanese yen; then, for a long time, a dollar bought 280 yen; then, 240; today a U.S. dollar is sometimes at pains to buy 100 yen. This reflects more change in the relationship between the United States and Japan, and in their respective political and cultural positions in the general world, than mere economics can indicate—Japan is not just richer than it was before, it now is more important, in many ways.

The same need not necessarily be said for Indonesia. Indonesia may not have become more important over time, relative to the United States or to any other nation, the way Japan has. What may have changed, however, is the way in which these things are measured.

Fritz Machlup posited some time ago the advent of an information society [4], and since then commentators from Peter Drucker to the Tofflers have observed that information—its production, its provision, its control—increasingly would be the primary occupation and locus of power in the society that now is emerging in most countries. To the extent that online digital information techniques have increased the amount of information about Indonesia that now is available, it may well have increased the global importance of Indonesia; and to the extent that this Indonesian information now is greater than that available for some other country, Indonesia's importance may have been increased relative to that other country as well.

National prestige and significance is a competition felt acutely by most people on the international scene despite any protestations to the contrary. It would be good news for participants in this race who are from economically poor countries if they were to learn that an entirely new factor—information—had suddenly become available to them to use instead of the frustratingly unavailable economic wealth that for so long has eluded their grasp. The same might be bad news—or good, perhaps—for economically wealthy countries.

Either way, what is true for Indonesia is also true for a vast number of relatively impoverished nations not usually counted among the economic leaders of the world. There is now a great deal of digital information available online about these places, information that never has been so available in such quantities before. Digital libraries are organizing all this and bringing it to users. The full impact of the global changes that this effort will bring has yet to be felt.

NOTES

[1]   Covarrubias, Miguel, *Island of Bali*, New York: A. A. Knopf, 1937.

[2]   http://www.w3.org/hypertext/DataSources/bySubject/Overview.html

[3]   Crawford, Walt, and Michael Gorman, *Future Libraries: Dreams, Madness &* *Reality*, Chicago: American Library Association, 1995.

[4]   Machlup, Fritz, *The Economics of Information and Human Capital*, Princeton, NJ: Princeton University Press, c1984.

Chapter 14

National government— the NSF digital libraries projects, in the United States

THERE ARE MANY digital libraries projects under way in the United States. There are so many, in fact, as to be literally uncountable—the projects change, and definitions twist, and most of all the numbers increase too quickly—like most current Internet statistics that are U.S.-based. This is not, furthermore, a book about the United States, but about the international development of digital libraries on the Internet. The emphasis here deliberately is on nations other than the United States, which was the Internet's birthplace and therefore understandably contains much more activity in these areas at the moment.

Nevertheless, there is one very clear-cut area in which U.S. digital libraries development is setting the pace, not only for the United States but also for non-U.S. settings. There is an overwhelming need for consolidation and focus of all the disparate threads of digital libraries discussion in order to provide some conceptual grasp of the underlying activity, as that activity goes through its frenetic changes and phenomenal growth. Whatever the eccentric differences are that might develop between one nation's digital libraries approach and another's, all share a common need for clarity of concept; it does not have to be the same concept, but there does have to be some sort of organized effort mounted to achieve clarity about it.

In the United States, the national government, through its National Science Foundation (NSF) agency, has created a mechanism for achieving this much-needed conceptual clarity about the digital libraries development that is taking place in the United States and elsewhere:

"The Initiative's focus is to dramatically advance the means to collect, store, and organize information in digital forms and make it available for searching, retrieval, and processing via communication networks—all in user-friendly ways. Funded through a joint initiative of the NSF/ARPA/*National Aeronautics and Space Administration* (NASA)" [1].

This collection of U.S. national government agencies has provided, since 1994, US$24 million to six projects—$4 million each—to try to investigate leading-edge issues in the construction and use of digital libraries: of any digital libraries, of any type and located anywhere—precisely the sort of conceptual underpinning the need for which just was noted. The result, in this U.S. context, has been the formation of six university-based consortia, each engaged in the collaborative research for which U.S. university and general research procedures have become famous.

1. Carnegie-Mellon University: "full-content search and retrieval of video";

2. University of California at Berkeley: "work-centered digital information services";

3. University of California at Santa Barbara: "spatially referenced map information";

4. University of Illinois at Urbana-Champagn: "federating repositories of scientific literature";

5. University of Michigan: "intelligent agents for information location";

6. Stanford University: "interoperation mechanisms among heterogeneous services."

In each case, the consortium involves a number of different departments and actors on the university campus—centering usually, but never exclusively, on the computer science department—plus numerous off-campus public (government) and private (corporate) sector partners.

The differences in aim and approach among the six NSF digital libraries projects are instructive and have received much comment. Several of the projects build upon undertakings that existed prior to the announcement of the NSF initiative, which somewhat explains their particular orientations. Another general factor is the "science" bias of nearly all the projects, at least in their practical application and approach if not in the general conclusions that they hope to achieve (a bias best explained, perhaps, by the origin of the money in government "science" agencies—there are no mechanisms for search and retrieval in a Shakespeare corpus under construction here).

All of the NSF digital libraries projects except one have an actual database under construction. At the University of Illinois at Urbana-Champaign, this is engineering and science journals and magazines; at the University of Michigan, it is Earth and Space Science materials; at the University of California at Santa Barbara, the database will contain maps, photographs, atlases, gazetteers; at the University of California at Berkeley, environmental information; at Carnegie-Mellon University, digital video.

Each NSF digital libraries project intends to generalize from its particulars, however. At Berkeley, for example, these investigators who are building a giant database of environmental information in fact intend something more broad:

> "The project's goal is to develop the technologies for intelligent access to massive, distributed collections comprising multiple terabyte databases of photographs, satellite images, videos, maps, full text documents, and multivalent documents."

but also

> "We propose developing a vision of electronic libraries in which large numbers of geographically distributed users can conveniently access the entire contents of very large and diverse repositories of electronic objects. These repositories will exist in locations physically near or remote from the users and will contain objects comprising text, images, maps, sounds, full-motion videos, merchandise catalogs, and scientific and business data sets, as well as hypertextual multimedia

compositions of such elements. Users will be able to browse and retrieve information from these repositories by content; both organizations and private citizens will be able to easily incorporate repositories of their own into this global system" [2],

decidedly a more general aim than that simply of putting up a database of environmental information, part of an attempt to define,

"Work-Centered Digital Information Services... library services that address a work group's information retrieval needs. These services differ in several ways from those required of digital libraries or information systems that meet, for example, education-or entertainment-related needs" [3].

If the Berkeley people can achieve these general aims, the application in other digital libraries projects—involving similarly geographically distributed users, but electronic objects consisting not of environmental information but perhaps of feature movies, retail sales offers, and perhaps even Shakespeare text quotations and films and soundtracks—seems obvious and valuable.

Stanford's NSF digital libraries project—the one concentrating nearly exclusively on the generalities and de-emphasizing the database/testbed—sums up the digital libraries general underlying conceptual task, as they see it, as,

"to develop the enabling technologies for a single, integrated and 'universal' library, composed from the large numbers of emerging individual heterogeneous repositories... Our technology will provide the 'glue' that will make this worldwide collection usable as a unified entity, in a scaleable and economically feasible fashion... The goal is to provide high-level concepts and protocols that can allow users to access information, through interfaces that hide the unimportant details of diversity of materials, and provide ways to navigate and manage the 'information space' in a consistent and unified way" [4].

Stanford's approach is one of "Using Distributed Objects for Digital Library Interoperability": "Distributed object technology can provide interoperability among emerging digital library services," they believe—provide the glue, in other words. The Stanford team has developed, among other things, devices procedures for organizing multiple online payment schemes to illustrate their distributed object/interoperability point [5].

One commentator on the NSF digital libraries projects recently ventured the general observation that, for all six,

"The shared vision is an entire Net of distributed repositories, where objects of any type can be searched within and across indexed collections... deep semantic interoperability—the ability of a user to access, consistently and coherently, similar (though autonomously defined and managed) classes of digital objects and services, distributed across heterogeneous repositories, with federating or mediating software compensating for site-by-site variations... the primary goal of networked digital libraries is to consider the entire Net as a single virtual collection from which users can extract relevant parts" [6].

In the international context, the U.S. national government's NSF digital libraries projects offer at least two fundamental contributions.

First undeniably is that of the substantive work that they are undertaking. If and to the extent that the NSF digital libraries will be able to achieve their lofty goals—they seem to be well in advance of similar projects, located elsewhere, at least in clarifying these goals if not necessarily yet in achieving them—their contributions may provide other projects with much-needed new tools, new concepts, and new methodologies.

For now, the mere clarification—and enunciation—of the issues involved in digital libraries work, as seen by the NSF projects, is a substantive contribution to work elsewhere; their formulations are not uncontroversial—there appears to be little mention in them of equity issues of user access, costs, transition questions in the shift from other media to digital, Shakespeare, or of books—but at least they offer rigorous defined starting points for inevitable debates. This is the current conundrum, mentioned initially here, between the exactness of definition in the *digital* side of the equation, and the continued uncertainties that surround the term *libraries*; the NSF people have a pretty good grasp of the problems of digital information, but libraries may be more than just putting all the digits together and serving their contents out seamlessly.

The second contribution offered by the NSF projects to the particularly international dimension of digital libraries development, however, is procedural. Once again, through the agency this time of the NSF, we find digital information being promoted and developed under the aegis of the U.S. national government. This is an indirect participation, in the U.S. tradition. The six participating universities, and certainly their private sector/corporate research partners, are not owned and operated by the national government, as France

Télécom was at the time that it developed the Minitel. The NSF projects constitute national government participation, all the same: that is, seed money, to its defenders in the traditional debate, for projects of great potential social benefit that are too risky initially for private enterprise to undertake—subsidy and competition, to the debate's critics.

The procedural question—the question of who owns, who pays, and how these rights and payments are to be arranged—is of far greater importance internationally than it is in the United States. Even in the United States, as just has been suggested, there can be some debate. The national government is seen in the United States neither as the owner/purveyor of all social goods nor as an entity totally removed from the process—the tideline between government participation and private enterprise control flows and ebbs with every change of U.S. general political opinion.

That line is pushed much further, however, in the government's favor in nearly all cases internationally. The United States has one of the planet's most private enterprise–oriented economies. In other nations, where the Internet now is spreading—and where other people dearly would like to mount digital libraries themselves, like these six of the U.S. NSF—national government control and spending generally are far more active and intrusive, particularly in an area of potentially such great national importance as digital information. Minitel was a French government project. The national government-owned Telekoms still control much digital information activity in European nations generally, despite recent European Union calls for their privatization and lessened control [7].

In Japan, government agencies and their intramural turf battles still condition much of what might develop in digital information. In China, the army, of all organizations, appears to be playing a significant economic development role. Translating up, then, to international applications, the significance of the U.S. NSF digital libraries projects may be not so much their substantive contribution but their procedural one.

Even in the free-enterprise U.S. context, other nations will see—as they often observe about the early Department of Defense involvement with the Internet's birth—that digital information development appears to require national government involvement. The real trouble with this analysis would be its next implication: National government involvement in non-U.S. contexts is rarely as passive, or permissive, or downright entrepreneurial, as it is in the case of the mere seed-money being provided by the U.S. national government in the NSF digital libraries case.

Notes

[1]   http://www.grainger.uiuc.edu/dli/national.htm

[2]   http://http.cs.berkeley.edu/~wilensky/proj-html/proj-summary/note1.html

[3]   http://www.computer.org:80/pubs/computer/dli/r50037/r50037.htm

[4]   http://Mjosa.Stanford.EDU:80/diglib/pub/abstract.html

[5]   http://www.computer.org:80/pubs/computer/dli/r50061/r50061.htm

[6]   http://www.computer.org:80/pubs/computer/dli/

[7]   The Bangemann Report—http://www.earn.net/EC/bangemann.html

Part III: Specifics—international

AT LEAST FOUR characteristics may be distilled from the above examples, characteristics that appear to address specifically international applications of the digital libraries idea:

1. Human language questions and problems;

2. Overt politics and political structure problems;

3. A need for propagating and disseminating technical standards that is far greater internationally than the similar need "at home";

4. A greater role for business, operating literally out of control in the international arena—self-control or external-control—in ways short-sighted for societies in general and perhaps for business itself in the long run.

Each of these specifically international questions will be explored in the four chapters that follow.

Chapter 15

Language

The world currently uses about 6,800 human languages [1].

There are, in addition, great numbers of past and future languages, both oral and written, that must be considered by any medium of communication. Ancient Greek script, faintly recalled Native American tongues, the patois of rap music, and rapidly evolving computerspeak, are all among the languages that need to be conveyed by communications media if history is to be preserved and if the medium itself is to keep up with current change.

The representation of human languages by online digital information systems—by symbols, that then can be stored and manipulated by the systems—is itself a complex and changeable task. One system that is trying to represent only all the language symbols currently in use—neither those used in the past, nor those used in the future, nor even those used only rarely now—has identified 34,168 characters, from 24 supported scripts, in need of representation (plus secondary scripts such as "diacritic marks, punctuation, mathematical and technical symbols, and dingbats" [2]).

These are only the symbols, that is, the representations of letters, numbers, and pictograms that human languages use. The syntax and semantics of expression impose many additional layers of complexity. Machine translation programs are attempting even this; but not—so far—too successfully. The best still rely on human translators and, ultimately, on users themselves to fill in the many gaps that still exist after the considerable ground that has been covered. Globalink, The Translation Company, for example, one of the most advanced, offers sophistocated digital translation services but finds it necessary to offer human intermediaries as well—albeit taking advantage of online and other digital techniques—when full translation actually is required.[1]

Human languages have a political dimension, as well. The definition of a people's language to some extent—and to them and at least their immediate neighbors, anyway—is an effort to define those people themselves. Like any such, it is taken very personally, and much is put into their own effort to define and defend it.

So the French insist on French, the French-Canadians on French-Canadian, the Bretons and the Basques and practitioners of the Langue d'Oc on their own local linguistic preferences. Britain has the Welsh and the Cornish and the Cockneys. Spain has choices of Catalan, Andaluz, Gallego, and Basque. In Mexico the Yaquis do not speak Spanish but Yaqui. In Asia, local linguistics and local orthographies are refined and insisted upon with an exactness that makes European attention to these appear general, simple, and even innocuous. In all cases, such local language differences represent and at times incarnate the political identities of those who practice them.

One political dilemma for information systems, then, is encountered in making any choices at all among competing human languages. First, the choice is whether to use one or another human language to represent a given concept. Should the system show a given piece of literature in modern French, in English translation, in its original Breton or Langue d'Oc or early-French?

Even given an ability to show all of these, however—an assumption of unlimited resources, in the most general case—the mere decision to do so involves politics. French political sensibilities can be seriously offended by a decision to offer a Breton text in translated English, even if the French is shown. Bretons can take to the streets in Brittany over the decision as well and even if the Breton is shown alongside the French and the English.

Moreover, more serious examples can be found elsewhere. In East Asia, a decision to prefer one type of language encoding scheme over another—or

---

1.   Globalink can be found via W3 at http://www.globalink.com

even to use them both—can bring about an international political incident. In Madras or Sri Lanka a decision to or not to render a text in Tamil can lead to loss of life.

So what, then, to do, in constructing digital libraries, given human language diversity and complexity and the political passions that lurk behind them?

The first step, for most systems, would simply be to recognize and accept the political dimension of the human language problem. There is much talk in systems design of human language diversity and complexity. But there is little discussion and less acceptance of its political dimension.

This rule is true in cultures that currently have a strong international linguistic presence. The United States has developed and is now exporting systems that accommodate, nearly exclusively, American English. England does the same. In France, the French make valiant attempts to learn and to use the American and English systems but build systems of their own that function primarily in French, despite the examples that we have seen here of their English-language flexibility.

The politics in all of this is at least implicit. Explicitly, these systems are under development and promotion in native languages—or in languages that are preponderantly native, remembering the Bretons, the Welsh, and the Chinese-speaking populations of the United States—for economic reasons; in the short run it is easier, and certainly cheaper, to produce systems that are monolingual.

If the result is the promotion of one culture over another, such is not the intention, argue the system's producers; these politics of language are implicit at most, they say. Intended or not, however, they encounter political resistance, and other problems, at the very least on export.

Cultures less confident in their international linguistic role are more interested in multilingualism. In Europe generally—including France—and in Canada, there is more interest in multilingual access than there is in the United Kingdom and the United States.

In Asia there is such an anxiety to learn and use English that native languages are neglected even in local system development. Again the explicit motivation may be economic. It is easier to sell a system if it speaks the customer's own language. Asians themselves have not embraced the faith in "the Asian economic miracle" that currently so captivates Americans and Europeans; Asians still are most concerned with selling in the United States and Europe, although this is changing. So learning English, and using English-language-based online digital information systems, enjoys a priority in Asia perhaps unique for its explicit economic role.

The politics implicit in multilingual systems development, however, bode well for their developers in the long run. As Asia itself discovers its own "Asian economic miracle"—as Asians increase their current strong tendency to buy and sell goods and services among Asians, without United States or European participation—the current Asian preference for English-language media will subside. Anyone who seriously believes that English has attained its current role as the international communications medium of choice securely, for any reason other than economic—or that this role one day might not change, with an economic shift favoring non-English-speaking nations—forgets that the *lingua franca* of the past was French.

A second strategic point for dealing with multilingual realities, in online digital information systems design, would be to build user choice, per se, into the systems, from their beginnings.

Systems design labors under the demands of a number of imperatives. Time—which often means simply bringing a product to market to get an income stream rolling in order to begin paying off start-up investors and creditors—is only one of these.

Expense is another concern. The design of a system to provide for multilingual capacities and choices adds expense, before the cost of the extra expertise needed in particular languages themselves even is factored in. A system must provide structures for multilingual access in addition to hiring people who know the initial foreign language such as French. Then Spanish and certainly Chinese will add other expenses, in both the languages themselves and in structural system change. A system that provides a place to "switch to Italian" so must provide support for "ISO Latin 1 / ISO 8859-1" character sets, design Italian help screens, and give careful and expensive thought to the logistics of connecting to Web servers located in Italy.

The addition of Chinese may be able to build upon the choice structures provided for the Italian access but will have to master the political and other delicacies of bitterly competing "GB" (PRChina) and "Big 5" (Taiwan) character sets, "pinyin" versus "Wade-Giles" and other romanization schemes, help screens designed for Chinese users, and the Byzantine logistics of connecting to Web servers located in China. No matter how, or how variously, Web servers located in Italy will connect to a system, Web servers in China will develop some entirely different form of connection. A digital libraries effort with pretensions of being truly international will have to become aware of all such issues and devote resources—more certainly than normally is anticipated—to their resolution.

Expense problems are being helped somewhat, however, by international access itself. The cost of reaching foreign resources and of discussing their use with their practitioners, themselves physically located overseas, has been reduced immensely by online access. The very ability to offer and work with online services that can reach from Italy to China and beyond bears with it the complementary ability to work with people in Italy and China on the problems of developing the service; email makes an entire world of international expertise available at a developer's fingertips, at very little expense.

The trick is to realize this and to use the capacity efficiently—email is a great devourer of otherwise cost-effective time—and to stay aware of the differences despite the apparent similarities of an email correspondent. An email user in Shanghai no doubt will have much in common with an online digital libraries developer in Bangalore; but the latter would err grievously in assuming that the former will be able to use a system designed for Bangalore users easily, simply by logging in. The systems designed for each should have the capacity, built in from the inception, to add the linguistic access of the other, at least eventually. Modular design can accomplish this—each system designed to accommodate additional language modules—but the necessity for this has to be driven home.

A third multilingual strategy point might involve an explicit recognition of process in the human language aspects of systems design so that systems can change as human languages do.

All that has been said here about the politics and the need for choice in multilingual international systems design is complicated, immeasurably, by the tendency of human languages to change. There is much in the teenage-American argot, which has constructed the Internet itself, that would have been unrecognizable in the American 1950s, let alone in the 1950s as they occurred in France, India, or China. A systems designer working at the turn of the twenty-first century, who wishes to construct online tools such as digital libraries that still will be useful by the end of that century's first decade—let alone by the year 2050 or later—has to become and stay aware of the rapidity with which human language, any human language, now is changing.

Much is being written about the effect of some modern trends on this rapidity of human language change, whether the rate of this change might be more or less than it has been in the past, and what might and might not be affecting it. Online digital information itself—the extensive and immediate global reach of digital libraries—may have become an important agent in such human language change. That certain human language vocabularies in Milan, St. Petersburg, and Taipei might all share a common understanding of terms like *geek* and *operating system* and *RAM* and *email* is a change from 10 years ago and is, no doubt, due in large part to the new availability of online digital information, although video and increasingly inexpensive international travel have much to do as well with this change.

Whatever the root causes that those who study it will eventually settle upon, however, the resulting phenomenon is the same; rapid change in human language must be addressed by online digital information systems design. This perhaps becomes most clear in a study of vocabulary in a country that has implemented online digital information broadly. A comparative study of technical vocabulary popular in the United States a decade ago and now would reveal such differences dramatically, as would a similar study undertaken in France.

The critical importance of this change to information systems design, however, might be even more dramatically underscored in an international study. A system designed to be aware of multilingual needs—and, further, that offered users choices in enabling multilingual access—quickly and dramatically would become obsolete, as nations and peoples newly arrived to online digital information picked up the specialized language and terms and adapted them, sometimes in translation and sometimes not.

An online catalog, for example, that offered access choices in several European "Latin" languages—as some in Europe now do, although the "choice" seldom extends yet beyond search screens, to indexing and to the contents of the records themselves—would have to be part of some sort of ongoing effort to monitor change in the local terminology used in connection with its system.

A multilingual OPAC in France that offered Italian access, for example, would have to know of and respond to a change in local Italian practice for describing *telnet* procedures for reaching the catalog; this includes a change in technique, such as the shift generally now from *telnet* to W3 sessions that effectively hide the *telnet client* operation from the user, as well as changes in the semantics, syntax, and vocabulary of its description in Italian.

All this is a tall order for information systems developers. To add, on top of the necessities for their staying abreast of their own technical disciplines and economic and other imperatives, the need to know when the word for telnet is going to change in Italy, increases their general burden well beyond the already frantic pace of online digital information development being sustained today.

But:

1. *This is a competition.* Those who figure out international needs quickly and successfully will succeed internationally, while those

who don't, won't—and international needs can directly translate down to competitive advantages at the local level as well.

2. *Online digital information service is already international by virtue of the Internet.* Those international users are out there and are online already, whether a provider wishes to acknowledge them or not.

3. *The digital information networks in fact make it easier to get international help in all of this.* All a developer need do to find assistance on an applications problem in reaching India is to ask someone in India, via email, the cost of the communication having been reduced via the information networks, in both directions.

Multilingual access is one of the more important international aspects of online digital libraries' development. Adding it to an already overburdened systems development schedule is a daunting challenge. But, (1) recognizing the need, (2) providing choices to users, and (3) building in mechanisms allowing for constant change can do much to provide a system with this and other necessities of providing service and competing, both in international arenas and to a great extent "at home."

NOTES

[1]   http://www.stonehand.com/unicode/standard/principles.html, citing Grimes, Barbara F., ed., *Ethnologue: Languages of the World*, 12th ed., Dallas: Summer Institute of Linguistics, c1992, ISBN 0883128152 (paper), 0883128233 (hardcover); see also http://www.sil.org/ethnologue/ethnologue.html and http://www.ala.doc.ic.ac.uk/~rap/Ethnologue/ .

[2]   http://www.stonehand.com/unicode/standard/general.html; also, The Unicode Consortium, *The Unicode Standard: Worldwide Character Encoding*, Version 1.0., Reading, MA: Addison-Wesley, c1991-c1992.; also Cain, Jack, "Linguistic Diversity, Computers and Unicode," paper presented to *Networking the Pacific: An International Forum*, conference of the British Columbia Library Association, May 5-6, 1995, Victoria, BC, Canada, http://www.idrc.ca/library/document/netpac/abs21.html; Jack Cain is "Senior Consultant, Trylus Computing, Toronto, Canada."

Chapter 16

Politics and political structures

THE SECOND OF the four characteristics of digital libraries international applications to be discussed here, after human language, is politics.

It is most important to realize and to admit, as we have seen, that the whole business of digital libraries—and the Internet, the WorldWideWeb, the Information Society, and technology in general—is only a small and relatively insignificant part of larger social trends. This is seen most easily in politics.

There are or can be political implications to nearly anything. Almost anything—a break in a dam, the birth of a baby, a style of handwriting, or a stellar event—can become someone's personal political cause. Scientific subjects have no immunity from this, although scientists have longed for the immunity. Scientists from Galileo to J. Robert Oppenheimer have discovered the political significance of supposedly "wertfrei"/*valuefree* scientific phenomena, in many cases both after the fact and in situations involving great personal and social unhappiness or even tragedy.

Human language is no exception, as just has been suggested. Few subject areas have enjoyed such intense and entirely scientific activity as have those of human language, and yet great personal successes and failures—and wars and revolutions—have been fought in the name of what a thing is called and how a word is spoken.

Political implications can be sidestepped or ignored but rarely for long for something significant. If it is significant, someone will care about it; and if someone cares about it, it will become political; someone will assert ownership, someone else will want it, they will fight, someone will be found to regulate it to prevent further fights, someone will contest the regulations, and so it goes.

Digital libraries fall squarely within this political conundrum and particularly in their international manifestation. They can be owned—or ownership of parts of them, at least, can be asserted—they can be fought over, and then regulated and contested and so on, like anything else. In the international arena—where laws, rules, courts, and political for a for resolving conflicts are inadequate or entirely lacking—the politics of digital libraries can become incredibly complicated.

A number of illustrations can be drawn simply from the examples described earlier here. Digital libraries servers for China, for instance—some physically located inside China, some not—currently face a complex political question regarding the representation of Chinese textual characters in online digital information systems. *Big 5* Chinese is the method favored by Taiwan and Singapore and many other "overseas" Chinese enclaves, but the *Guo Biao* Chinese system is used in China itself—decisions made by a server such as that described earlier at China's IHEP site may not be made upon simply technical considerations, as one system may be mandated politically irrespective of its technical superiority or inferiority to another.

Nonlinguistic politics is also present in online digital information's development. India's digital libraries services have been described here, and some allusion has been made to the immense social and political problems of that country's relatively recent *Partition* between Hindus and Moslems.

There still are sizable Moslem populations residing on Indian territory; the northern Indian states of Jammu and Kashmir are predominantly Moslem. Two large Moslem nations, which themselves retain bitter memories of Partition, border modern India—impossibly impoverished and entirely surrounded Bangladesh, in the east, and wealthier and strategically placed and perhaps nuclear arms–producing Pakistan, just to the west. Regardless of what language one uses, an Indian digital libraries designer ventures into literally dangerous territory either addressing or even in some cases ignoring certain groups in India's volatile politics, such as Tamils in the south, Moslems in the north and west and east, and "untouchables" anywhere in the country.

Even in politically more-tame Australia, overt politics plays a role. The Australians, for all of their excellent attention to digital libraries development, are still engaged in a long sea change from a Eurocentric culture to one more cosmopolitan and even aimed toward Asia. Yet their digital libraries still speak only English. Even far away in France, the digital libraries servers are designed to speak more than just the national language. Australia runs a grave risk at missing the market at which it is aiming, simply through a failure literally to speak the intended customer's language—a marketing failure only, perhaps, but the old description of trade as being "warfare by peaceful means" points out the ultimate political consequences, for Australia, that such short-sightedness might one day have.

This overt role of politics in online digital information is not recognized, or perhaps admitted, in much current Internet development, for reasons that are understandable. The rarefied political atmosphere in which the Internet was engendered did not lend itself to overt political controversy. The common distinction between "political" and "Political" applies to the Internet; certainly there were internal "political" turf wars among academic departments in developing the original Internet testbed and fierce contests for initially scarce resources—but rarely until recently did local and national politicians, who themselves knew nothing about online digital information, feel constrained to take positions on it, in a "capital-P," "Political," sense.

Now this has changed. General public access has given rise to great numbers of Political causes associated with online digital information. Censorship and pornography already have become national Political issues in the free speech–minded United States. Control of online digital information in general—for Political and other reasons—has become a preoccupation in certain European nations, Asia, and any society that has less-than-perfect faith in its ability to control unruly populations. Issues of equal access to the new resource—cost, availability, intellectual as well as simple physical access, guarantees to minorities, lowest and highest common denominators of quality for majorities—are rapidly becoming issues for politics and politicians.

Furthermore, digital libraries applications may create the occasion for politics to really come to the fore in online digital information development. As a social good—perhaps an imprecise and ill-defined one—"libraries" are able to bring to the political issues of the online digital information debates all of the rich experience of centuries of dealing with questions of censorship, pornography, control, and equal access in regard to printed materials. In these matters the medium may have changed but the issues have not much.

These are the same users—with the same enormous range of interests, alliances, biases, and degrees of concern or the lack thereof. The information that they seek to obtain, or with which others seek to provide them, is pretty much the same, although the medium has changed. Much of the political ideas of thinkers such as Sun-Tzu and Aristotle, filtered through digital libraries experience, might be brought to bear upon online digital information.

There could also be other occasions for political involvement in online digital information arriving soon. General public access, for example, could create the economic interests necessary to make a political cause out of a technological development, simply by virtue of the immense political power that those economic interests will represent.

If and to the extent that the Internet attains the immense economic size, as an industry, that some of its supporters predict, selected players in that indus-try—and perhaps certain industry organizations—could come to wield the political influence, through advertising, political contributions, and other means, now enjoyed by other large media and industry moguls. The overt political influence of a Ted Turner in Washington or of a Rupert Murdoch in several world capitals may be enjoyed by a Bill Gates today but could be transferred to a Steve Case (America Online), Jim Clark (Netscape), or Larry Ellison (Oracle) tomorrow.

As with other factors in online digital information development, these overt political possibilities are magnified when they are transferred to the interna-tional arena. The example discussed in Chapter 11 of George Soros and his Open Society effort is only one such. Soros will be in an obvious position to wield immense political power in Eastern Europe if online digital information truly expands there, as currently predicted, and if the Open Society Foundation is to be the primary agent in that expansion in the future, as it currently is becoming.

Other international examples are plentiful, however. From the group or individual who supplies the telecommunications cable to Vietnam, to the unit inside China that succeeds in dominating Internet access there, to whatever element of the bureaucracy controls telecommunications and consumer elec-tronics importing in any number of small countries, the possibilities for exerting overt political control simply by virtue of control of online digital information appear to be limitless at the international level.

There are means of controlling things like general public access, however, before they develop so as to distribute political power in unpredictable ways. These means are not so obvious in the enormous and complex United States or in Europe, where many layers of checks and balances exist to impede any attempt to control anything completely. A smaller nation, however, with a less-advanced infrastructure, might simply restrict telecommunications access. When it becomes apparent that telecommunications access is needed for the nation's general economic development, the ruling authorities then might restrict access to specific equipment needed for online digital information applications.

Moreover, there always is the price mechanism. It is not necessary to forbid a thing—one need only price it out of the popular market, which any quasi-controlled economy can do. In a country in which the very small elite that rules also possesses the only significant education and owns nearly all the economic wealth—the situation of most countries internationally—such simple price control would be significant.

There is, finally, the threat of political intimidation. Countries that enjoy basic political rights and freedoms find it difficult to imagine the very immediate and very personal terror that even highly selective enforcement of censorship regulations can inflict. The United States—a nation in which laws can simply disappear through lack of use, as the Internet's own *acceptable use policies* did (see Chapter 1)—would understandably have trouble appreciating the chilling effect that a bureaucrat's mere threat to investigate might have upon information use in a society that takes its laws a bit more seriously. Skeptics might consider Haiti or South Africa of only a few years ago—or Burma or any number of Middle Eastern, African, and Latin American nations still—as examples of nations where political control by simple intimidation might have a pronounced effect on the use of online digital information.

Digital libraries development involves the interactive use of information—via digital media—between users and providers. It involves intelligence. Intelligence, however—a byproduct of that general information society that commentators have been describing now for several decades—is an impossibly difficult commodity to control, monopolize, or tyrannize. A totalitarian government can take over and control or suppress any number of potentially subversive social phenomena; printing presses can disappear, customs borders can be strictly regulated or even closed, economic wealth can be confiscated, and political activity can be stifled. But intelligence is difficult to identify, much less to control politically once it has taken root.

One possibly very difficult aspect of online digital information's rise, for many national governments, is that intelligence appears to be essential to its processes. Thus, suddenly, this most intractable of social constructs—intelligence—is being carried along in an explosive growth pattern by the increases in online digital information technology. As the Internet grows, wildly, so does the interactive use of information upon it and so does the difficult-to-manage intelligence of its users.

A few priorities do exist that some governments would prefer over having a smart and well-informed population—such as a well-fed one, for example, or one that is healthy or at peace with itself and its neighbors. Bosnia, Somalia, and Nigeria, at the moment, arguably could do with things other than the Internet and the greatly increased information and intelligence and potential for political unrest and violence that it might bring.

Political developments, furthermore, can be conscious or unconscious. There can be political actors and political victims. Any member of an apathetic majority knows this, as does any critic who has decried that apathy. It rarely is the case that any political development is less than a two-edged sword, having at least some deleterious consequence accompanying any advantages that it brings: more often the sword has three, four, or many more edges—significant political changes rarely produce the results originally predicted.

So when political aspects of online digital information are examined today, it is extremely difficult to analyze them in workable categories for predicting results, even at a national level. At an international level such analysis is impossible. The Internet, more information, and a more intelligent population for Japan may be *either* a good or a bad thing politically, probably will be both, and may be several other things besides; the same can be said for its growth in France, India, or Indonesia.

It is difficult even to identify the political outcomes of online digital information's introduction and growth internationally. Will this mean more democracy or less, more stability or more unrest, greater frustration from greatly heightened expectations? Young Balinese on their scooters in Denpasar tell a very different story of the level of social happiness in their society than that told by the mostly foreign hotel tourist guides: what will the Internet mean politically for Bali, and will it necessarily be good?

Is the Internet and all its online digital information an immense force for political change or merely a new tool for control and manipulation in its political contexts overseas? Consciously or unconsciously, then, various political consequences of online digital information's development could be under way. They undoubtedly are under way, in fact, given the universal human ability and tendency to politicize anything and everything.

Our inability to predict the outcomes of this politicization need not deter us. Politicization is as healthy, natural, and unavoidable a process as breathing. The fantasy, however, that all this technical development, including the development of digital libraries, can occur without overt political consequences is perhaps the greatest danger against which to guard. Just as there is no need to defend science against the charge that it is political—everything is or can be, and science is no exception—so there is great need to examine these political effects of science. In the case of online digital information, much work must be done to understand its political effects. In the international arena, even more work is needed.

Chapter 17

Technical standards

T HE THIRD OF the four characteristics of digital libraries international
applications to be discussed here, after human language and politics,
is the special international need for technical standards.

Among the chief weapons possessed by the information community, at least
in making explicit what otherwise might be hidden, beneath technology-driven
confusions like information overload and techno-babble, are technical standards. Technical standards are not value-free. Nothing is. But technical standards do enjoy the twin virtues, in a political arena, of being at least primarily
technical in nature—rather than simply motivated from self-interest and irra-
tional bias, like much of politics—and of being consensus-driven.

The technical standards process is one of the messiest and most aggravating
but—therefore, perhaps—one of the most promisingly democratic forms of
cooperation functioning on an international level today. At a time when the
United Nations and NATO have difficulty meeting budgets, when they fight
between themselves over issues like Somalia and Bosnia, and when international
trade indulges in winner-take-all battles for market share and shifting terms of

trade, the lobbying, consensus-building, and organized meetings of the various national and international standards bodies seem positively sedate.

The general purpose of technical standardization appears eminently obvious and logical. "Technical standards describe how to do a particular procedure, in a particular way. In the retail marketplace the use of technical standards guarantees that parts produced by different manufacturers will work together. The goal in using technical standards in information services, libraries, and publishing is to achieve compatibility and therefore interoperability between equipment, data, practices, and procedures so information can be made easily and universally available" [1].

At the international level, the purpose of technical standards becomes even more obvious and logical. "The adoption of technical standards by those who develop and sell products and services offers the prospect of expanded markets domestically and abroad. Producers and service providers can realize economies of scale and efficiencies as they address larger markets" [2]. "The existence of nonharmonized standards for similar technologies in different countries or regions can contribute to so-called technical barriers to trade. Export-minded industries have long sensed the need to agree on world standards to help rationalize the international trading process" [3].

If trade is "war by peaceful means," then standards can be an important part of not only world trade but also world peace.

Technical standards, however, can appear Byzantine to an outsider. "ISO, OSI, JPEG, MBIG, MPEG, SGML, ODA, SDIF, DSSSL, SPDL, SDML, ODIF, CCITT, CALS, MHEG, CG46, CN4, DIS 10585, ISO/TR 8393, Z 44-000, and other sign(s)—this perhaps is not an inventory à la Prévert [Jacques Prévert—French writer who lampooned such things], but certainly a world à la Perec [Georges Perec—another]… 'By what succession of miracles does one arrive, in a practical sense and throughout the entire world, at the agreement that 668.148.2.099 designates the definition of toilet soap?'" [4].

Perec knew this succession of miracles well; he was making fun for a purpose, but only making fun. The process by which human language comes to represent concepts is well known to poets. Only a poet like Perec, however, might begin to understand the incredible complexities that contribute to technical standards making.

Technical standards-making processes might best be viewed from the two directions from which they normally proceed, that is, from the top down and from the bottom up. In the first case, there is an enormous and well-developed superstructure of organizations, committees, and procedures for industries and nations and even at the international level in and through which experts in different areas debate and agree upon technical standards.

The International Organization for Standardization (ISO)

At the most global—if not necessarily the "highest"—level, ISO passes judgment on the products of long and tortuous national, regional, and industry negotiations. The caché of status as an ISO standard is not necessarily conclusive, but it certainly endows any particular technical approach with the maximum amount of professional legitimacy that the general standards-making process can supply (Figure 17.1).

Today ISO organizes and oversees the meetings and agreements of member and observer organizations coming from over 100 nations. An ISO standard, when it is finally completed, "can be anything from a four-page document to a 1000-page tome, including twice the weight of the standard itself in informative annexes. It may specify the tasks that a certain range of equipment must be able to perform or describe in detail an apparatus and its safety features. It may contain symbols, definitions, diagrams, codes, test methods, etc." [5].

Examples of ISO standards include:

- m, kg, s, A, K, mol, cd are the symbols representing the *seven base units of the universal system of measurement* known as SI (Système international d'unités). The SI system is covered by a series of 14 International Standards.
- *Paper sizes*. The original standard was published by DIN in 1922. It is now used worldwide as ISO 216.

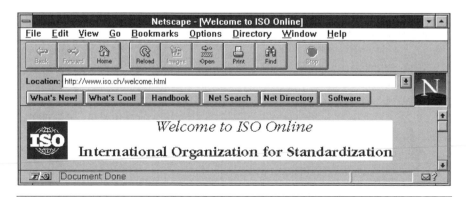

Figure 17.1   Standards: international—ISO. © 1996 Netscape Communications Corporation.

- A well-designed symbol conveys a clear-cut message in a multilingual world. The same *symbols for automobile controls* are displayed in cars all over the world, no matter where they are manufactured.

- *Safety of wire ropes* used, for example, on oil rigs, on fishing vessels, in mines, in all types of building operations, for lifts and cable cars. ISO international standards systematically define basic characteristics such as size, surface finish, type of construction, tensile grade of the wire, minimum breaking load, and linear mass.

- The ISO international codes for *country names, currencies, and languages* help to eliminate duplication and incompatibilities in the collection, processing, and dissemination of information. As resource-saving tools, universally understandable codes play an important role in both automated and manual documentation.

- The ISO *film speed* code, among many other photographic equipment standards, has been adopted worldwide, making things simpler for the general user.

- The internationally standardized *freight container* enables all components of a transport system-air and seaport facilities, railways, highways, and packages-to interface efficiently.

- The diversity of *screw threads* for identical applications used to represent an important technical obstacle to trade. It caused maintenance problems, and lost or damaged nuts or bolts could not easily be replaced. A global solution is supplied in the ISO standards for ISO metric screw threads [6].

Via W3 to: http://www.iso.ch/welcome.html

The U.S. National Information Standards Organization

At the national level, standards organizations like the French *Association Française de Normalisation* (AFNOR) and the U.S. *National Information Standards Organization* (NISO) are busy formulating technical standards that apply specifically to online digital information and the development of digital libraries and that in some significant cases are already in operation. Examples from the U.S. case include the following.

- *Information Retrieval* (Z39.50), a computer protocol that can be implemented on any platform, defines a standard way for two computers to communicate for the purpose of information retrieval. A Z39.50

implementation enables one interface to access multiple systems providing the end-user with nearly transparent access to other systems.

- *Electronic Manuscript Preparation and Markup* (NISO/ANSI/ISO 12083) provides off-the-shelf *document type definitions* (DTD) for books, articles, serials, and mathematics. 12083 is an application of SGML (Standard Generalized Markup Language, ISO 8879) and can be used with the majority of SGML software without modification. Simple HyTime links have been included in 12083, so documents implementing 12083 can be used as hubs of HyTime webs.

- *Information Interchange Format* (Z39.2) sets the standard communication format for exchanging information about books, serials, and other library holdings. This standard was first agreed on over twenty-five years ago and has made possible the wide-scale application of automation in libraries. National bibliographic utilities and the vendors of library systems have benefited immeasurable from the introduction and implementation of this standard.

- *Paper Permanence* (Z39.48) sets the specifications for permanent and durable papers. Alkaline (nonacid) paper produced according to the specifications described in this standard will last several hundred years. In the first ten years since the introduction of this standard, a growing number of manufacturers are producing papers meeting the requirements of Z39.48. The potential cost savings to libraries is enormous, as libraries will be able to reduce the amount of money devoted to preservation microfilming and deacidification programs. An added benefit is that alkaline paper mills produce less pollution and contribute to a cleaner environment for all.

- *CD-ROM Volume and File Structure* (NISO/ANSI/ISO 9660) sets out a standardized way to organize data stored on a CD-ROM, much like a table of contents organizes the chapters and sections of a book. Standardizing this information allows a common retrieval software to locate the information you want on a CD-ROM.

- *Common Command Language* (Z39.58) standardizes an agreed-upon set of terms and commands for automated bibliographic systems. When every online library catalog or database is accessible through this language, it will be much easier for users to find the information they need.

- *International Standard Serial Numbers* (Z39.9) or ISSNs are unique eight-digit code numbers that identify a serial publication. Today, ISSNs are assigned to over half a million journal publications worldwide. The assignments and use of the ISSN has made possible the creation of a unique international database that makes it easier, faster, and less expensive to identify and access serial publications [7].

Via W3 to: http://www.niso.org

The second case, though—the second direction from which technical standardization normally proceeds—is even more complex and problematic than the first. High technology is a new, exciting, and volatile area. It does not lend itself to highly organized, bureaucratic, "from-the-top-down" discussion and decision making of the type that generally characterizes industry, professional, national, and international standards making. It can take five years to agree upon an international standard, but an entire model series, methodological approaches, and ranges of applications can now go out of date in the computer industry in five months.

So much in high technology is still generally the product not of long, thoughtful, processes that are amenable to patient rationalization by technical standards committees, but of spontaneous creativity, or nearly so—the product of shafts of insight and brilliance, of the odd combination of unanticipated things and events, of accidents. As Isaac Asimov is said to have observed about scientific discovery generally, "The most exciting phrase to hear in science, the one that heralds new discoveries, is not 'Eureka! I found it!', but, 'That's funny... '"

This means, for online digital information generally and for digital libraries, that much of the development process, and most of the innovation, which is coming along in great seemingly inexhaustible quantities, not only cannot be anticipated and planned for but even will come from totally unexpected sources. The world library and publishing communities, let alone their standards organizations, could not reasonably have anticipated several decades ago that two engineers working on a U.S. defense-related computer project might revolutionize their professions and industries simply by designing an internetworking telecommunications code.

An industry giant busily manufacturing mainframe computers—and itself setting the standards for the process—could not anticipate that the development of little stand-alone personal computer chunks of its larger mainframes' capacities might one day threaten the core of its basic business, let alone that the software operating system of the little PC might become more important than all the machines themselves.

Just so, today few are willing to admit the possibility that a single Internet application might, one day soon, so capture market share as not only to set the standard for all online digital information communication but possibly replace both the hardware and the software of the telecommunications machinery that until now has seemed so important. The idea that all this might occur, furthermore, using a next-generation machine and system that will have much less rather than any more technical capacity—an *NC*, or *Network Computer*, already dubbed *Noncomputer*—is simply unimaginable to many of those who already are entrenched within the technical standards-making process.

And yet this is often the point from which standards originate, particularly in the case of new and unsettled technique and industry like those involved with online digital information. The inventors and the market set the standards, ultimately, no matter what the standards-making organizations might decree. One recent but already classical example has been termed "The Protocol Wars": the protracted battles between the advocates of a comprehensive, international solution to digital telecommunications questions—OSI—and the inexorably exploding Internet industry that is based on only a subset, and to some extent an alteration, of OSI fundamentals—the more practical standard that has become the default by virtue of its success, TCP/IP [8].

In the same manner, IBM—once so successful with its mainframe business—for years set the standards for computing, and standards-making bodies followed. The personal computer and personal computer software revolutions brought other default standards setters to the fore, as recent Mosaic/Netscape and NC/Network Computer/Noncomputer developments are now doing again [9].

But technical standards making can be a from-the-bottom-up process as well. Critics of the general process point out that, "standards can be either beneficial or a hindrance… the key to a rich and affordable information and knowledge-based economy and society… is through the prudent development and use of a diverse and competing set of alternatives and solutions," quoting with approval Clifford Lynch's contention that, "the era of Standards as an end product has ended" [10].

The two approaches to making standards are not in opposition to one another. A combination of approaches—from-the-top-down regulation by industry, national, and international organizations and from-the-bottom-up spontaneity by those who actually are making the online digital information revolution—not only is needed but is the only thing that will work, as the example of the OSI vs. TCP/IP protocol wars may provide.

The Internet Engineering Task Force

The standards organization most specifically concerned with the Internet, the *Internet Engineering Task Force* (IETF), is a curious combination of both the national and international and top-down and bottom-up standardization approaches. The IETF describes itself as, "… the protocol engineering and development arm of the Internet. The IETF is a large open international community of network designers, operators, vendors, and researchers concerned with the evolution of the Internet architecture and the smooth operation of the Internet. It is open to any interested individual" [11].

Originally a combination simply of interested individuals—more of a club than anything elaborate or formal—the IETF has evolved into an enormous and highly complex organizational structure, which holds various physical meetings throughout the year and nearly innumerable ongoing discussions among its participants online. The force of IETF pronouncements is voluntary and consensual. They are promulgated through the online posting, and online and print circulation, of Drafts and *Requests for Comment* (RFCs). These sometimes do but very often do not go on to become national or international standards, that is, through the NISO and the ISO processes. An RFC nevertheless may become a default Internet standard by being adopted by Internet developers, usually by virtue of its having been extensively and exhaustively peer-reviewed by the highly influential IETF itself, of which most Internet developers are a part.

Whether this hybrid IETF structure and procedure will survive, in an Internet era now opening to the far more formalized general public commercial and international arenas, remains to be seen. The commercial world that now is entering online digital information in full force, to capture and exploit that new general public market, is very inclined to ignore engineering dictates where they conflict with marketing considerations, as numerous examples from the history of the computer's development already indicate; the technically superior machine, software, or systems approach is not always the commercial winner.

Many of the considerations of international scale presented in this book, moreover, become political issues on the international scene—issues for which the technical considerations and expertise represented in the current IETF considerations largely are irrelevant. The problem at the international level, for example, may be not so much giving country A a better solution than its neighboring and inevitably competing country B but giving country A some different solution even if it is an inferior one.

The engineering hope is that the careful work and weeding done by the IETF for Internet standards will continue. It certainly involves a more democratic process than do several of its more overtly political or commercial alternatives. But politics and commerce do not always give way to good engineering, particularly when overwhelming political and commercial marketing considerations are at stake as they are increasingly with the Internet.

Via W3 to: http://www.ietf.org

17.1 Summary

The standards process is messy but thus far appears to work well for online digital information. The systems are proliferating; online digital information is prospering. Some of the greatest advances are being made in human language areas, described in the previous chapter, where the activities of the Unicode Consortium and others have been helping developers to rationalize that particularly complex and political process.

Some future critic may be able to look back and decide whether standardization in this area was in fact beneficial or a hindrance. For now, though, it would seem that standards making—even at local and national levels, where so much must be done to avoid costly duplication of effort and to ensure that all voices are heard, not to speak of the international level, where there are so many voices to be heard and so much to be lost in adopting approaches which will not scale up—is a, and perhaps the, activity of primary importance in further developing online digital information and international digital libraries.

NOTES

[1] http://www.niso.org/whatare.htm

[2] http://www.niso.org/whatare.htm

[3] http://www.iso.ch/infoe/intro.html

[4] Perec, Georges, *Penser, Classer*, [Paris]: Hachette, c1985; quoted in "Editorial," *Bulletin des Bibliothèques de France*, Vol. 38, No. 5, 1993, p. 9, Paris: Direction des Bibliothèques de France; Text extract shown here translated by Jack Kessler.

[5] http://www.iso.ch/infoe/intro.html

[6]   For all ISO examples just listed—http://www.iso.ch/infoe/intro.html

[7]   For all NISO examples just listed—http://www.niso.org/whatare.htm

[8]   Salus, Peter H., "Protocol Wars: Is OSI Finally Dead?", *Connexions: the Interoperability Report*, Vol. 9, No. 8, p. 16, August 1995, Foster City, CA: The Interop Company, ISSN 0894-5926.

[9]   Pelline, Jeff, "IBM, Oracle, Sun to Create NC Standard," *San Francisco Chronicle*, Saturday, May 11, 1996, p. D1.

[10] Aiken, Robert J., and John S. Cavallini, "Standards—When is it too much of a good thing?", *Connexions: the Interoperability Report*, Vol. 8, No. 8, p. 19, August 1994, Foster City, CA: The Interop Company, ISSN 0894-5926; quoting from Lynch, Clifford, "Interoperability: The Standards Challenge for the 1990s," *The Wilson Library Bulletin*, 1993.

[11] The Internet Engineering Task Force / IETF—http://www.ietf.org

Chapter 18

Business

T HE FOURTH AND FINAL of the particularly international characteristics of digital libraries applications to be discussed here, after human language and politics and the special international need for technical standards, is the role of business.

The greatest difficulty with improvements to online digital information language techniques, with improvements to political structures, and above all with improvements to technical standards, is that they all take a long time to develop. They may indeed offer the only effective means of scaling up the Internet to international applications in the long run. In the short run, however, Internet usage is already exploding. The world is not waiting for the perfections of language access, user-friendly political structures, and sophisticated technical standards, before going online.

The people who know this best are those in business. While the academics argue over linguistic niceties, while the politicians posture, and while the engineers refine technical standards often far beyond anything reasonably necessary, business has to make a profit off it, or so goes the classical business argument. The art of the possible, the practical solution, balances and compromise: businesses—local, national, and international—have to and get to make do with whatever the current state of affairs is, well before any ideal solution is reached in access, linguistic or other, in politics, democratic or other, or in standards, necessary or other.

There are two results: one perhaps good, one perhaps not so. Business solutions—the art of the possible—above all tend to be pragmatic. Computer-operating systems produced and marketed in the commercial environment may not be the best in terms of theoretical purity or even basic functionality, but they do reach users and promote the industry that pays for research. Nutrition experts debate balancing and ratios endlessly; business people get hamburgers sold in the meantime. Subtle nuances of telecommunications policy are debated in political arenas; business firms build networks.

The problem, however, is that business solutions too often "boil down to a single common denominator"—not necessarily the lowest common denominator, although this argument often is made by business' detractors, but a denominator in common nevertheless. The outstanding single common denominator in business is return on investment—money—business firms do not stay in business for long without it. The primary difficulty with online digital information's current efforts' falling solely into the business arena—if only by default, because problems like access, political structure, and technical standards simply have not yet been solved—is that all of these problems get funneled, in a business situation, toward the same single monetary standard.

Technical standards perhaps are amenable to such a funneling. The presence or absence of industry standards can be quantified, and evaluated monetarily, in their effects upon an individual firm. Gray areas, such as the increased social concord or discord achieved by having an accepted standard, or the greater or lesser chance that a particular firm might manipulate its domination in a particular standard to monopolize a market, are harder to quantify. But a firm can judge the need for a technical standard generally and quantify it, as can its competitors, its regulators, its consumers, and those who wish simply to understand it.

Quantification is not so easy, though, with a phenomenon like politics. How might even a business firm quantify, in monetary terms, the presence or absence of an efficient government regulatory agency for controlling information? Where, in a purely business environment, is there room for consideration of interest group politics, minority representation, equity and democratic—one person, one vote—representation?

Linguistic factors, finally—merely among those identified here as specific concerns of online digital information—are perhaps the most difficult to quantify and represent monetarily. How might a firm quantify, for any purposes much less those of monetary evaluation, the differences among old, middle, and modern English usage; between one type of modern Chinese and another; or among the various assortments of pictograms and representational schema that different groups advocate—all to gauge their preference for particular reasons?

Monetary calculations truly might strike only a lowest common denominator here—that which is only most common, also only easiest, leaving out vast ranges of human expression and means of information access, which might be of as great importance to civilization as is any common tongue.

Would American English be richer without the Southern or New England accents or the New Orleans "Cajun" patois? Would a system offering only the currently popular "pinyin" romanization be useful for Chinese scholars? What about the minority of users in need of some means of transcribing Wade-Giles and other methods? What of any linguistic minority, present, past, or future: are they to be excluded from access to online digital information simply because their particular language method at the moment does not sell?

The purely business solution could have this result, the problem with the popular view that "any valid need will create a market" being that in business all too often it is the market that determines the validity of a need in the first place: a circular situation—nonmainstream applications excluded from the mainstream because they are not mainstream—has been the fate of many good digital applications that simply have failed to establish the all-important market share, sufficiently, or in time.

The consequence for digital libraries of this purely business development would be simultaneously a benefit and an impoverishment. The business applications currently under way—the general international online digital information development, being spurred on now increasingly and untrammeled by private sector business—certainly appear to be able to promote online digital information growth far faster and far more efficiently than similar efforts of either national or international government. The growth engine of the Internet for now is the commercial firm, not the government agency.

The great impoverishment of such a growth model, however, results from its neglect of the nonquantifiable, nonmonetary factors that business traditionally is ill-equipped to address; issues of equity, of political preference of any kind, and of minority interest group protections of the type represented by linguistic preferences are dealt with poorly if at all by a commercial market.

Much can be lost, furthermore, in the constant ebb and flow of commercial trends and development. Business has a short memory: yesterday's solutions, if they no longer sell, are liquidated and forgotten. But there are others in society—students, researchers, historians, writers—who are interested in preserving the long-term record. The present commercially driven explosion in online digital information has been singularly unable to assist them in this—most of the development record of its own past twenty years already simply has disappeared—and international digital libraries development driven by a purely commercial model might result in similar historical short-sightedness.

There is one final problem in the purely commercial development pattern currently driving online digital information: things do not work this way so well outside the United States. The commercially oriented high-technology juggernaut that now is developing the online digital information revolution in the United States is a specifically U.S. response to a problem, one even less likely to translate up to international application in predictable ways than is the online digital information revolution itself.

The idea that several hundred (perhaps several thousand) privately owned, nearly unregulated, profit-minded commercial firms should compete with each other—often stealing each other's ideas and eventually and repeatedly absorbing, re-absorbing, and mutually bankrupting each other—all in order to develop and promote a communication technique of such profound commercial, political, and social importance, is at best an odd idea to most people in most countries outside the United States. In most other nations, the government would do it; in most other nations, this is one fundamental reason why they have a government.

So perhaps the strangest idea internationally of the online digital information revolution—the idea least likely to translate up internationally—is that private firms will do it. Imagine Moslem countries, where the will of Allah is so much more important than the profit motive; or Asian societies in which social harmony and control play at least an equal if not greater role than American-style entrepreneurial freedom in most people's imaginations; or any regime in which overt political control has highest priority for whatever reason—this describes far more regimes than they themselves, or than most Americans, would care to admit; a scenario under which any of these societies would blindly adopt a Silicon Valley/Leesburg Pike independent-entrepreneur and commercial-development approach to anything so socially significant is hard to imagine and unlikely.

So there is a great leveling force—profit, return on investment, money—that resolves many seemingly intractable business debates. Difficult though the technical issues of online digital information's development have been, few have proved impossible to solve in application. This perhaps is the measure of the success of the online digital information revolution. Had the idea—John von Neumann imagining human brains to be like vast linkages of electric light switches, Cerf and Kahn imagining internetworked computer systems protocols—been less visionary, or perhaps less lucky pace Asimov, the issues and the ideas would have been left on the drawing boards, for they would have failed in application.

That they did not so fail does not mean, however, that they were solved. Making do is not resolution. There are researchers in online digital information who will pursue ideas long past their practical utility, like the scholastic philosophers who counted angels on the heads of pins long after that had ceased being interesting to anyone else. But in online digital information something practical does appear to have been produced.

The problem of theoretical investigation versus practical application to some extent has been posed, in network information development, by the term *scaling up*. This might in fact be better characterized as a *scaling down*: The general public—and the commercial market that to some extent tries to serve and to some extent tries to dictate to them—perhaps has no need for and quite possibly will not be getting those sophisticated but impractical full solutions to the fundamental problems of online digital information. The additional layers of complexity involved in scaling up or down to the international market, developed as a purely business solution, may only ensure an even greater degree of practicality and even less sophistication. Digital libraries, in any event, partake of this additional complexity, far more than purely business solutions ultimately can provide.

Chapter 19

International organizations

F EW TYPES OF organizations have resisted the temptation to become involved in online digital information. The Vatican, the General Motors Corporation, the National Library of Russia, the Whole Earth 'Lectronic Link, *Wired* magazine, and the French Ministry of Culture, all have their own W3 services, many of which contain and offer enough structure and information to be described as digital libraries.

International organizations are no exception.

The European Union

The European Union, as an example of an international organization, has assembled online a vast and fantastically useful body of information about Europe. EU news, projects, and great varieties of other information can now be reached like other online digital information, by anyone from anywhere (Figure 19.1).

via W3 to http://www.echo.lu

Figure 19.1   The European Union. © 1996 Netscape Communications Corporation.

RLG and OCLC

Among the most significant international efforts in online digital information, also, are several digital libraries that have existed for some time. RLG and OCLC were both born, in the 1970s, from the efforts of many academic libraries first to use computers in finance, then to use them for the inventory control that librarians call cataloging, then to present that cataloging to the users and the outside world in what came to be known as OPACs. The idea of cooperating in cataloging to share expenses—exchanging records between one institution and another, and building common union databases that all might use—occurred early (Figure 19.2). These two organizations—and several others like them—arose from that original cooperation idea. Over the years the databases maintained by RLG and OCLC have grown to be among the largest in the world, and the reach of both has come to include libraries, archives, and other institutions located in many countries.

There has been the threat, recently, that distributed computing applications, such as the minicomputer, the personal computer, and the Internet, might undermine the highly centralized and essentially mainframe environments that both inhabit. The dream of some libraries was to avoid even RLG and OCLC costs by building their own local catalog databases—or by capitalizing upon the

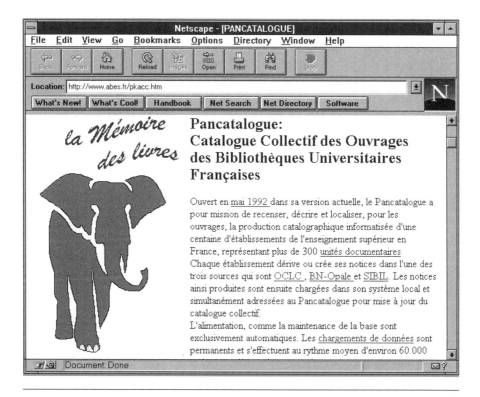

Figure 19.2   France's Pancatalogue—digital union cataloging outside the United States. © 1996 Netscape Communications Corporation.

one that they already had—and sharing resources with others only when necessary over the Internet. Great strides, in fact, have been made in improving and unifying cataloging standards and in smoothing the wrinkles in the various data transfer procedures that are offered by the Internet.

Now the dream of complete bibliographic independence has run its course, however. First came the financial crunch of the early 1990s, which saw all libraries and grant-funded institutions, on both sides of the Atlantic, severely hit by funding cuts. Cooperative cataloging efforts such as RLG and OCLC represent were hurt in this, but library expenditures on capital equipment and mainframe computer personnel were hurt even more. The retrenching, which cut into the bone in so many areas, cut into the bone in library systems offices as well—few libraries are in a position now to mount any significant new experiments in cataloging, databases, or large capital projects.

Then too, recently, the computer industry has offered a development that sounds the death knell of bibliographic independence as much as it guarantees the futures of digital libraries and of the futures of cooperative efforts like those of RLG and OCLC. Online digital information generally just is taking a further step, from the distributed—personal computer and minicomputer based—processing models of the 1980s back to an internetworked, terminal-and-mainframe-based (or, better, client-server-based[1]) processing model for the coming decade. This is the significance of the Internet and of the NC/Network Computer/Noncomputer, both of which are rushing into commercial development and enormous expansion now in the mid 1990s.

The Internet and the NC represent a return, to a great extent, to the mainframe-and-terminal systems environments of the 1970s. Now, as then, time-sharing and other cooperative models based on large machines and systems will be the economy measures taken, as they were then. During the 1980s, numerous minicomputers and personal computers were purchased in lieu of larger and supposedly more expensive mainframes. The 1990s focused on the duplication of effort and expense involved in such purchases and the fact that such a small percentage of the full capacity of the minicomputer packages, and certainly of the personal computer package, ever truly was put to use.

The general computing environment of the late 1990s and the beginning of the next century, as well as the financial problems of the beginning of the present decade, dictate a necessary change of approach for libraries. Much of this change will be toward internetworking, inexpensive terminals/clients/NCs, and the cooperative and economizing approaches represented currently by RLG and OCLC (Figure 9.3).

Via W3 to: http://www.rlg.org
            http://www.oclc.org

International cooperation goes much further than the formal efforts of organizations like RLG and OCLC, however. One of the essential characteristics of online digital information techniques is their ability to enable such cooperation. Many hundreds of major efforts, and tens of thousands of smaller projects, already are under way that use online digital information to assemble what are becoming at least the kernels of future digital libraries.

The general picture can only be grasped by perusing Internet indexes and discussions, that is, by surfing the Internet. There one can find vast lists and

---

1.   I am indebted to Walt Crawford for this distinction.

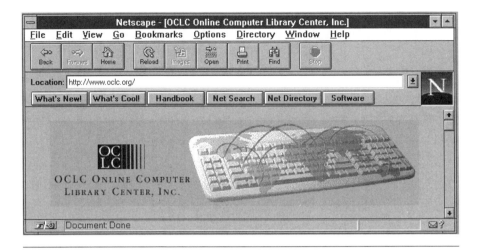

Figure 19.3   OCLC—digital union cataloging inside the United States.
© 1996 Netscape Communications Corporation.

hypertext links referring to the great numbers of projects—some involving large institutions themselves located in several countries, others strictly personal efforts involving only a few individuals—that are assembling online digital information into digital libraries, and parts thereof, on the Internet.

It might be said that every college professor's and researcher's hard disk, located anywhere, contains at least several potential online digital information projects, most of which now will be international if they happen at all, thanks to the Internet—and no small few of which have the potential for becoming valuable resources for digital libraries, and in a few cases digital libraries themselves.

The Consortium of European Research Libraries

One specific example of a highly organized international digital libraries effort is the Consortium of European Research Libraries (CERL) (Figure 19.4). This is a cooperative project of about fifty major European national libraries and other institutions to share bibliographic and other resources over the Internet. Already, this organization has mounted a database that pools the various institutions' records from the Hand Press Book (HPB) period (c1450–c1830), and other cooperative projects are under way and planned.

The Internet and the NC/Network Computer/Noncomputer make all of this much easier. New members of such an international cooperative

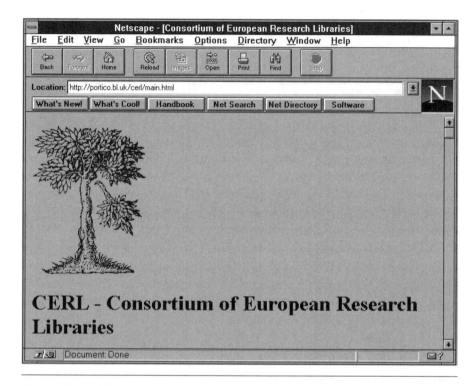

Figure 19.4   CERL—international cooperation in union cataloging.
© 1996 Netscape Communications Corporation.

consortium—from southern and eastern Europe and from Russia—need not make the prohibitive expenditures formerly required for minicomputers and staff workstations. All they will need will be inexpensive NCs and Internet access to their Consortium's mainframe computer, and that mainframe may itself be located, at this point, nearly anywhere in the world.

via W3 to http://portico.bl.uk/cerl/main.html

19.1 Summary

The particular balance struck so far in the development of online digital information, between private enterprise and government regulation, seems unlikely to go much further. The specifics of international digital libraries development reveal needs—in linguistic access, political structure, and technical standards—that will not be met satisfactorily by the private enterprise model that is currently driving the development in the United States.

This is not to say that private enterprise–led development will not occur internationally or will not continue its current explosive growth pattern there. It cannot even be said that private commercial firms—many of them American, increasing numbers of them foreign—will not continue to be the primary agents of all of this. But the results—the way in which things develop overseas—will be different; the process may be the same, but the outcomes will not be. Silicon Valley infrastructure may appear similar in Cupertino, Sophia Antipolis, and Malacca, but what it produces in France and Malaysia will not be identical to or perhaps even resemble what it produced in Silicon Valley's California.

Ultimately the fundamental reasons for this difference lie not so much in specifics, like the language applications and regulatory mechanisms and technical details just discussed, but in generalities—about the societies overseas that are spawning or accommodating this communications revolution, and the role of technology generally played within each of them—several of which are presented and discussed in the section that follows.

Part IV: Generalities

AT LEAST THREE general problems confront international digital libraries efforts, even if their four specific characteristics outlined above—language, politics, technical standards, and business expediency—are dealt with successfully:

1. Certain mythologies of objectivity that accompany science generally, and digital science even more, impede many efforts to understand them and it.

2. One outstanding such impeding mythology concerns antiquated paradigms for information service, which are ill-suited to a world inhabited even in small part by online digital information.

3. Human users do not necessarily like and even more necessarily are not always interested in technology, so that the goods and services that a new technology offers must somehow be fit in to human lives that are often busy elsewhere.

All three of these general problems are difficult at the national level as well. But they become acute in situations involving international applications. Each will get brief consideration in one of the final chapters.

Chapter 20

Media and messages—
is the pipe neutral?

I T IS ONE OF THE enduring fantasies of science that somehow scientific effort can be morally, ethically, and politically neutral. Scientists since the early Greeks have claimed objectivity and value-free status for their work. These claims and fantasies are not so much inaccurate as naive; they greatly underestimate the human capacity for complicating what very often ought to be simple issues.

Digital libraries media have been no different from any other scientific effort in this, up until now. The antiseptic quality of bits and bytes and electronic impulses has encouraged those researchers who, impatient with politics and philosophical arguments, have claimed that their work is above the fray, value-free, scientific, and objective and that the Internet pipe somehow is neutral.

The information pipe that they have been creating, they claim—its computers, cables, switching equipment, protocols, and digital techniques generally—can carry any sort of information: good or bad, right or wrong, safe or dangerous, approved or subversive, pornographic or nonpornographic. The associated claim—that they, the Internet researchers, as scientists are not responsible for the misuse of their creation by others—has followed the claim for objectivity closely [1].

The issues raised by the claim to objectivity made by digital techniques become very clear in application, in digital libraries. In application, the techniques become associated with substance, the procedures with content; substance and content are more undeniably value-laden than are technique and procedure. It is possible for research to argue for objectivity in relation to bits, bytes, and electronic impulses, but much less so when such data is organized into value-laden text, images, and multimedia, as it is now in digital libraries.

So the scientific experiment, and the scientists, are increasingly confronting unfriendly philosophical—and, ultimately, political—territory, in the effort to develop digital techniques into digital libraries. Such confrontations are common now in local experiments. Even on a single U.S. college campus, issues of the inherent bias of online digital information and access are arising. Student and community groups muse about the unequal access to such information afforded underprivileged minorities, and the scientists involved retreat behind their objectivity, protesting that they cannot control the information and that their information pipe itself is neutral.

Difficult as such issues are at home, where their context is familiar, their debates become intractable overseas, where many of the presupposed ideas about technology and objectivity and information and its biases are less familiar and certainly less commonly accepted. If agreement about bias and the extent to which it creeps into online digital information is hard to achieve in Cambridge, Massachusetts, how much more difficult might it be to achieve in the case of a Cambridge, Massachusetts, database suddenly purveyed, thanks to the Internet, to digital libraries users in Shanghai, China?

Suppose the database contains local election return statistics, bibliographic citations to religious materials, or information on the evils of smoking. China's views on all three are radically different from those of Massachusetts. The perceptions about the role of science and its claims to objectivity are not similar in the two places; ideals regarding the role of free information in a society perhaps could not be less alike.

Such political and philosophical differences between Massachusetts and China are not new. But the instantaneous and widespread accessibility of the information assembled by citizens of the former to the citizens living in the latter, thanks to online digital information and the growth of digital libraries, is something very new.

Fifty years ago it sometimes took weeks for researchers in Massachusetts to learn of their own local voting trends. These had to be tallied, reported, and analyzed and the analysis distributed, reviewed, and often analyzed again—a printing and distribution process that took some time to accomplish. Now it takes—or appears to take—minutes, and, most importantly, those voting results may be seen at the end of those few minutes by viewers in Shanghai as easily as they may be seen in Massachusetts.

This instant access to information is a phenomenon that is hard to control. It is hard to prohibit, hard to control once it has begun, difficult to channel, and nearly impossible to censor. And yet prohibition, control, channeling, and censorship are among the duties considered fundamental by most governments around the globe.

The mere fact of this instantaneous and universal access puts online digital information techniques, and the digital libraries that are trying to develop it, into immediate conflict with such governance principles and such governments. There is no neutrality in the pipe; the pipe itself is essentially and importantly biased in favor of the broad and unregulated dissemination of information.

This is not to say that the information disseminated cannot itself be channeled and controlled, however. Vance Packard's *The Hidden Persuaders* [2] taught us long ago that advertising was able to control mass media in ways actually imperceptible to most of us. Hidden frames in movie credits persuaded us to consume soft drinks, and suggestive slogans clicked buttons in our brains that might otherwise have been unaffected by political campaign messages. Cassandras, from Aldous Huxley in *Brave New World* [3] to George Orwell in *1984* [4], have warned of the ability of massive amounts of information to become a force for evil—as propaganda, and as numbing, overwhelming, mind control.

The basic point for online digital information generally, though, and for digital libraries in particular, is that the online digital information pipe emphatically is not neutral but is a tool, like any other, that can be used for bad or for good by whomever wields it. A tool is neither value-free or value-laden—this is another "category mistake," like looking for "the university" in the middle of the town of Oxford—it is simply a tool, having nothing whatsoever to do with values, and can bring upon its users great amounts of good or great amounts of harm.

In the international context of online digital information this has not yet been perceived. There is a roseate glow emitted by the Internet and by all things associated even vaguely with it and with the computers and digital techniques that accompany it. The Internet, overseas, signifies not just the technology that it represents in California's Silicon Valley but a plethora of associated and equally foreign images, such as those young and eager pocket protector-equipped California Silicon Valley technologists who invented and now promote it; the wealth that they represent in the popular imagination overseas; and their democratic, tolerant, and often self-indulgent political ideals. This association of these latter ideals with the technology is an idea that must be overcome, or at least understood, before it shapes an outcome at best unintended and perhaps at worst cloaking the actions of those who would manipulate this wonderful new tool for their own personal ends.

NOTES

[1]   Dewey, John, *The Quest for Certainty: a Study of the Relation of Knowledge and Action*, New York: Minton, Balch, 1929.

[2]   Packard, Vance Oakley, *The Hidden Persuaders*, New York: D. McKay Co., [1957].

[3]   Huxley, Aldous, *Brave New World*, London: Chatto & Windus, 1938.

[4]   Orwell, George, *1984: a Novel*, New York: New American Library, 1950, c1949.

Chapter 21

Libraries and information—warehouses and services?

A SECOND, GENERAL, problem in the international application of digital libraries, after the most general problem of the value-free media, involves the current identity crisis of libraries themselves.

21.1 A crisis of identity for libraries

One general and global current trend in libraries is the tendency to separate information warehousing from information service.

The two have long been combined in traditional library activity. Librarians have long wrestled with the twin duties of preserving information and providing access to it—the problem with the first being that media containing information have been fragile and impermanent, the problem with the second being users' dirty fingers and various bad habits in mistreating the media.

Collection development in librarianship, in addition, has long been bedeviled with the 80/20 rule; like any commercial inventory, the library collection is never used entirely—20% might be, but a remaining 80% might not, or 70/30, or 90/10. Librarians, and their space planners, budgeters, and college administrators, have worried long and hard in the past over that supposedly dormant 80%: whether it should have been bought in the first place, whether to catalog it, whether to hold it in open stacks or store it, and whether to retain it at all.

One particular problem now of digital libraries is that digital techniques are largely accentuating the differences between extremes in these traditional and ongoing library debates. Suddenly, for example—with the advent of the Internet—the potential general public is not just the unwashed and uninitiated masses of the library's own locale, but all of the general public, that is, everyone and anyone, anywhere, who possesses the wherewithal to use a computer and particularly a modem.

Just as suddenly, both the composition of the reading public and readers' habits are changing, and thus so is the 80/20 rule; not only is that dormant 80% being made to appear far more dormant, but the remaining 20% is suddenly facing CD-ROM and W3 and other forms of attractive and exciting multimedia competition for potential book-readers' attention, making the books seem less and less interesting. Library collection development no longer is being challenged just in its weak points but is facing challenge in what it had supposed were its strong points as well.

Such problems, in fact, have occurred before, and the crisis of identity through which libraries are suffering now, in this era of online digital information, has been long in coming. The process inaugurated by Gutenberg at the end of Europe's fifteenth century has been remarkably long-lasting. Other characteristics of the modern printed word—its production on bound leaves rather than in scrolls, its presentation on the page, the linear organization of the texts that it presents—have been even more durable. People have been reading things in books, organized in fairly standardized and in some ways rigid patterns, well prior to Gutenberg, for well over a thousand years.

Techniques for organizing, preserving, and circulating these books themselves have a history that is nearly as old. Library classification schemes still are in use in Europe that owe much to medieval Latin systems of organizing and labeling knowledge.

Many of the modern problems of librarianship—particularly those of the relationship between the librarian/guardian of the text and its potential user—merely restate old debates regarding the access to knowledge and scholarship that derive from the Middle Ages. The ancient French kings wanted to borrow the books, possibly never returning them, in the incidents described earlier here, in much the same way as a recent French president borrowed one and gave it away for reasons of his own, in both cases to the outrage of the librarians involved.

The power of the printed text for changing society, violently, during the European Reformation is precisely the power feared by modern Asian authorities, who look askance at looming Internet development: Better to classify some things as off-limits, to limit the forces of change, say some—better to let them loose, say others—an old debate.

The traditional library medium itself, moreover—printed text—has faced challenges from other media prior to the digital age: dire predictions of the demise of print were associated with the advents of television and radio, which took place some time ago.

Things are changing rapidly for traditional print libraries now, though, more rapidly than they did under pressure from previous challenges. For example, academic library collections are increasingly finding themselves being shunted off-campus, out to the periphery, out to where costs are less, storage capacities are greater, but user access and visibility in budget battles, among other things, are also much less or are even nonexistent.

Many large library collections in the United States and elsewhere now have built surplus facilities, physically located far from their former central locations, in often purpose-built, modern, latest-warehousing-technique storage facilities that do not resemble even remotely the old bookstacks that they once inhabited.

These new storage facilities organize their holdings, like any warehouse, by size, weight, and frequency of use, rather than by age-old user access techniques of traditional library classification systems. Choices of *last in, first out* (LIFO) or *first in, first out* (FIFO) are far more interesting in such a facility, as they are in any modern distribution facility, than is any notion of their visitation by the nonexistent users.

Perhaps the most current, and significant, of such storage facility projects is that planned for the new Bibliothèque Nationale de France, which must move over 10 million books across Paris to its new site during 1996 and 1997. At Marne la Valée, far to the east in the suburbs of Paris, a not-insignificant 50,000-ft^2 technical facility was planned for the new BNF, expandable from the beginning to 600,000 ft^2.

As the years of that particular library project have gone by, the pretense of the Marne la Valée center being merely a technical facility gradually has been dropped, and now it is referred to even in official BNF literature as a surplus facility. One wonders how many, eventually, of the 10 million books that the BNF must move—particularly of its perhaps 8 million dormant books, will make it across Paris to the new, very expensive, city-center location at Tolbiac, and how many simply will be shunted out to Marne la Valée? It would seem illogical, in fact financially irresponsible—if entirely terrible from some other points of view—if all the dormant books were to go to the expensive new downtown location.

This is one library tendency that does appear to be international. It could be caused—certainly exacerbated—by a growing international preference among users for newer and more exciting digital media over the older printed collections. At least as likely, though, are international urban economic trends, and library financial difficulties, that are making it increasingly impossible to pay for the space and labor necessary to maintain large and bulky inventories of anything in the central city: All inventory-heavy industries are moving out to the suburbs, after all, not just libraries—and the library 80/20 rule has been around a long time, longer than digital techniques, and might have dictated these moves even if the computer never had been invented.

21.2 International developments

The international focus makes both types of library change—the shift to broader publics and the shift in the nature of the collection—more clear.

It is difficult at times to see advantages of one medium over another—print over digital or vice versa—in a society in which both are plentiful. Within the city boundaries of Cambridge, Massachusetts, one can find nearly any book, and certainly any computer database or interface—so there much can be taken for granted. In Lagos, Nigeria, where books rot quickly even if they are available, issues of choice between printed and digital media take on different meanings than they do in Cambridge.

Library techniques, too, take on new meanings in their international application. A book-classification system subdivided endlessly for the convenience of the Protestant Christian falls short in an Asian Buddhist country; assumptions about general public access to library information by a well-disciplined public readership run aground in societies that not only do not favor but actively discourage information access by their more unruly general publics.

The trend does seem to be clear, however—the books are moving to the suburbs—and it appears to be international. The same thing that is happening in Northern California and New England is happening in Paris, apparently for many of the same reasons. Even more interesting, then, is a similarly international trend that appears to be accompanying it.

At the same time as the books are moving to the suburbs, internationally, the need for information service of the type traditionally provided by the reference librarians who used to accompany the books is increasing, also internationally. There are rising needs, in Paris and New England and Northern California—any place where the books are being shunted off-campus, and elsewhere—for people to help in organizing and finding information.

This might be because of the Internet and the rise of online digital information. Perhaps, though, the need is arising for other reasons as well, such as the exhaustively documented rise of the information economy generally or the structural shift in modern societies into service and therefore information-reliant industries. For whatever reason, the need is there, that is, the growing need for information service at precisely the same time as the books are disappearing.

This has created a tension within the library community, and between the library community and the public that it hitherto has served. On the one hand, the demand and support for traditional library warehousing activities—acquiring, cataloging, storing, searching, retrieving, and otherwise managing great collections of books—is diminishing quickly. Schools of librarianship are closing or changing their names to drop the library appellation entirely and become schools of *information*. Such trends are seen on both sides of the Atlantic, and they are gathering momentum.

On the other hand, the demand and support for library service activities—service activities that have been just as traditional as those of library warehousing—are soaring. Information indexing and abstracting services multiply weekly; it seems that a new *initial public offering* (IPO) in Yahoo, Inktomi, or Magellan rocks the financial markets every few months now. Information reference services, in which both online automated services and actual middlemen assist users in finding and using information, are not far behind; the Information Broker profession may be one of the U.S. economy's fastest growing industries.[1]

Indexing, abstracting, and ready-reference are very traditional, very old, library functions, easily as old as library warehousing. Many of these new

---

1.   One leading industry group, *National OnLine* (NOL), now boasts 6,400 attendees at its annual meetings, in a telecommuting profession the members of which often try to avoid personal travel—these are information brokers and service providers, largely ex-librarians; see http://www.infotoday.com/nom.html .

information indexing, abstracting, and particularly reference service people are moonlighting or former librarians.

Arnold Toynbee used to refer, however, to a time of change for a society as a time of troubles; there was a stimulus, the grand historian thought, and there was a response, and out of that reaction might spring both pain and pleasure but inevitably transition. The question in the library time of troubles case is whether the pain might kill the patient before the arrival of the pleasurable aspects of the transition.

Most of the work being done in information as opposed to library book warehousing still is being done by individuals, that is, either former librarians or librarians still uncomfortably trying to exist within a primarily library book warehousing world. The tensions for the latter are severe: turf battles within organizations and the profession, frustrating attempts to continue offering services that increasing numbers of users no longer want to receive. The organized professional response has been hesitant, while the *digital* side of the digital libraries equation has forged unhesitatingly ahead. Library organizations in the United States have tried desperately to keep both book and digital information within the same fold, but in the meantime the information and the users are leaving and the library schools are closing.

International comparison can be a help in this respect as elsewhere. The documentalist movement that developed in France has coexisted, uneasily at times, with the *bibliothécaire* profession for nearly a century. The latter represents traditional librarianship, concerned primarily with books. The former represents more what digital information work is concerned with today, namely the information contained, irrespective—and at times regardless—of the container. Documentalists in France find the information for you or help you to find it, whether the document is a book—new or old—a magazine, a newspaper, a photograph, database, bird collection specimen, or even an antelope [1].

The uneasiness that bibliothécaires in France feel toward documentalists and the fluidity of the demarcation between the responsibilities of the two professions continue today. As late as May 1996, somewhat agonizing discussions of these subjects again is taking place online, in the French librarians' e-conference, the archives of which may be consulted for a very full and complete current picture [2].

The point for librarianship and information work generally, however, whether these are located in France or in the United States or anywhere else, is that the French distinction between bibliothécaire and documentalist may contain some possibilities for resolution of the dilemma in which digital libraries currently are placing the traditional library profession. As digital libraries, or at least things that call themselves or are called digital libraries, proliferate on the information networks, the difficulty of defining the libraries half of the equation, referred to in the beginning here, might be eased by thinking of books and information much as the French think of bibliothécaire and documentalist. A librarian, in the sense used in the United States, might do both, that is, warehouse and manage books and help people to find information.

But if there is a split developing between the two functions now, with a decline in the use of library book collections accompanied by vast increases in the need for information service, the distinctions developed by the French between bibliothécaire and documentalist might also help U.S. and other librarians see how their own profession might develop to accommodate the split. The definitional problems of digital libraries, then—the lack of definition currently of libraries—might be helped greatly by the increased clarity. Digital libraries, we have seen, are being developed to assist both book collections and information searching; it would be good for digital libraries developers if there were greater clarity from the *libraries* side, going forward, as to which purpose was being served by a given technique on a given occasion.

NOTES

[1] Buckland, Michael, and Ron Day, "The Semiotics of 'Document' and the Antelope of Suzanne Briet," paper presented to the *Fifth Congress of the International Association for Semiotic Studies*, 1994, citing, Briet, Suzanne, *Qu'est-ce que la Documentation*, Paris: EDIT, 1951.

[2] http://www.univ-caen1.fr

Chapter 22

Human users—fitting something new in—wine and bottles, chickens and eggs

O NE OF THE twentieth century's most extraordinary and perhaps most significant achievements, online digital information, now finds itself entering its most remarkable stage of development; it is expanding outward, now, from its original academic-user U.S. base, to reach general public users at the international level.

Among the earliest applications designed to achieve this expansion are digital libraries. Whatever the term means—however the exact term *digital* may be balanced against the inexact term *library*—all of the digital libraries efforts described and analyzed here have had in common one basic thing. They are concerned with users—for the most part normal, human, nontechnical users—far more than digital technology applications until now ever have been.

22.1 The phenomenon of the un-interested user

Online digital information systems and services are trying to fit something new in—the users—and they are having trouble. The digital revolution—computers, and all that they mean—has been under way for some time, as have the application of digital techniques to information and its transmission over telecommunications channels. But human users are proving to be more unpredictable and intractable than the many hardware, software, systems, and basic conceptualization problems that online digital information thus far has encountered in its astonishingly rapid and highly successful development.

There is a strand in philosophy that refers to any highly complex, multifaceted, ill-defined question as a "wicked" problem. The user is online digital information's new and very wicked problem. Nowhere is the wicked problem of how to accommodate the human user more dramatically apparent than in the international arena. There, questions of human language, human politics, and the difficulties involved in engineering human compromises on complex questions of technical standards—among many other problems—obscure the partial successes that have in fact been made in these areas at the national level.

International development appears, moreover, to be taking the lead in online digital information development generally. Growth curves abroad are overtaking growth curves in the United States, where the development was spawned originally. International applications, in the much-changed twenty-first century, could have a far greater impact even on national applications than ever was possible during the less fluid and less telecommunications-dominated twentieth century.

There is some despair to be found in the immense variety of online digital information applications found currently at the international level. It does appear, some days, as though the differences never may be reconciled; as though Bangalore and Bordeaux never will have much in common, and differences of language and politics will always separate the people in them. Variety can offer a greater assortment of solutions, however, and presumably—such is the democratic hope, anyway—from a greater assortment, some better solutions might be found than would be available otherwise.

22.2 Implementation strategies

The short-term question appears to be who will implement the expansion: which, among many competing commercial, government, and other social entities, will take the lead in bringing online digital information to the general public. What works in this effort at the local and national levels does not necessarily work, it is suggested here, internationally; online digital information solutions in Schenectady will not necessarily resemble online digital information solutions in Singapore, and neither may look much like what users eventually will see in Shanghai. The battles in this—for commercial market dominance, for effective government control, and for social filtering of various kinds and at various levels—are only beginning to be fought.

One more long-term question appears to be who will be left out—perhaps temporarily, but perhaps temporarily for very long periods of time—while the short-term solutions are arranged among these businesses and government and other actors who are currently competing for control of the online digital information market. One old and recurring theme in traditional librarianship has been the problem of the *information poor* [1], the segments of society either deprived of or simply raised without adequate access to information; in the modern *Information Society*, in which society as a whole—and its values, rewards, and power—appears increasingly to be centered on information, the disadvantages of the information poor are far more keenly felt.

It seems unlikely that the grassroots, democratic, and highly chaotic pattern that has characterized online digital information development so far in the United States will translate up effectively to general public usage even in that country, let alone internationally. If there is free information in some places, will this create political chaos there? If there is repressively controlled information in other places, will this mean the exclusion of some users there from information that they need or from information techniques altogether?

Even in the supposedly free United States, will the transition to general public access and commercial applications create a two-class information society, in which substantive and empowering information reaches the elites while only entertainment-based vapidity reaches the masses? The information society could have its information poor, in the long run, in the international arena that is about to adopt it but also even in the supposedly free nation that invented it. Online digital information is not out of the woods yet in either place.

There is a faith, however, that broader dissemination of a technique—like the broader dissemination of information—will result in better solutions to its problems. At least, runs the argument, more people will examine and apply online digital information in more and more varied situations, as the technique translates up and out to international applications.

22.3 Wine and bottles, chickens and eggs

Better solutions, however, do not resemble necessarily—often cannot resemble necessarily—solutions taken from the process of solving an earlier, narrower problem. The greater exposure changes even the old, accepted, wisdoms. A Sophoclean play, performed on a Greek stage, changes fundamentally when it is performed in English in a modern New York City theater-in-the-round, even more so when it is presented in a printed book text, as a Hollywood movie, or as part of a CD-ROM video game. Understanding the last requires approach and thought processes that are entirely different from those used in understanding the first, or so goes the argument. New wine, it is often observed in discussions of the online digital information phenomenon, requires new bottles.

Or does it? The same discussions that bring up the "wine and bottles" metaphor fall apart on the effort to characterize online digital information as "old" or "new" wine, even when they achieve rare agreement on whether to call online digital information techniques an "old" or "new" bottle. It is the digital libraries argument in a different mold: some saying as to both that the world is being remade anew, others saying that the sun has nothing new beneath it. It seems at times as though the advocates of either position would hold their views whatever the reality that they confront.

Their debates might be helped, however—like any debate—by a search for commonality. The common ground that both sides share is, now, users. Digital techniques, particularly those of online digital information and telecommunications, now for the first time are encountering un-interested users in massive numbers. The world of traditional information has much experience with users, and continuing interest in them, to offer. It is the suggestion here that library techniques, evolved over centuries for assisting users with information, combined with the new digital techniques, would provide the most useful applications for addressing the new common ground that both have found, of meeting the demands of online digital information's new un-interested users.

Such a claim has a long and respectable pedigree—more than just the force of an interesting suggestion. If Lewis Mumford is right and users came before techniques [2], the current reorientation of digital techniques toward users simply is a return to the fold: digital technique going back to its roots, touching base again with the "practical" and human world from which it arose.

Pure scientific research, though, has a claim to originality, similar to the claims of an art form or a literary style. Certainly human societies create science, as they do art and literature, but to some extent the reverse also is true, and literature, art and science create society. Would our modern society that is coping with online digital information be the way it is if not for Victor Hugo and Picasso, as well as digital pioneers such as John von Neumann, Vannevar Bush, Paul Otlet, Doug Engelbart, Robert Kahn and Vinton Cerf, and all the others? The process works both ways—in both directions—the wine influences the bottle, the bottle the wine, whether either is "new" or "old."

22.4 Digital libraries and the problem of designing for change

What is needed, perhaps, is a bit more dynamic view of the entire process than usually is presented in current debates about it. *Digital* and *libraries* both have their often-fierce partisans. Some want to wire schools; others say this begs and even distracts from the crucial questions of education. Some say that information, "wanting to be free," necessarily will be so once it is digitally and telephonically available; others scoff that "the pipe is not neutral" and that totalitarians always will find a way to exert control. There are people who believe now, fervently, that telecommuting and the information society will solve all the world's work problems; others that all this is a recipe for digital downsizing, family disruption, and alienation of a type and to an extent that not even Marx could have anticipated. There are those who believe in the *media,* and there are those who advocate the *message.*

It seems clear, however, that in application at least both sides are needed. The developers of digital techniques might be able to avoid the wicked problem of dealing with human users at least at the pure research levels of digital technique and information work. The messy world of providing information to human users arguably could continue, as it has for centuries, without the benefits of digitization. If the two are colliding now, however, more than just a virtue might be made from the necessity of their combination, by combining them rather than choosing between them, as so many still are attempting to do.

Any organization, such as a corporation, school, government agency, or even a family, might view the introduction of new digital techniques, like computers and online digital information and telecommunications, as a dynamic process of integrating these with older information-gathering and information-using techniques—dynamic in the sense that an old technique might be suitable for one purpose, while a new technique might be suitable for another, an old approach and way of thinking as valid and useful as a new one, rather than the one being a replacement for the other.

Societies rarely change precipitously, although technique does. Society evolves, very slowly. Revolutions in technique, which overturn decades or centuries of practice in scientific domains, are more slowly integrated into social practices that depend on so much more than just science.

In the scientific revolution under way now thanks to digital techniques, one of the earliest meeting grounds for this relationship—the social frontier—is its application in information. To some extent, the success of this particular revolution will be measured by the extent to which it convinces society to absorb it, and societies always have been interested in information. The revolution appears to be on its way to a remarkable success; but there is much ground still to be covered. The digital libraries efforts described and analyzed here provide a meeting ground in which this uneasy courtship between very new scientific techniques and very old social needs may be examined before the marriage is completed. It hopefully will be both successful and, like any successful marriage, a constantly changing and evolving relationship. But it would be best at least to get it started off right, by looking at it now as closely as we can before it gets fully launched.

NOTES

[1]   Childers, Thomas, and Joyce A. Post, *The Information-Poor in America*, Metuchen, NJ: Scarecrow Press, 1975.

[2]   Mumford, Lewis, *Technics and Civilization*, New York: Harcourt, Brace and Company [c1934].

Appendix A

French libraries online

F<small>RENCH LIBRARIES</small> online represent the vast range of possibilities for digital libraries access outside of the United States, including some not on the Internet but nonetheless digital and accessible—simply for one nation, France (adapted from a file that appears every six months, updated, in the *FYI France* electronic newsletter, ISSN 1071-5916). Other nations can and are doing the same.

A.1 MINITEL kiosk libraries

These libraries now may be reached from nearly anywhere via Minitel. Minitel is generally available in Europe. Free MAC or DOS diskettes and emulation software for Minitel may be obtained in the United States and Canada from voice telephone 1-800-MINITEL (they will fax you a form) or via telnet from anywhere to minitel.fr . Access policies do change from time to time. Access to all of these libraries is very inexpensive.

3615 ABCDOC	Archives, Bib.s, Centres de Documentation (directory)
3614 ATLIVRE	Atelier du livre, Inspection Académique (Seine&Marne)
3617 BIUP	Bibliothèque Inter-Universitaire de Pharmacie
3615 BIBNAT	Bibliothèque Nationale (for opac see Internet, below)
3615 BPI	Bib. Publique d'Information (Centre Pompidou, Paris)
3617 CCN	Catalogue Collectif National des Publications en Série / MYRIADE (nat'l union catalog project, serials)
3614 BMDIJON	Dijon, Bibliothèque Municipale
3616 DOCTEL	La Documentation Française
3615 BIBLI38	Echirolles, Bibliothèque Municipale d'
3617 BIBENSPTT	ENSPTT / Ec.Norm.Sup. of the PTT, Bibliothèque
3615 BIBLI38	Fontaine, Bibliothèque Municipale d'
3614 MADOC	France Télécom, Bibliothèque Professionelle de
3614 BIB	Grenoble, Bibliothèque Municipale de
3614 TELMER	IFREMER / Inst. Fr. pour l'Exploitation de la Mer, Bibl.
3614 INJA	Inst.Nat.Jeunes Aveugles: Base de Données Bibliogr.
3615 BMLIM	Limoges, Bibliothèque Municipale de
3615 LIONS	Lions Club, liste des bibliothèques sonores
3615 BMLYON	Lyon, Bibliothèque Municipale de
3615 MARSEILLE	Marseille, Bibliothèque Municipale de
3615 MIRADOC	Metz, Bibliothèque, Université de
3615 MESR	Ministère de l'Enseignement Supér. et de la Recherche
3614 NANCY	Nancy, Bibliothèque Municipale de
3617 PANCA	Pancatalogue (national union catalog project, books)
3615 DASTUM	Phototèque Dastum, Breton culture
3615 BIBLI38	Le Pont de Claix (Isère), Bibliothèque Municipale
3615 BRISE	St. Etienne, Bibliothèques de
3615 BIBLI38	Saint Martin d'Hères, Bibliothèque Municipale de
3615 SF	Sibil-France (university libraries using the Sibil system)

3615 BNU	Strasbourg, Bibliothèque Nationale & Universitaire de
3614 VDP14	Vidéothèque de Paris (also 3615 VDP15)
3614 MEDVIL	La Villette, Médiathèque, Cité des Sciences (Paris)
3614 VINBIB	Vincennes, Bibliothèque Municipale de

A.2 MINITEL "V23" direct-dial libraries

The following French library services are among a quickly increasing number that may be reached by a telephone call, either from a Minitel that can do so (European terminals can, but North American Minitel service distributed per the above cannot) or using a V23bis modem, available in European computer stores. French scholars will be pleased to see a number of famous resources appearing here. Even cheese connoisseurs will find something familiar. Public librarians everywhere will be pleased to see some very tiny and obscure institutions appearing here, and they might note the extraordinary breadth of the French "Bibliothèque Municipale" (not quite a "public" library, but the closest thing) offerings online.

39.11.10.04	Achères, Bibliothèque Municipale de
79.37.17.22	Albertville, Bibliothèque Municipale d'
22.97.11.11	Amiens, Bibliothèque Municipale d'
41.86.18.00	Angers, Bibliothèque Municipale d'
50.87.06.96	Annemasse, Bibliothèque Municipale d'
75.67.90.50	Annonay, Bibliothèque Municipale d'
90.49.38.88	Arles, Bibliothèque Municipale d'
(en travaux)	Auxerre, Bibliothèque Municipale d'
90.82.97.08	Avignon, Bibliothèque Municipale de
59.25.51.75	Bayonne, Bibliothèque Municipale de
44.06.36.17	Beauvais, Bibliothèque Municipale de
21.56.69.72	Béthune, Bibliothèque Municipale de
43.77.01.22	Bonneuil sur Marne, Bibliothèque Municipale de
75.43.13.10	Bourg les Valence, Bibliothèque Municipale de

48.24.72.72	Bourges, Médiathèque de
74.28.64.93	Bourgoin Jallieu, Bibliothèque Municipale de
98.34.30.47	Brest, Bibliothèque Municipale de
31.86.14.14	Caen, Bibliothèque Municipale de
56.89.88.89	Canejan, Bibliothèque Municipale de
92.98.19.19	Cannes, Bibliothèque Municipale de
56.38.39.10	Carbon Blanc, Bibliothèque Municipale de
56.78.16.18	Cestas, Bibliothèque Municipale de
51.68.39.91	Challans, Bibliothèque Municipale de
50.53.28.70	Chamonix, Bibliothèque Municipale de
43.78.27.94	Charenton le Pont, Bibliothèque Municipale de
92.64.01.80	Chateau Arnoux, Bibliothèque Municipale de
80.51.98.91	Chenove, Bibliothèque Municipale de
64.48.60.07	Chilly-Mazarin, Bibliothèque de
46.48.38.38	Clamart, Bibliothèque Municipale de
64.88.64.04	Combs La Ville, Bibliothèque Municipale de
70.64.55.82	Commentry, Bibliothèque Municipale de
98.50.84.85	Concarneau, Bibliothèque Municipale de
34.90.04.89	Conflans Ste. Honorine, Bibliothèque Municipale de
49.05.36.10	La Crèche, Bibliothèque Municipale de
92.31.09.69	Digne, Bibliothèque Municipale de
69.39.35.00	Epinay sous Senart, Bibliothèque Municipale de
69.10.05.57	Epinay sur Orge, Bibliothèque Municipale de
78.70.60.38	Feyzin, Bibliothèque Municipale de
43.48.53.65	La Flèche, Bibliothèque Municipale de
33.64.97.24	Flers, Bibliothèque Municipale de
63.81.20.24	Gaillac, Bibliothèque Municipale de
92.51.76.35	Gap, Bibliothèque Municipale de
35.68.93.72	Grand Quevilly, Bibliothèque Municipale de

28.65.59.43	Gravelines, Bibliothèque Municipale de
57.93.11.84	Le Haillan, Bibliothèque Municipale de
35.19.55.50	Le Havre, Bibliothèque de l'universite' de
59.20.42.27	Hendaye, Bibliothèque Municipale de
31.44.46.60	Herouville, Bibliothèque Municipale de
42.77.19.16	IRCAM, Institut de Recherche et Coordination Acoustique/Musique, Centre Pompidou, Paris
47.57.51.51	Levallois, Bibliothèque Municipale de
64.91.05.07	Limours, Bibliothèque Municipale de
43.88.17.17	Livry Gargan, Bibliothèque Municipale de
67.44.35.30	Lodève, Bibliothèque Municipale de
96.28.64.99	Loudeac, Bibliothèque Municipale de
83.26.18.28	Ludres, Bibliothèque Municipale de
76.41.20.21	Meylan, Bibliothèque Municipale de
58.09.42.98	Mimizan, Bibliothèque Municipale de
76.35.64.82	Moirans, Bibliothèque Municipale de
60.60.21.86	Moissy Cramayel, Bibliothèque Municipale de
88.38.06.15	Molsheim, Bibliothèque Municipale de
43.51.20.30	Montfermeil, Bibliothèque Municipale de
21.76.21.25	Montigny en Gohelle, Bibliothèque Municipale de
98.88.19.29	Morlaix, Bibliothèque Municipale de
78.91.60.05	Neuville sur Saône, Bibliothèque Municipale de
49.73.23.30	Niort, Bibliothèque de
37.52.50.15	Nogent le Rotrou, Bibliothèque Municipale de
38.64.13.11	Olivet, Bibliothèque Municipale de
78.50.11.35	Oullins, Bibliothèque Municipale de
98.05.45.00	Plouzane, Bibliothèque Municipale de
97.27.97.97	Pontivy, Bibliothèque Municipale de
30.32.21.71	Pontoise, Bibliothèque Municipale de

75.64.68.98	Privas, Bibliothèque Municipale de
61.75.72.33	Ramonville St. Agne, Bibliothèque Municipale de
(en travaux)	Reims, Bibliothèque Municipale
40.04.08.43	Rezé, Bibliothèque Municipale de
69.25.99.17	Ris Orangis, Bibliothèque Municipale de
77.75.99.99	Rive de Gier, Bibliothèque Municipale de
75.05.18.08	Romans sur Isère, Bibliothèque Municipale de
50.01.04.96	Rumilly, Bibliothèque Municipale de
45.12.80.77	Rungis, Bibliothèque Municipale de
50.58.57.85	Sallanches, Bibliothèque Municipale de
90.56.28.49	Salon de Provence, Bibliothèque Municipale de
46.02.70.61	St. Cloud, Bibliothèque Municipale de
78.86.82.31	St. Genis Laval, Bibliothèque Municipale de
38.86.35.85	St. Jean de Braye, Bibliothèque Municipale de
55.02.18.23	St. Junien, Bibliothèque Municipale de
33.72.00.46	St. Lô, Bibliothèque Municipale de
76.38.31.78	St. Marcellin, Bibliothèque Municipale de
74.86.49.04	St. Maurice l'Exil, Bibliothèque Municipale de
69.25.19.96	Ste. Geneviève des Bois, Bibliothèque Municipale de
46.61.61.61	Sceaux, Bibliothèque Municipale de
74.05.06.62	Tarare, Bibliothèque Municipale de
62.34.38.38	Tarbes, Bibliothèque Municipale de
49.66.24.94	Thouars, Bibliothèque Municipale de
20.25.43.50	Tourcoing, Médiathèque de
93.58.31.05	Vence, Bibliothèque Municipale de
54.80.25.59	Vendôme, Bibliothèque Municipale de
39.76.12.59	Le Vesinet, Bibliothèque Municipale de
74.60.64.44	Villefranche sur Saône, Bibliothèque Municipale de
69.96.94.06	Viry Chatillon, Bibliothèque Municipale de

A.3 Telnet (that is, from the Internet)

(en travaux)	Auxerre, Bibliothèque Municipale d'
(en travaux)	Besançon, Bibliothèques Municipales
opale02.bnf.fr	Bibliothèque Nationale, login opale *see also http://www.bnf.fr
caen1.unicaen.fr	Caen, Bibliothèque Universitaire; username: Bibliotheque or Library
FRMOP22.CNUSC.FR	Centre National Universitaire Sud de Calcul, Montpellier, provides access to PANCATA-LOGUE and SIBIL and numerous other French services, account required (fax, in French, to 67-52-37-63, at Montpellier); also available via Minitel (see above) or French Transpac #134022271494 (account required)
IFBIBLI.GRENET.FR	Instit. Fourier, St.Martin d'Hyères, login bib
134.214.24.3	Lyon, Bibliothèque Municipale de
LIMVX4.UNILIM.FR	Université de LIMOGES, user id: GRACE
STROPH.UNIV-ST-ETIENNE.FR	Université de St. Etienne; Username: brise; At %PAD-I-COM, enter <return>
CRISV2.UNIV-PAU.FR	Université de Pau; login: grace
FRPOLY11.POLYTECHNIQUE.FR	École Polytechnique, Paris: at userid screen hit <enter> , type DIAL VTAM , at Menu des Applications screen type DIAL VTAM. (tn3270 only).
FTP.IRCAM.FR	Ircam-CNRS library catalog—login: libquery—to switch to english, type: l=e

As with the Internet and digital libraries generally, it is nearly impossible to keep up with the phenomenal growth of French online resources. Nearly every library in France has some sort of informatisation/digitalisation project under way now, at least in cataloging: certainly any library, such as those listed here, that provides dialup access.

The Minitel's own "Guide de Services" now lists nearly 20,000 services, while published accounts claim more than 25,000 currently in operation; and these numbers do not begin to account for the many online services that rely on the omnipresent Minitel "boxes" found throughout France—and Minitel

"V23bis" norm emulation software now found throughout France and increasingly elsewhere—to act as simple terminals for their connections. Many new library services (see the list at item 2) use this latter function—untabulated and unindexed—so that until libraries go into the marketing business no one really knows how many French digital libraries there are online.

Appendix B

Electronic conferences

ELECTRONIC CONFERENCES represent professional development possibilities online—the future for digital libraries, in any country. The largest electronic conferences have thousands of participants in dozens of countries—one of the largest now claims over 13,000 readers, in over 67 countries—and they are increasingly becoming indispensable in research and the professions, as much for their growing online and searchable archives, and contacts possibilities, as for the discussions themselves.

In most cases, an email message to the address shown, saying, exactly:

subscribe <confname> <yourfirstname> <yourlastname>

will obtain a subscription. Subscriptions are free.

A good, well-moderated, e-conference will guarantee email discipline: It will send a maximum of 15 messages per day, a maximum of 250 lines per message; messages will always be on the conference topic and will contain none of the profanity, and sometimes-entertaining but always time-consuming idiocy, often found on Usenet and elsewhere on the Internet. Such an e-conference also will accept your own messages via email, distributing them, again via email, to all of the other subscribers. Imagine—in one case, your words to 13,000+ readers in 67+ countries around the world, in an instant. (That largest list does hold things one day, to edit them and generally to be careful. Most others repost nearly immediately.)

Several electronic conferences, again just for a single international example (adapted from a file that appears every six months, updated, in the *FYI France* electronic newsletter, ISSN 1071-5916) include:

ADBS-INFO   "Association Française des Documentalistes et Bibliothécaires Specialisés"; documentalists' and Special Librarians organization;subscribe to adbs-info-request@univ-rennes1.fr; for ADBS members, unmoderated.

BALZAC-L   "French, Québecois & Francophone literature and culture"; subscribe to listproc@cc.umontreal.ca; French/English; 700 subscribers.

BIBLIO-FR   "Bibliothécaires Français"; librarians in France; and France-specialist librarians elsewhere; subscribe to listserv@univ-rennes1.fr; in French; 400 subscribers, archive: http://www.univ-rennes1.fr

BIBLIO-FR-A   same as BIBLIO-FR but with accents!(?)

H-FRANCE   "List for French history scholars" (formerly FRANCEHS); 418 subscribers; subscribe to listserv@VM.CC.PURDUE.EDU; in French and English.

LAW-FRANCE   "The law of France"; subscribe to law-france-request@amgot.org with "Subject: subscribe"; send message with "Subject: ARKIV" for file-list including "MTL / law-oriented Minitel servers in France."

There are many others, just for France. The most useful tool for locating professional online discussion of a particular topic is the list maintained by Diane Kovacs, of Scholarly Electronic Conferences (there are many thousands more that are unscholarly—Ms. Kovacs and her team perform an invaluable filtering service). The Kovacs list, now on its tenth edition (1996), is available in many places online.

The excellent "list of lists"that follows is an example of the *meta-indexing* that many digital libraries and librarians are now undertaking: the online service provided by the University of Rennes 1, at http://www.univ-rennes1.fr/listes/. It shows a rampant eclecticism: there is an "ISOC Internet Good Conduct Code discussion" e-conference, and even one on "1950s rock 'n' roll and rockabilly."

France is a leader. But if the French can assemble this sort of variety, so quickly, using what is essentially to them a technology that is foreign (linguistically, culturally, and in so many other ways), so can—and so have—Thailand and Indonesia and Mexico and Japan. There is no better way of developing skills and knowledge—particularly in computer and online digital information areas, but also in anything else at all verbally oriented—than by the use of a well-moderated online electronic conference, such as those shown here. One, in fact, might do a sociology of online digital information's development, simply from an analysis of the following, perhaps comparing it to similar lists from other countries. Each entry of the list which follows is backed up by an extensive and searchable online archive, any one of which in itself might constitute an increasingly invaluable *digital library*.

Electronic Conferences Using the French Language [descriptions translated and abbreviated and annotated, a little, by JK]

4D-forum@jca.fr	"SGBDR 4eme Dimension" databases
abg-jobs@grenet.fr	Employment offers for young researchers
acticem@univ-rennes1.fr	Freinet teaching method
adbs-info@univ-rennes1.fr	Documentalists' association
adest@grenet.fr	Bibliometry
afc-list@lmcp.jussieu.fr	Cristallography
afnor-posix@hsc.fr	A French technical standards group
aiesfran@serveia6.u-3mrs.fr	Business students
algerie-diplo@ina.fr	Algeria and Human Rights
amimac@univ-rennes1.fr	Macintosh networking
archi-www@univ-rennes1.fr	Webmasters of architecture sites
biblio-fr@univ-rennes1.fr	Librarians and Documentalists [see above]
biosym-list@jussieu.fr	Biosym/MSI (molecular modeling) users
cogni-discussion@univ-lyon1.fr	Cognitive science—discussion
cogni-info@univ-lyon1.fr	Cognitive science—information

cogni-publication@univ-lyon1.fr	Cognitive science—publications
comics@exmachina.be	Comics [logical]
consultation@senat.fr	French Senate outreach to students
cru-ann@univ-rennes1.fr	Higher education
cru-multinet@univ-rennes1.fr	Multinet software
cru-news@univ-rennes1.fr	Usenet implementation discussion
cru@univ-rennes1.fr	Networking for higher education
csiesr@lmcp.jussieu.fr	Computerization for higher education
cuisine-fr@univ-rennes1.fr	Cooking and culinary culture [France!]
dns-fr@univ-rennes1.fr	DNS/Internet discussion
doc-ma@univ-rennes1.fr	Documentalists of one large organization
ecrivains@uquebec.ca	A writers' group in French Canada
edudoc@vm1.ulg.ac.be	A documentalists' group in Belgium
edufrancais@univ-rennes1.fr	Education in France
euroback@vm1.ulg.ac.be	Exchange of duplicates by libraries
forum-je@serveia6.u-3mrs.fr	"Forum Junior Entreprise France"
france_langue@culture.fr	The French Language
france_langue_assistance@culture.fr	The French Language #2
francopolis@univ-lyon2.fr	Politics/current events
freenix@hsc.fr.net	UNIX users
freinet@univ-rennes1.fr	Freinet teaching method #2
frenchtalk@list.cren.net	French expatriates
freud-lacan@imag.fr	Freud and Lacan (bilingual fre/eng)
frgo@sophia.inria.fr	Go (the game)
frogjobs@list.cren.net	Science jobs in France
ftp-fr@univ-rennes1.fr	List of ftp server managers in France
G7-forum@univ-lyon2.fr	The G7 summit: Lyon June 1996
gen-ff-l@mail.eWorld.com	French genealogy

gestprod@univ-rennes1.fr	Research in production management
graphique-l@univ-lille1.fr	"graphisme"
GroumF@ext.jussieu.fr	Mathematica users
gut@ens.fr	TeX users
harvest-fr@pasteur.fr	Harvest users
humains-fr@univ-rennes1.fr	Humanities
immersion-fr@sfu.ca	French language "immersion" (Canada)
ip@univ-rennes1.fr	IP networks
ipv6@imag.fr	"IPv6" [?]
isf@lails1.ec-lille.fr	Ingénieurs Sans Frontières
isoc-code@univ-rennes1.fr	ISOC Internet Good Conduct Code discussion
issi@crrm.univ-mrs.fr	Scientometrics and Infometrics
java@u-strasbg.fr	Java
kgb-users@univ-rennes1.fr	"Kits Garde-Barrière du CRU" [?]
list-oc@cict.fr	Langue d'oc culture
list.monde@regards.fr	"Regards" magazine
lmb-actu@univ-rennes1.fr	News bulletin—computers/information
lmb-list@univ-rennes1.fr	CNRS computer news bulletin for research
loess-info@univ-rennes1.fr	Loess soil—geology
mac@u-strasbg.fr	Mac users
media-diplo@ina.fr	Journalists
medievale@uqam.ca	Moyen Age—history and culture
metafont@ens.fr	Metafont users
mimearis@cli51ak.der.edf.fr	MIME users
mm-fr@univ-rennes1.fr	Multimedia networks
nag@thot.u-strasbg.fr	NAG science library
nature@kwak.isem.univ-montp2.fr	Environmentalism
nms@u-strasbg.fr	Digital information networks management

nsnet-diplo@ina.fr	North-South politics and the Internet
opax@univ-rennes1.fr	"Projet pilote français"
oracle@univ-rennes1.fr	Oracle databases
paradis@u-strasbg.fr	Parallel and distributed processing
pc@u-strasbg.fr	PC users
phigksbx-l@univ-lille1.fr	"Club PHIGKSBx (graphisme)"
pilot@univ-lyon1.fr	Pilots [as in airplane]
pm@istia.univ-angers.fr	PETRI Maker users
poesie-fr@univ-rennes1.fr	Poetry—publishing
prog-logique@irisa.fr	ALP (Association for Logic Programming)
r:r@grenet.fr	Econ./Soc. research
ra-l@bred.univ-montp3.fr	Anarchism research
rare-atm@univ-rennes1.fr	RARE working group on ATM
renater-cache@univ-rennes1.fr	network http caching
renater-forum@univ-rennes1.fr	RENATER (French Internet program)
renater-imagerie@univ-rennes1.fr	RENATER / networked imaging
renater-info@univ-rennes1.fr	RENATER—information
rescol-fr@univ-rennes1.fr	Schools network—primary / secondary
reseau-iris@univ-rennes1.fr	IRIS Network Provence
rge@u-strasbg.fr	Grand Est [eastern France] network
rockabilly@u-strasbg.fr	1950s rock 'n' roll
sas@edelweb.fr	Internet security
sator-l@bred.univ-montp3.fr	Narrative fiction
sec@pasteur.fr	UNIX and network security
smtp-fr@pasteur.fr	SMTP email
sybylfr@univ-lyon1.fr	SYBYL users (molecular modelling)
test@univ-rennes1.fr	Rennes1 network testing
tlsfrm@uhb.fr	"Terminologie" [?]

transrech@univ-lyon2.fr	Transportation and Regional Development
tulp-fr@grasp.insa-lyon.fr	TULP users (List management)
UfloMat@ext.jussieu.fr	MathWorks users
vpac-internationale @cunews.carleton.ca Politics	
wais-fr@univ-lyon1.fr	WAIS users
windows-nt-fr@univ-rennes1.fr	Windows NT and NTAS
www-fr@univ-rennes1.fr	The WorldWideWeb
yre@univ-rennes1.fr	"Young Reporters for the Environment"

Appendix C

A small statistical "essai"

A TRY OR ATTEMPT, in the French sense of the *essai* term, at not answering but at least asking a few general questions about the phenomenally expanding international use of the Internet, based loosely on some brave statistics gathering and analysis efforts that others have undertaken, follows.

The greatest problem with the Internet's general development today—for digital libraries as well as for any other online digital information application—is the lack of reliable statistics. No one appears to know the answers to questions like "Where is the Internet?", "How many users?", "What are they doing, how often, and for what?" There is no lack, however, of people willing to supply unreliable answers to all of these: Recent figures cited in news media, for example, place the number of Internet users at around 10 million—other figures place it at approaching 100 million—and neither is correct.

The following two sources are the best of which I am aware for methodologically thorough, statistically accurate, and thoughtful analysis of online digital information: These are the only two places I know to get reliable Internet statistics. If others exist I would like to hear, but in the meantime I feel that no book about online digital information and the Internet is complete without some reference to the few known facts:

1. Mark Lottor publishes Internet statistics online through his firm Network Wizards, at http://www.nw.com . These include actual numbers and links to other useful statistics sites, but also—invaluably—much of the detail necessary to explain and verify his procedures.

   Internet Domain Survey

   - Latest Survey Results (Jul. 96)
   - Survey Definitions
   - Host Count History (text)
   - Host Count History Graphs (Linear and Logarithmic)
   - ISO Country Codes
   - RFC 1296: Internet Growth (1981–1991). How the survey works.
   - Archive Data

   Lottor's/Network Wizards' latest survey shows, for example, that as of July 1996, there were nearly 13 million "hosts" connected to the Internet, with phenomenal annual growth rates. The following chart is adapted from Network Wizards' chart, "Number of Internet Hosts", http://www.nw.com/zone/host-count-history .

Date	Hosts	Change per Annum
08/81	213	
05/82	235	110%
08/83	562	239%
10/84	1,024	182%
10/85	1,961	192%
02/86	2,308	118%
11/86	5,089	220%
12/87	28,174	554%
07/88	33,000	117%

Date	Hosts	Change per Annum
10/88	56,000	170%
01/89	80,000	143%
10/89	159,000	199%
10/90	313,000	197%
01/91	376,000	120%
01/92	727,000	193%
01/93	1,313,000	181%
01/94	2,217,000	169%
01/95	4,852,000	219%
01/96	9,472,000	195%

A *host* is not a single human *user,* however, a fact that bedevils Internet statistics, particularly now that public service and commercial applications, like digital libraries, are developing and must justify their activities with numbers. Various attempts have been made to estimate the number of human users from these "host" counts, most relying upon some arbitrary number of "users per host": "1" would yield 10 million users, "10" yields 100 million—but some hosts support hundreds of users, and some users (developers, for example) make exclusive use of several hosts.

Lottor himself is extremely careful: "A host is a domain name that has an IP address (A) record associated with it. This would be any computer system connected to the Internet (via full or part-time, direct or dialup connections), that is, nw.com, www.nw.com ."

2. John Quarterman is as careful as Lottor—he makes acknowledged use of Lottor's data—but is concerned with different things. Quarterman's 1990 book defined "The Matrix" as including all interconnected online digital information systems: "The Matrix is a worldwide metanetwork of connected computer networks and conferencing systems... " (p. xxiii, please see full citation in the Bibliography).

At his online *Matrix Information and Directory Services, Inc.* (MIDS)—http://www.mids.org—he presents, for sale, a vast and growing array of sophisticated maps and various graphic depictions of the Internet and its growth and usage. MIDS services include:

a. *Matrix Maps Quarterly* (MMQ): a quarterly color map publication, available both in print and online, that contains graphic depictions of Internet/Matrix growth and characteristics (I highly recommend one called "Internet Latency, A Diagram of Cyberspace") that make wildly exciting additions to any presentation on the subject;

b. *Matrix News* (MN): a monthly newsletter;

c. A poster, presentation packages, and individual maps;

d. MIDS Internet Demographic Surveys: precisely the type of methodologically respectable polling and statistical analysis, much needed to extend and apply Mark Lottor's careful figures and to counter the vast number of not-so-respectable generalizations that float around in Cyberspace about the size and character of the Internet. "The Internet has about 26.4 million users as of October 1995..."; but there were 39 million users in the full global online digital information "Matrix," and 16.9 million users in something called the "Core": see Quarterman's full report, and a very nice graphic at http://www2.mids.org/ids3/pr9510.html;

e. MIDS Internet Weather Report: when the whole thing is going to grind to an information-overloaded halt—find out ahead of time, here—also, the local weather in Zilker Park.

Appendix D

Digital libraries

L ACKING ANY ACCEPTED definition, one approach to defining digital libraries might be to see how the term currently in fact is used, in some sort
of statistically acceptable sample. MELVYL, the University of California's very large—nearly nine million records—general U.S. academic bibliographic database, finds the following entries on the search, "find tw digital
library." The entries include discussions of many assemblages of scientific
research datasets, a library catalog, preservation and imaging, among other
things.

1. Digital typeface library. New York, NY: Digital Typeface Library
   Co., c1985.

2. Gardels, Kenneth. CERES and ELIB: a distributed digital library of
   environmental information/Kenneth Gardels. IN: Geo information
   systems. Vol. 5, no. 5 (May 1995).

3. Groman, R. C.
   The digital data library system: Library storage and retrieval of digi-
   tal geophysical data/by R.C. Groman. 1974. Series title: Woods
   Hole Oceanographic Institution Reference; 74–68.

4. International Hydrographic Bureau. Digital deep-sea sounding library: description and index list = Collection de sondes oceaniques
   digitalisees: description et liste index / International Hydrographic
   Bureau. Monaco: The Bureau, 1969. Series title: Special publication
   (International Hydrographic Bureau); no. 45.

5. Olsen, Wallace C.
   Digital storage of an academic library book collection—nontech-
   nological information to aid consideration [by] Wallace C. Olsen.
   Boston [Educom] 1969. Series title: Educom Staff paper.

6. Public use of Earth and space science data over the Internet: a cooperative agreement notice soliciting proposals for 1) innovative remote sensing database applications, 2) digital library technology
   development, and…Washington, D.C.: Office of Aeronautics, National Aeronautics and Space Administration, 1994.

7. SOUND RECORDING
   Re-tooling academic libraries for the digital age: missions, collec-
   tions, staffing: San Francisco, CA, October 20–21, 1995/CARL;
   ACRL; California Academic and Research Libraries. Garden Grove,
   Calif.: InfoMedix, [1995]. 12 sound cassettes (ca. 50 min. each) in
   folder: mono.

8. Reilly, Kevin D., 1937–
   Digital computer simulation models of library-based information re-
   trieval systems: a paper delivered at the 3rd annual symposium Com-
   puter Science and Statistics Symposium, Los Angeles, California,
   January 30–31, 1969 /… Los Angeles: Institute of Library Research,
   University of California, [1969?].

9. A Testbed for advancing the role of digital technologies for library
   preservation and access: a final report by Cornell University to the
   Commission on Preservation and Access, October, 1993/Anne R.
   Kenney…[Washington: The Commission], c1993.

10. Tobler, Waldo Rudolph.
    A digital terrain library: technical report/Waldo R. Tobler, Charles
    M. Davis. Ann Arbor: University of Michigan, College of Literature,
    Science, and the Arts, Dept. of Geography, 1968.

11. The U.S. Geological Survey, digital spectral library/Roger N. Clark...[et al.]. Version 1:0.2 to 3.0 um. [Denver, CO]: U.S. Geological Survey: [Books and Open-File Reports Section, distributor], 1993. Series title: U.S. Geological Survey open-file report; 93-592.

12. Videodisc and optical digital disk technologies and their applications in libraries: a report to the Council on Library Resources/by Information Systems Consultants Inc. Washington, D.C.: The Council, [1985].

13. Waters, Donald J.
From microfilm to digital imagery: on the feasibility of a project to study the means, cost, and benefits of converting large quantities of preserved library materials from microfilm to digital images: a report...Washington, D.C.: The Commission, c1991. Series title: Report (Commission on Preservation and Access)

14. Wilkes, M. V. (Maurice Vincent)
The preparation of programs for an electronic digital computer, with special reference to the EDSAC and the use of a library of subroutines, by Maurice V. Wilkes, David J. Wheeler, and Stanley Gill. Cambridge, Mass., Addison-Wesley Press, 1951.

15. Wilkes, M. V. (Maurice Vincent)
The preparation of programs for an electronic digital computer: with special reference to the EDSAC and the use of a library of subroutines/by Maurice V. Wilkes, David J. Wheeler, and Stanley Gill; with a...Los Angeles: Tomash Publishers, c1982. Series title: Charles Babbage Institute reprint series for the history of computing; v. 1.

A MELVYL search of "fin tw digital libraries"—truncated and combined searches with the previous reach system load limits—then yields additional entries.

1. DISSERTATION
Beckwith, Herbert Henry.
Applications of automatic punched card and digital machines in libraries.. 1959.

2. Conference on the Theory and Practice of Digital Libraries (1st: 1994: College Station, Tex.)
Proceedings of Digital Libraries '94, the first annual Conference on the Theory and Practice of Digital Libraries: June 19–21, 1994, Col-

lege Station, Texas, USA/edited by John L. Schnas... [et al.]; sponsored... College Station: [Texas A&M University]: Additional cop-
ies of these proceedings may be ordered from Hypermedia Research
Laboratory, Dept. of Computer Science, Texas A&M University,
[1994].

3. Digital Libraries '95 (1995: Austin, Texas)
    Proceedings of Digital Libraries '95: the Second Annual Conference
    on the Theory and Practice of Digital Libraries, June 11–13, 1995,
    Austin, Texas/edited by Frank M. Shipman, Richard Furuta, and
    David M. Levy. College Station, TX: Hypermedia Research Labora-
    tory, 1995.

4. Digital libraries: current issues: digital libraries workshop DL '94,
    Newark NJ, USA, May 19–20, 1994: selected papers/Nabil R.
    Adam, Bharat K. Bhargava, Yelena Yesha, eds. Berlin; New York:
    Springer, c1995. Series title: Lecture notes in computer science;
    916.

5. GIS approach to digital spatial libraries. Redlands, CA: Environ-
    mental Systems Research Institute, Inc, 1994, c1993. Series title:
    ESRI white paper series.

7. Miller, David C.
    Special report—publishers, libraries & CD-ROM: implications of
    digital optical printing/by David C. Miller; client, Library and Infor-
    mation Resources for the Northwest, Portland, Oregon, a Fred
    Meyer Charitable... [Benicia, Calif.?]: DCM Associates, c1987.

10. International Symposium on Digital Libraries (1995: Tsukuba,
    Ibaraki, Japan) Proceedings of the International Symposium on
    Digital Libraries 1995, August 22–25, 1995, Tsukuba, Ibaraki,
    Japan/ sponsored by University of Library and Information Science.
    Kasuga, Tsukuba, Ibaraki, Japan: University of Library and Informa-
    tion Science, 1995.

In MELVYL, "fin sw digital libraries" then yields, in addition:

2. Study to identify measures necessary for a successful transition to a
    more electronic Federal Depository Library Program: as required by
    Legislative Branch Appropriations Act, 1996, Public Law 104-53:
    report to the...Washington, DC: U.S. G.P.O., [1996].

<u>3</u>. International Essen Symposium (18th: 1995)
Electronic documents and information: from preservation to access:
18th International Essen Symposium, 23 October–26 October
1995: Festschrift in honor of Patricia Battin/edited by Ahmed H.
Helal, Joachim W. Weiss. Essen: Universitatsbibliothek Essen,
1996. Series title: Veroffentlichungen der Universitatsbibliothek Essen; 20.

<u>5</u>. The Evolving virtual library: visions and case studies/edited by Lav-
erna M. Saunders. Medford, NJ: Information Today, 1996.

<u>6</u>. Die Unendliche Bibliothek: digitale Information in Wissenschaft,
Verlag und Bibliothek/[herausgegeben von] Borsenverein des Deut-
schen Buchhandels, die Deutsche Bibliothek, Bundesvereinigung
Deutscher Bibliotheksverbande. Wiesbaden: Harrassowitz, 1996.
Series title: Gesellschft fur das Buch (Series); Bd. 2.

Altavista, the also very large ("30 million pages ['Web' pages] found on
225,000 servers and three million articles from 14,000 Usenet news groups. .
. accessed over 12 million times per weekday"), U.S. nonacademic assemblage,
of perhaps less-random entries—Altavista's tend to be more focused on things
digital than Melvyl's, and so might be more likely to mention "digital libraries"—finds, for an "Altavista advanced search":

digital and librar*	=	100,000 entries
digital and libraries	=	60,000 entries
digital and library	=	100,000 entries
digital near librar*	=	40,000 entries

These might be analyzed someday as well, in an attempt to determine what
current English/American linguistic usage on the WorldWideWeb, at any rate,
considers digital libraries to be. It seems as unlikely, though, that such analysis
yet will obtain any greater agreement about this "fuzzy" term, as it is that any
agreement thus obtained will last very long, given the current rapid rate of
change both in the digital world and in libraries.

Glossary

THE FOLLOWING INCLUDES terms and abbreviations that may not be readily available in standard dictionaries, particularly in certain specialized senses used here, and particularly for non-U.S., non-American-English, readers.

abstracting	Summarizing of information, for reference work
acceptable use	Internet usage restrictions in the United States
AI	Artificial intelligence, nonhuman
algorithm	Formula executing a particular search approach
annuaire	French national telephone directory
ANSI	American National Standards Institute
arena	Particular political decision-making process
armarius	Chest (Latin), used for Medieval book storage

ARPA	Advanced Research Projects Agency (US)
ARPANet	ARPA Internet, Internet precursor
artifical intelligence	Nonhuman intelligence
ASCII	ANSI Standard Code for Information Interchange
AT&T	American Telephone and Telegraph Company
BabyBells	Former divisions of AT&T, now independent
backbone	Telecommunications support, Internet hi speeds
banalisation	French term, digital system acceptance by users
BBS	Bulletin Board System
Berkeley	University of California, Berkeley campus
bibliographic	Describing books, as in "bibliographic record"
bibliothèque	Library (French)
bibliothèque municipale	"State" library in France, not always public
binary	Math notation using only 1 & 0, ie. "2" = "10"
bit	Unit of data, recorded using binary procedures
BNF	Bibliothèque Nationale de France
Boolean	Logic system for online searches ("and/not/or")
bps	Bits per second, speed measurement flow of bits
Bulletin Board System	Internet multiple-user conversation system
byte	Unit of digital information, composed of bits
card catalog	Library catalog, records printed on paper cards
catalog	Cardfile/database of bibliographic records
CD-ROM	Compact Disk, Read-Only-Memory
character set	List of characters used in depicting language
client	Computer using data / system of a "server"
client-state	Nation-state dependent upon another
closed reserve	Unavailable for borrowing, even by the king
codex	Mediev. Eur. book-binding method (sing.)
codices	Mediev. Eur. book-binding method (pl.)

cognitive	Human knowledge, perception, understanding
collection	Books, etc. owned/stored by a library
convergence	Similar development of different technologies
cybernetics	Study of relation between humans and machines
Cyberspace	Imaginary world of interconnected communication
DARPA	Defense Advanced Research Projects Agency (US)
data	Digital "bits" without intelligence, cf. information
data-loading	Putting data into a computer
data set	Related data assembled together
database	Software creating files like library catalogs
de-accessioning	Selling or otherwise disposing of, that is, books
deacidification	Removal of acid, that is, from wood-pulp paper
diacritical	Editing, nonalphabetic marks
dial-in	Users connecting via normal telephone lines
Diderot's Encyclopédie	Eighteenth-century French printed encyclopedia
digit	Common term referring to information "bit"
digital	Binary representation of text, images, anything
distributed processing	Single processing by several computers
distribution facility	Warehouse—politically correct term
domain	Segment of an IP address
DOS	Disk Operating System (Microsoft Co. software)
downsizing	Shrinking, as in the no. of employees
e-conference	Electronic conference
e-journal	Electronic journal
electronic conference	Email system allowing multiple users
electronic journal	Journal published electronically
email	Electronic mail, that is, via Internet or Minitel
FIFO	First in first out inventory, item received earliest used first

First Estate	Members of nobility, prerevolutionary France
forum	Political arena for making a decision
francophile	France/French-loving
francophobe	France/French-hating
francophone	Able to speak and use French language
ftp	File Transfer Protocol, Internet file transfer
fulltext	Entire text of a document versus catalog record
gateway	Non-Internet network Internet connection
geek	American slang term for technology-enthusiast
gigabyte	One billion bytes
gopher	Internet text indexing and storage software
graphical user interface	User-system connections tool using graphics
grey literature	Research literature not commercially published
GUI	Graphical User Interface
hardware	Computer equipment, not programming or systems
hierarchical	Nonhypertextual (see hypertext)
host	Internet-connected machine(s) with IP address
html	HyperText Markup Language
http	HyperText Transfer Protocol
hypertext	Nonlinear presentation of information
illuminated manuscripts	Handwritten and illustrated texts, that is, Medieval
imaging	Digital representation of something as an image
incunabula	Any early printed work, made c. 1450–500
indexing	Abbreviations for works organized for reference
information	Digital "bits" with intelligence, cf. data
information broker	Professional online information searcher
information overload	Too much information to be useful
information science	Systematic study of information
informatisation	Computerization plus information (French)

Initial Public Offering	First corporate stock sale to general public
interconnectivity	Connection capacity among several systems
interoperability	Capacity of systems to operate one another
interface	Tool for user _ system connections
Internet	Interconnected telecom networks using tcp/ip
Internet architecture	Design/structure of Internet operations
Internet host	See host
Internet Relay Chat	Internet multiple-user conversation system
Internet Service Provider	Internet middle man providing user accounts
IP address	Internet Protocol address, Internet address
IPO	Initial Public Offering
IRC	Internet Relay Chat
ISBN	International Standard Book Number
ISDN	Integrated Services Digital Networks
ISOC	Internet SOCiety
ISP	Internet Service Provider
ISSN	International Standard Serial Number
IT	Information Technology
journal	Publication that appears daily, cf. periodical
keyword	Identifying, indexed term used in searching
kilobyte	One thousand bytes
kiosk	Minitel centralized online billing system
library	Amorphous term sometimes meaning only books
library service	Service rendered by librarians
LIFO	Last in first out inventory: item received most recent used first
link	Hypertext interface jump, one source to another
logging in	Connecting to a computer or system
Mac	Macintosh personal computer, not DOS-based

mainframe	Largest stand-alone computers, cf. mini, PC
MARC	MAchine Readable Cataloging rules
market share	Commercial market served by single firm
markup language	Rules for indicating structure in text
Matrix	All interconnected telecom networks
Mbone	Television-via-Internet, *multicasting*
megabyte	One million bytes
meta-data	Data about or which describes other data
meta-indexing	Indexing of indexes, that is, a "list of lists"
mini	Minicomputer, mid-sized, cf. mainframe, PC
Minitel	Non-TCP/IP French online information system
MIT	Massachusetts Institute of Technology
MNC	Multinational Corporation
Mosaic	First leading World Wide Web GUI/interface
multimedia	Currently anything both digital and saleable
nation-state	International political actor with land, people
NC	Network Computer, simple Internet device
Netscape	Leading commercial version of Mosaic interface
Network Computer	Simple Internet terminal, some intelligence
NSF	U.S. National Science Foundation
Numèris	France Télécom ISDN service
object	Digitally treatable thing, most general term
online	Active, not in storage; also, on the Internet
online chat	Human conversations using digital systems
online conferencing	Multiple-user conversations on the Internet
OPAC	Online Public Access Catalog, in libraries
pagination	Page numbering, as in a book
papyri	Papyrus plant used by Egyptians as paper
parallel processing	Single processing by several computers at once

parchment	Competitive "paper" substitute for papyrus
PC	Personal computer (all, or just DOS-based)
periodical	Publication that appears regularly cf. journal
probabilistic	Search algorithms based on probabilitistic math
protocols	Rules, here for telecommunications design, etc.
Provençal	Concerning Provence, France's southern province
PX	U.S. military commercial supplies system
RAM	Random Access Memory in a computer
Random Access Memory	Computer's memory available whenever needed
RBOCs	Regional Bell Operating Companies (see BabyBells)
ready-reference	Librarians' on-demand reference service
remote users	Online system users not physically on premises
Renater	Internet access program for schools in France
romanization	Language depiction using "Latin" characters
scaling up	Expanding to larger size, using same system
script	Written depiction of a language, cf. oral
search engine	System for search and retrieval of information
Second Estate	Members of clergy, prerevolutionary France
seed money	Funds necessary to start a project
serial	Item published in series, ie. magazines
server	Computer functioning as data / system home base
SGML	Standard Generalized Markup Language
software	Computer programming, not equipment or systems
spreadsheet	Software creating files like accounting sheets
stand-alone	Unconnected to other systems
surfing	Browsing of online information
system	Entire operation including hardware & software
Tamil	Ethnic group and language, India's south coast
tape-loading	Data-loading using magnetic tape media

TCP/IP	Transmission control protocol/internet protocol
teasers	Excerpts published to entice buyers
techno-babble	Too many technical terms to be useful
TEI	Text Encoding Initiative—standards effort
telecom	Telecommunications (also "telekom")
telecommunications	Communication via telephone techniques
telecommuting	Telecommunications instead of physical travel
telcom	Telecommunications
telnet	Internet computer to computer connection
terabyte	One trillion bytes
terminal	Interface hardware with little intelligence
testbed	Project to test a theoretical idea
Third Estate	The bourgeoisie, prerevolutionary France
time-sharing	Independent users sharing a single computer
tn3270	Telcom method requiring special software
translating up	See "scaling up," plus a "translation" element
TTY	TeleTYpe, simple terminal emulation (see VT100)
turf battle	Competition, in bureaucracy: much, in high-technology
Usenet	Internet multiple-user conversation system
user-friendly	Easily used by an average user
V23bis	Minitel telecommunications standard
vacuum tube	Switching device used in early computers
valuefree	Independent of moral / ethical values
video game	Entertainment "game" software used on computers
Videotex	Visual-image-based information system
virtual	Anything having to do with cyberspace
VT100	Most common terminal emulation (see TTY)
W3	Non-U.S. term for the WorldWideWeb
Wars of Religion	Sixteenth-century civil wars in France

Web	Common abbreviation for the WorldWideWeb
Web Service Provider	Internet middleman providing user accounts
what-if scenario	Management tool: "what if X, then what?"
word processor	Software creating files like typing sheets
WorldWideWeb	Hypertext organization of the Internet
WSP	Web Service Provider
WWW	WorldWideWeb

Annotated bibliography and resource list

THIS CHAPTER is not intended to be comprehensive, as currently too much is written about many aspects of the digital libraries topic, while too little is written about digital libraries as a whole and almost nothing is written about their international development. The following is intended more to provide a starting point—a "bibliographic and resource essay."

Digital—the meaning

Classics

The following are still readable. It is even more interesting to see what the original idea was now that we think that we know so much. (Someone said that "anyone who forgets his ends and still pursues his means has become a fanatic.")

- Bush, Vannevar, "As We May Think," *The Atlantic Monthly*, July 1945.

This highly-influential article proposed the melding of information and computational machinery into something called *Memex:* "a device in which an individual stores all his books, records, and communications, and which is mechanized so that it may be consulted with exceeding speed and flexibility. It is an enlarged intimate supplement to his memory." The fulltext of the article may now be found in thousands of places online: among these sites, one in Japan:

http://www.notredame.ac.jp/ftplib/Articles/CMC/bush45.txt

- Lasswell, Harold Dwight, *Propaganda Technique in the World War*, New York: Alfred A. Knopf, 1927.

Origin or at least precursor of content analysis: the idea that quantitative techniques might aid in the analysis of human discourse.

- Von Neumann, John, and Oskar Morgenstern, *Theory of Games and Economic Behavior*, 2nd ed., Princeton, NJ: Princeton University Press, 1947.

The idea that numbers have something to do with human behavior.

- Von Neumann, John, *The Computer and the Brain*, New Haven, CT: Yale University Press, 1958 [repr.1964].

The above idea applied to computing machines.

- Wiener, Norbert, *Cybernetics; or, Control and Communication in the Animal and the Machine*, Cambridge, MA: Technology Press, 1948.

The none-too-modest but eminently-readable founder of Cybernetics. See also his:

- Wiener, Norbert, *The Human Use of Human Beings; Cybernetics and Society*, Boston: Houghton Mifflin, 1950.

- Salton, Gerard, *Automatic Text Processing: the Transformation, Analysis, and Retrieval of Information by Computer*, Reading, MA: Addison-Wesley, 1988.

Information science as truly a science.

- Shannon, Claude Elwood, *The Mathematical Theory of Communication*, Urbana, IL: University of Illinois Press, 1949.

Information as a thing that flows, oddly sort of like electricity, and the idea of *feedback*.

Recent titles: some very technical, some not

- Blahut, Richard, ed., *Digital Transmission of Information*, Reading, MA: Addison-Wesley, c1990.
- Das, J., S. K. Mullick, P. K. Chatterjee, *Principles of Digital Communication*, New York: Wiley, c1986.
- Jones, Scott [et al.], *Developing International User Information*; Scott Jones [et al.], Bedford, MA: Digital Press, c1992.
- Eisenhart, Douglas M., *Publishing in the Information Age: a New Management Framework for the Digital Era*, Westport, CT: Quorum Books, 1994.
- Lebow, Irwin, *The Digital Connection: a Layman's Guide to the Information Age*, New York: Computer Science Press, c1991.
- Schroeder, M. R., *Number Theory in Science and Communication: with Applications in Cryptography, Physics, Digital Information, Computing, and Self-Similarity*, 2nd enl. ed., corr. printing. Berlin, New York: Springer-Verlag, 1990, c1986.

Libraries—the meaning

Classics

- Shera, Jesse H., *Introduction to Library Science: Basic Elements of Library Service*, Littleton, CO: Libraries Unlimited, 1976.

Eloquent modern statement of some very fundamental and very ancient ideas about libraries.

- Otlet, Paul, "Traité de Documentation: le Livre sur le Livre," *Théorie et Pratique*, Bruxelles: Editiones Mundaneum, 1934.

The same, for information in general.

Recent work

- Buckland, Michael K., *Library Services in Theory and Context*, New York: Pergamon Press, c1983.
- Buckland, Michael K., *Information and Information Systems*, New York: Greenwood Press, 1991.
- Cronin, Blaise, *Library Orthodoxies: a Decade of Change*, London: Taylor Graham, c1991.
- White, Herbert S., *At the Crossroads: Librarians on the Information Superhighway*, Englewood, CO: Libraries Unlimited, 1995.

Looming Issues

- Neely, Teresa Y., and Khafre K. Abif, *In Our Own Voices: the Changing Face of Librarianship*, Lanham, MD: The Scarecrow Press, 1996.
- Childers, Thomas (assisted by Joyce A. Post), *The Information-Poor in America*, Metuchen, NJ: Scarecrow Press, 1975.

Still looming: much information is online, more and more will be only online—and only 37% of U.S. households currently own a "computer"—the new general-public-oriented "NC/Network Computer/Noncomputer" may help this?

International librarianship

- Danton, J. Periam, *The Dimensions of Comparative Librarianship*, Chicago, IL: American Library Association, 1973.

- Foskett, Douglas J., *Introduction to Comparative Librarianship*, Bangalore, [India]: Sarada Ranganathan Endowment for Library Science, 1979.
- Simsova, Sylva, *A Primer of Comparative Librarianship*, London: Bingley, 1982.

http://www.nlc-bnc.ca/ifla/

The International Federation of Library Associations and Institutions.

The Internet

Classics

- Gibson, William, *Neuromancer*, New York: Ace Books, c1984.

Locus classicus for the term *matrix* to refer to the entire global network-of-information networks-of-networks: the idea of global information networking itself, back at a time when most people still were troubled by the idea of "computer A" being able to communicate with "computer B." Inspiration in fiction for many of the concepts later realized in cyberspace fact: such as *The Matrix* and *microsofts* and a less-than-rosy picture of the future of online digital information. Perhaps fittingly, *Neuromancer* is "punk" science fiction: not good reading for those with sensitive stomachs.

- Quarterman, John S., *The Matrix: Computer Networks and Conferencing Systems Worldwide*, Bedford, MA: Digital Press, c1990.

The bones for which Gibson's *Neuromancer* provided the flesh. Beginning with an acknowledged debt to Gibson for the idea, Quarterman describes the engineering that went into the construction of interoperability, internetworking, and *The Matrix*. Still unsurpassed for its breadth of coverage.

Recent Work

- LaQuey, Tracy, foreword by Al Gore, *The Internet Companion: a Beginner's Guide to Global Networking*, 2nd ed., Reading, MA: Addison-Wesley, 1994.

Among the thousands of handy pocket guides that can give an overview of the Internet to the novice, I personally think this one is the best. I wish she would update and re-issue it.

- Kumar, Vinay, *MBone—Interactive Multimedia on the Internet*, Indianapolis, IN: New Riders, c1996.

Mbone is television-via-Internet: fascinating more for the graphic demonstration it provides of Internet capacities—video on your computer tube, from/to Tasmania—than for the complex and backbone-backbreaking technical features that it represents. If multimedia/entertainment industry applications are the wave of the Internet's future . . .

- Huitema, Christian, *Routing in the Internet*, Englewood Cliffs, NJ: Prentice-Hall, c1995.
- Salus, Peter H., *Casting the Net: from ARPANET to Internet and Beyond*, Reading, MA: Addison-Wesley, c1995.

Libraries now: reaching new roles

- Valauskas, Edward J., and Nancy R. John, *The Internet Initiative: Libraries Providing Internet Services and How They Plan, Pay, and Manage*, Chicago, IL: American Library Association, 1995.
- Smith, Neil, ed., *Libraries, Networks and Europe: a European Networking Study*, [London]: British Library Research and Development Department, 1994.

Some digital library work in Europe.

- Kahin, Brian, and James Keller, eds., *Public Access to the Internet*, Cambridge, MA: MIT Press, c1995.

The first of the two great online digital information questions of the 1990s: Will the Internet scale up/down (1) to the general public or (2) internationally?

- Barron, Ann E., and Karen S. Ivers, *The Internet and Instruction: Activities and Ideas*, Englewood, CO: Libraries Unlimited, 1996.

The Internet's more pedestrian but ultimately most productive side: teaching for the future. Multimedia/entertainment industry applications may have a lockhold on the immediate future now, but the real future as always belongs to the children . . .

- Barnes, Bill [et al.], Shinohara, Mayumi, Richard Wenn, and Art Sussman, eds., *Tales from the Electronic Frontier: First-Hand Experiences of Teachers and Students Using the Internet in K-12 Math and Science*, San Francisco: WestEd, c1996.
- Crawford, Walt, *Future Libraries: Dreams, Madness & Reality*, Chicago, IL: American Library Association, 1995.
- Waters, Donald, and John Garrett, co-chairs, *Preserving Digital Information: Final Report and Recommendations*, Washington DC: The Commission on Preservation and Access and the Research Libraries Group, May 20, 1996, http://www-rlg.stanford.edu/ArchTF/ .

Psychology and culture

- Turkle, Sherry, *Life on the Screen: Identity in the Age of the Internet*, New York: Simon & Schuster, c1995.

Turkle does one of the more responsible jobs of thinking about the psychology of long-term digital information use, in a literature not yet populated with too much that is very responsible.

And two others:

- Moore, Dinty W., *The Emperor's Virtual Clothes: the Naked Truth About Internet Culture*, Chapel Hill, NC: Algonquin Books, 1995.
- Dery, Mark, *Escape Velocity: Cyberculture at the End of the Century*, New York: Grove Press, c1996.

There are some identifiable problems cropping up already:

- Ahuja, Vijay, *Network and Internet Security*, Boston: AP Professional, c1996.
- Hoffman, David S., *The Web of Hate: Extremists Exploit the Internet*, New York, NY: Anti-Defamation League, c1996.

Money

- Cronin, Mary J., *Global Advantage on the Internet: from Corporate Connectivity to International Competitiveness*, New York: Van Nostrand Reinhold, c1996.

As with psychology, so with money. There is a lot of irresponsible talk about both floating around now, associated with the Internet and the WorldWideWeb and digital libraries—Cronin's is a salutary exception.

International: a literature is beginning to build

- Gabbard, C. Bryan, and George S. Park, *The Information Revolution in the Arab World: Commercial, Cultural and Political Dimensions: the Middle East Meets the Internet*, Santa Monica, CA: RAND, 1995.

Further research, library-related: but most discussion, and increasingly, will be online.

- Liu, Lewis-Guodo, *The Internet and Library and Information Services: a Review, Analysis, and Annotated Bibliography*, Champaign, IL: Graduate School of Library and Information Science, University of Illinois at Urbana-Champaign, c1995.

Synthesis

Gurus: no one really knows where any of this is headed, but each of us follows someone. In my own case I have several whom I follow as religiously I can, reading everything they turn out, and whom I can recommend to anyone interested in the evolution of these general subjects.

Clifford Lynch

Dr. Lynch is head of the University of California's Division of Library Automation, which produces the MELVYL online library system, one of the world's largest and best-organized digital libraries so far. Lynch currently (1996) is President of ASIS. He also is a latter-day "wandering scholar," who pops up in nearly every conceivable public-speaking venue on the planet, delivering inevitably-eloquent and erudite and—particularly—careful disquisitions on the topics treated here and many others. He has a background in both engineering and librarianship and has written extensively. His writing is immensely readable. The papers often appear in obscure journals, but nearly all of them appear to have been posted somewhere on the Internet by someone. The best source for a running bibliography of Clifford—he produces new material at a phenomenal rate—is an Altavista search on his name: that currently produces 700 matching entries, only a few of which are entirely false drops—many are fulltext papers that can be read directly online.

Pierre Lévy

The premise of this book is that objectivity requires not only a second opinion but one which is foreign. Even if this were not the case, the writings of Pierre Lévy would fascinate. He approaches digital information from an entirely different perspective than does Lynch, and Lévy is French. Altavista shows 300 entries for "pierre near levy": some are false drops—"Pierre" is a far more common cyberspace name than "Clifford"—but those that are not are well-worth reading. The multilingual indexing of Lévy online gives an indication of the immense power of the Internet's reach for a writer. Levy has written a book entitled, "Of programming, considered as one of the decorative arts":

La machine univers : création, cognition et culture informatique. Paris: La Découverte, 1987.

[with Michel Authier, and a preface by Michel Serres], Les arbres de connaissances, Paris: La Découverte, 1992.

De la programmation considerée comme un des beaux-arts. Paris: La Découverte, 1992.

L'Intelligence collective: pour une anthropologie du cyberspace. Paris: La Découverte, 1994.

Qu'est-ce que le virtuel? Paris: La Découverte, 1995.

James Fallows

Fallows is becoming/has become one of the United States' leading journalists. His writing is readable and interesting. He also brings a journalist's skeptical interest to computers and the use and abuse of online digital information. Finally, Fallows is an expert on Asia. He is my one personal hope, so far, for obtaining objective, realistic, appraisals of the development of digital libraries and of online digital information generally, as these explode in both use and abuse in Asia during the coming decade. Like so much else, Fallows's writing is to be found increasingly online: http://www.TheAtlantic.com, and he is in the process of joining a new publication. I suppose he hopes that everyone will be able to reach what he writes online, but I have my fears that this increasingly may not be so for many, unless digital libraries increase and improve their techniques.

About the author

J ACK KESSLER studied philosophy, politics, law, and library and information science at Yale, Oxford, and the University of California. He spent 15 years in international trade in Asia, the United States, and Europe. At the University of California he was introduced to email and the Internet and became convinced not only that digital information would be a marvel, but that it would become marvelous in entirely unpredictable ways. His primary interests are in general public and international access, both of which are relatively new and the most unpredictable aspects of online digital information's development. He has worked since 1989 as an Internet trainer and consultant for libraries, other organizations, and individuals in the United States and Europe. Since 1992, he has published *FYI France*, a monthly electronic newsletter on French and European library and online digital information news. He can be reached via email at kessler@well.sf.ca.us .

Index

The Artech House Computer Science Library

ISBN: 0-89006-740-6   *X Window System User's Guide,* Uday O. Pabrai

For further information on these and other Artech House titles, contact:

Artech House
685 Canton Street
Norwood, MA 02062
617-769-9750
Fax: 617-769-6334
Telex: 951-659
email: artech@artech-house.com

Artech House
Portland House, Stag Place
London SW1E 5XA England
+44 (0) 171-973-8077
Fax: +44 (0)171-630-0166
Telex: 951-659
email: artech-uk@artech-house.com